I0810340

IMAGES
of America

GREENHILLS

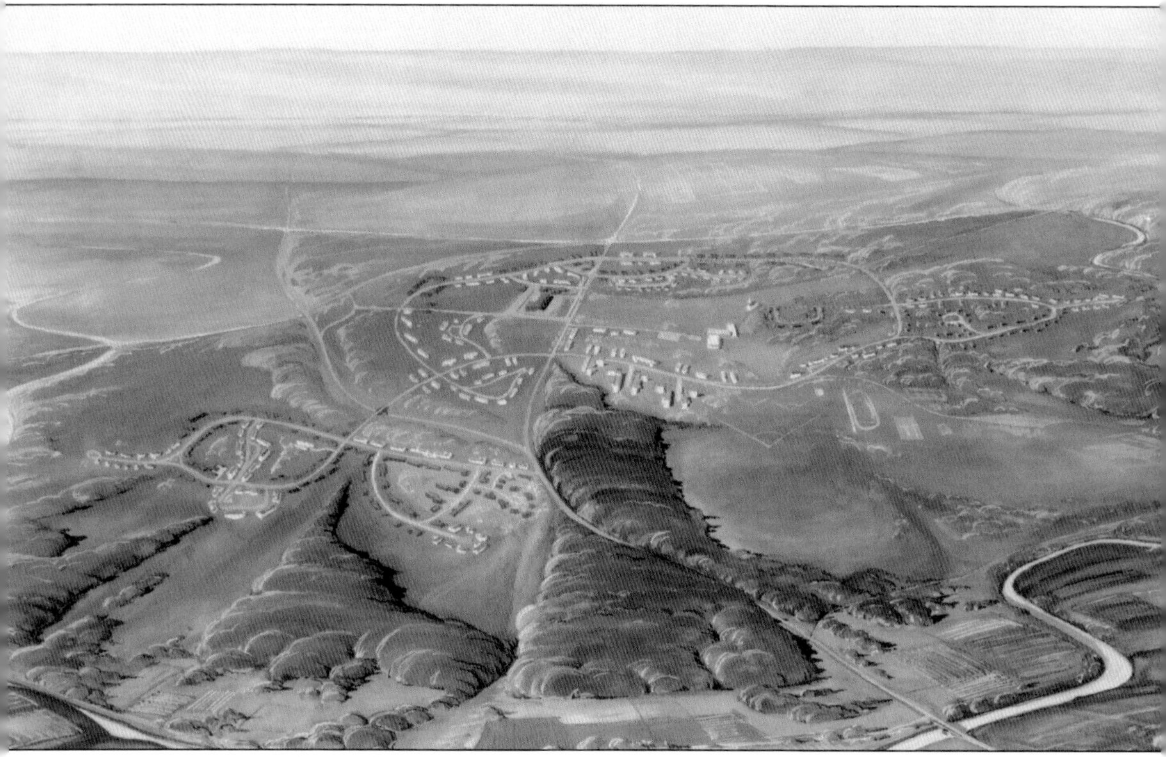

This is a watercolor rendering of the dream of Rexford Tugwell that became Greenhills. Over time, it has been the epitome of "the good life" for thousands of residents. The rolling hills and open land was a good starting point to build a community. This rendering was painted by an unknown artist or architect in the very early planning stages of Greenhills, when it was called the Cincinnati Project. Immediately after Pres. Franklin D. Roosevelt gained approval for the greenbelt towns in 1935, architects, planners, and draftsmen in Washington, DC, went straight to their drawing boards to start creating. (Courtesy of the Library of Congress.)

ON THE COVER: This view shows Andover Road, with its hipped and flat roofs. The curvilinear lines of the streets add interest in comparison to the usual square block plan of the period. Note the stylized bench, which was included in the original street and open space design, complete with blueprints. (Courtesy of the Library of Congress.)

IMAGES
of America

GREENHILLS

Debbie Mills and Margo Warminski
with the Greenhills Historical Society

ARCADIA
PUBLISHING

ISBN 978-0-7385-9886-4

Published by Arcadia Publishing
Charleston, South Carolina

Printed in the United States of America

Library of Congress Control Number: 2013934880

For all general information, please contact Arcadia Publishing:
Telephone 843-853-2070
Fax 843-853-0044
E-mail sales@arcadiapublishing.com
For customer service and orders:
Toll-Free 1-888-313-2665

Visit us on the Internet at www.arcadiapublishing.com

This book is dedicated to all past and present citizens, and to those who remain passionate admirers of Greenhills.

Contents

ACKNOWLEDGMENTS

We wrote this book in honor of the first residents of Greenhills, who were appropriately named pioneers. They endured the Great Depression and had the courage to take the chance to live a new life in Greenhills. These first citizens of the greenbelt town paved the way for what became a better place and a better way of life.

Thanks are due to the dedicated volunteer members of the Greenhills Historical Society, who feel the passion as much as we do to help share the story of Greenhills for future generations. We are also grateful to Betty Senior and the late Fran Wolf, who started organizing the Greenhills Historical Society's archival collections; to dedicated volunteers Wendel Fisher and Jackie Seymour, for their generous patience and continued hours of organization of the archives; to Paul Richardson, whose artistic talents have helped add polish to the Greenhills Historical Society; and to Karen Richardson, who can edit like no tomorrow.

Thank you to the Village of Greenhills and the keeper of records, Kathy Lives; to the Winton Woods School District, for sharing their archives; to the Greenhills Alumni Association and Bobbe Kugele, who told us who was who and what was what as we rifled through the old photographs and documents; and to the families who shared and donated photographs from their collections. We thank Chris Russo, vice president of the Greenhills Historical Society, who discovered Greenhills, moved here after falling in love with its beauty, became passionate about its history, and then dropped everything to help with the research and writing for this book. Our gratitude also goes to Terri Treinen, the current president of the Greenhills Historical Society, who contributed her expertise in writing chapters three and four.

Lastly, thanks are due to all the people who have rallied to save this precious place for future generations by fighting against further loss of our special, unique heritage.

INTRODUCTION

The Great Depression was one of the worst economic catastrophes in US history. Vast numbers of people were in need. One-third of the nation was ill-fed, ill-housed, out of work, and out of hope, which overwhelmed private charities. When Franklin Delano Roosevelt was inaugurated president in 1933, his New Deal program launched government-run relief programs. The public relief agencies studied the people they helped and compiled a wealth of statistics as never before. This information showed the nature and extent of rural and inner-city poverty, as well as the degraded state of the middle class. Until then, most in government had no idea, even in good times, how many people lived close to the poverty line. This information helped shape New Deal relief policies. The Suburban Resettlement Program was formed under the Resettlement Administration (RA) to solve this dilemma, thereby creating the concept of greenbelt towns.

Greenhills was one of the three model greenbelt towns of the Roosevelt administration that came to fruition in 1938. It all started from a group of talented individuals known as the brain trust, whom President Roosevelt hired to cure the ills of the Great Depression. That group developed many programs, but the program most influential to Greenhills was the RA. The Suburban Program, under the RA, carefully created and began the construction of three greenbelt towns. It was the most daring endeavor in post-depression planning that the country had ever seen, and it helped build the dreams of many families in the mid-to-late 1930s.

The experiment not only made quality housing affordable for those with moderate and low incomes, but it also put people back to work on a massive scale and even helped families who still wanted to keep the dream of a family farm alive. The greenbelt town concept was totally planned before the first shovel was put to earth. The plan was to separate the residential, commercial, and transportation function into distinct zones, with a buffering outer ring of forest and outlying farms. These zones all worked in harmonic interplay to provide a good life for the people.

More than 100 potential areas of the United States were surveyed for this endeavor, and northern Cincinnati eventually received the honor of being one of only three places in America to be built that met all of the criteria. On a cold December morning in 1935, the first shovel was put to the earth to build Greenhills.

According to the 1938 RA report, "Greenhills was more than just a simple housing venture. It was planned so that the occupants may enjoy the advantages of an urban community and at the same time have all the benefits of rural life." In other words, it combined the convenience of the city with the health and beauty of rural land. It was well situated outside a metropolitan area for commuting to work, but it included a buffer zone of forest. To this day, travelers through the greenbelt can feel the temperature drop on a hot day and appreciate the dampening of sounds from the outlying areas.

Irene Connerman, who moved to Greenhills as a child, remembers, "It was almost like a miracle. The fact that we were moving into a brand new place. It had never been lived in . . . It was like heaven for the kids. They had a sandbox, swings and slides." There is a misconception that Greenhills was built to provide slum clearance, which is simply not true. The planners of Greenhills saw the opportunity to provide good housing in a good neighborhood, allowing the possibility of a good life for people of moderate and low income.

Even though Greenhills has had some changes in the last 75 years, it remains a monument to the community development strategy of the 1930s and 1940s, which upheld the idea that place and culture were the primary shapers of individual behavior. It was designated a National Planning Landmark in 1987 and was placed in the National Register of Historic Places in 1989. To this day, Greenhills is still studied by architects, planners, and social scientists from all over the world.

Our wish is that the reader will appreciate the importance of Greenhills in this very small snapshot of the book. Hundreds and hundreds of pages could be dedicated to explaining its importance. We can only hope that the organizations and individuals who make the decisions for the future of Greenhills conduct themselves as stewards to honor the historical uniqueness of the landmark plan.

One

The Resettlement Administration

The source of our wealth is our land, and our civilization and national well-being rest upon it.

—Anonymous

After Roosevelt's inauguration in 1933, Rexford Guy Tugwell was appointed undersecretary of the Department of Agriculture. He helped create and direct the Agricultural Adjustment Administration (AAA), which included a domestic allotment program that paid farmers to voluntarily reduce their production by roughly 30 percent, funded with a tax on processing companies that used farm products as inputs. Tugwell's department managed the production of key crops by adjusting the subsidies for nonproduction. Another creation of Tugwell was the 1933 Soil Conservation Service (SCS), which restricted and restored poor-quality land. The program was critically important due to the devastating 1930s Dust Bowl.

In the first months of 1935, President Roosevelt, in a message to Congress, proclaimed that the nation was embarking on phase two of the New Deal. Many of the existing New Deal programs were continued under the umbrella of the newly created Resettlement Administration (RA). Tugwell subsequently became the RA's first director. The RA had four focus areas: the Land Use Program, the Resettlement Program, the Rehabilitation Program, and the Suburban Program.

In 1935, under the Land Use Program, President Roosevelt issued Executive Order 7027, consolidating several farm programs under the RA. The object of the Resettlement Program was to provide adequate homes and good farmland for those who proved their worth under the administration's loan program, and to offer eligibility for resettlement on better farms. The Rehabilitation Program offered help by granting small loans to enable farmers to replace working capital, like equipment and livestock, which had been wiped out during the Depression.

The fourth phase of the RA was the Suburban Program, which worked with nearly 200 communities on projects throughout the New Deal years. Soon, a new idea for special communities came to the fore. The much-needed idea of the greenbelt towns was the brainchild of Rexford Guy Tugwell.

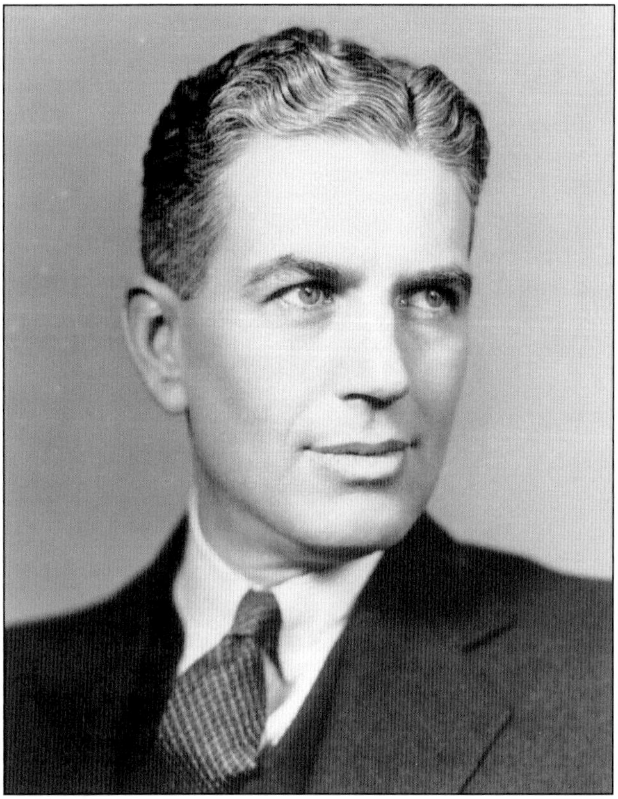

Rexford Tugwell, an agricultural economist and professor, was invited to become part of Pres. Franklin Roosevelt's first brain trust, a group of Columbia University academics, in 1932. They helped develop policy recommendations to advise Roosevelt and continued to be a huge influence in the New Deal years. (Courtesy of the Library of Congress.)

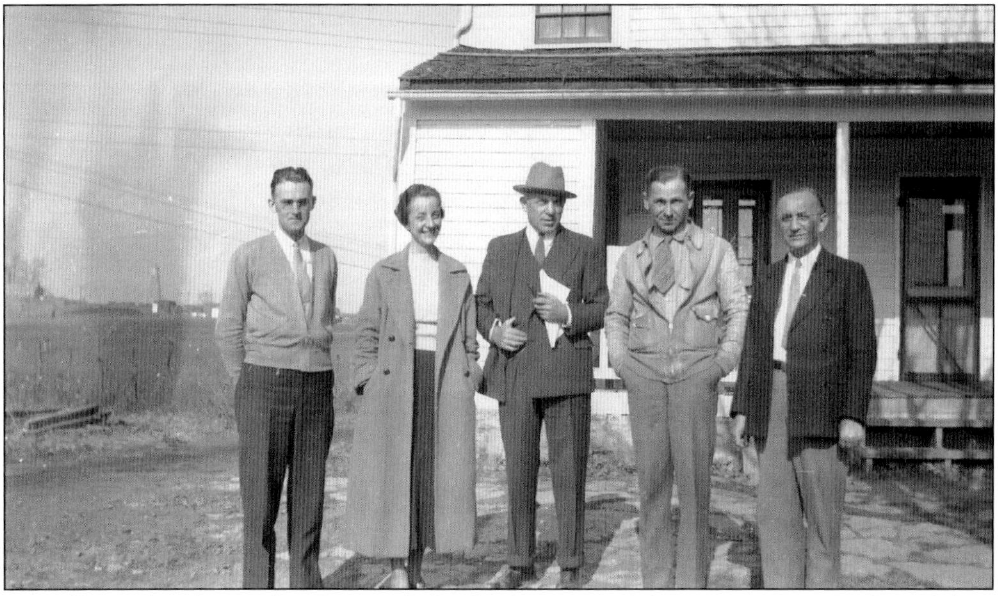

Tugwell stayed with President Roosevelt for the first years of the growing New Deal. He left in late 1936 after facing enormous criticism and attacks from legislators for his poor management of the RA. He thought that if he left, the criticism would die down, giving the program a chance to prove the legislators wrong. Tugwell (center) is seen here visiting the Greenhills project staff. (Courtesy of the Johnstone family.)

The RA logo and symbols were an important part of the New Deal era. They commanded immediate recognition to citizens symbolizing that the government program was the mediator of their ills. Notable symbols included the blue eagle of the National Recovery Administration (NRA); the bold, red, white, and blue, horizontally striped Works Progress Administration (WPA) sign; and this logo, which was put on every RA work truck and vehicle of the time. (Courtesy of the Greenhills Historical Society.)

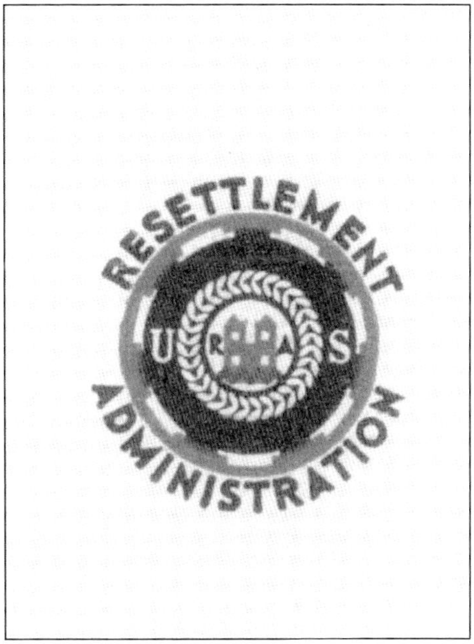

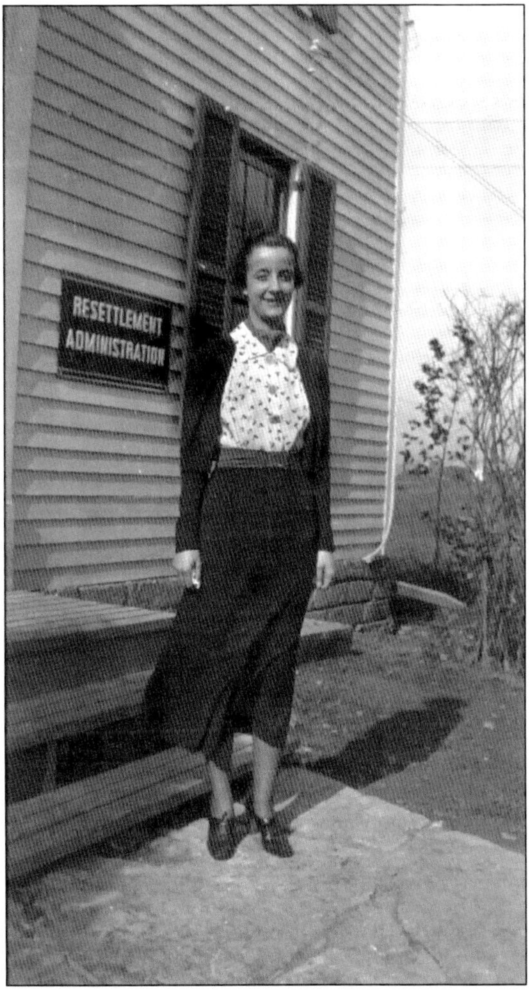

A member of the RA staff stands in front of a Greenhills project field office. A former farm building, like many of the existing buildings on the lands acquired for the project, it was repurposed for office use. Some buildings were also used for materials storage. (Courtesy of the Johnstone family.)

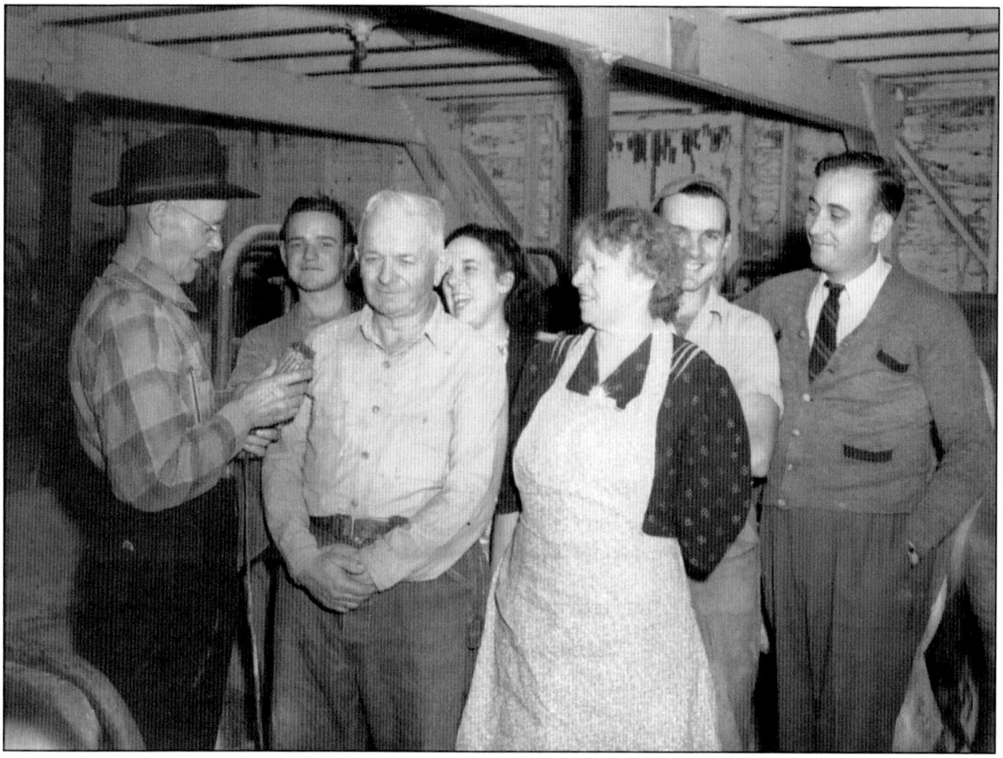

Due to the Depression, more than one million rural families were already placed on relief rolls. Soil was often depleted due to habitual over-farming and overgrazing, the clear-cutting of forests without subsequent replanting or conservation methods, and the lack of careful land planning. Despite subsidies from the former Rural Rehabilitation Division of the government, these problems were still causing hardship and devastation on the land. The Land Use Program reached ever further, taking millions of acres of land that had been exhausted by deforestation, over-farming, and drought, and moving farm families into government-owned planned communities, including model farms and model housing. Above, farmers are guided and trained by government experts on site, who helped them implement modern farming methods on land capable of producing good crops. The eroded field below shows how overgrazing devastated pastures. (Above, courtesy of the Palma family; below, courtesy of the Library of Congress.)

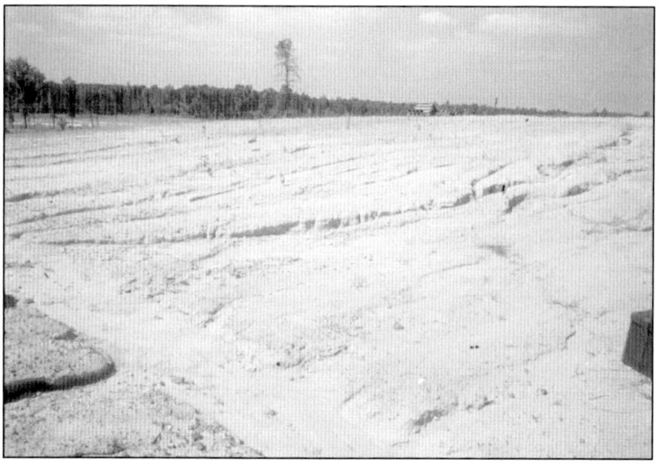

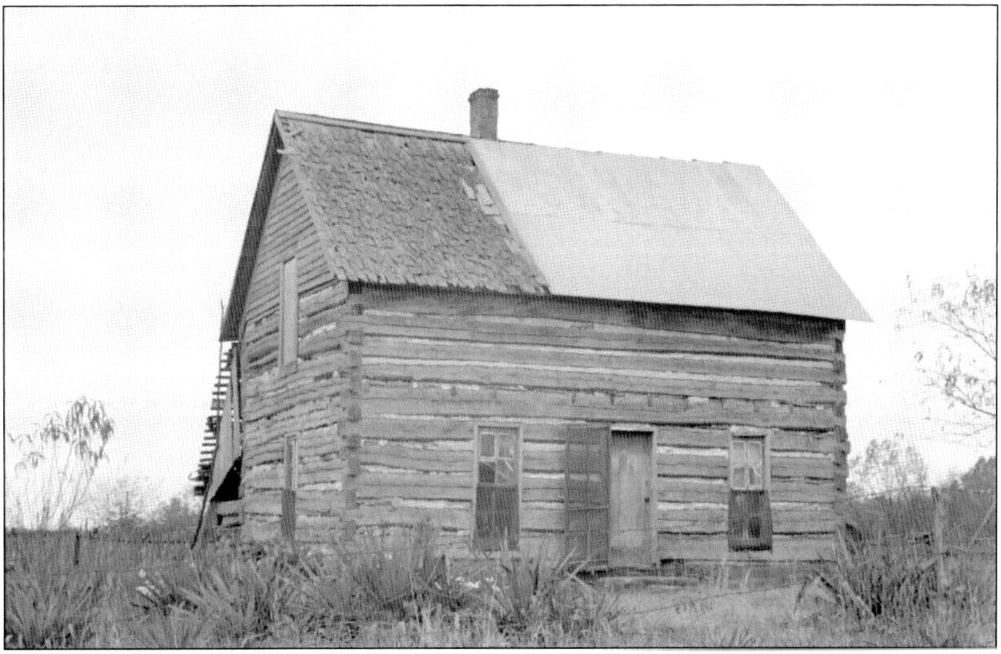

The Resettlement Program, under the RA, provided adequate homes and good farmland for those who had proved their worth under the administration's loan program, offering eligibility for resettlement on better farms. It helped spur better land use by buying up the land of these families, allowing them to move and create new farms elsewhere. The purchase of their land sometimes financed their resettlement unaided, decreasing considerably their need for government subsidies. If the housing was in disrepair, sometimes new farmhouses (below) were built right next to old ones (above). (Both, courtesy of the Library of Congress.)

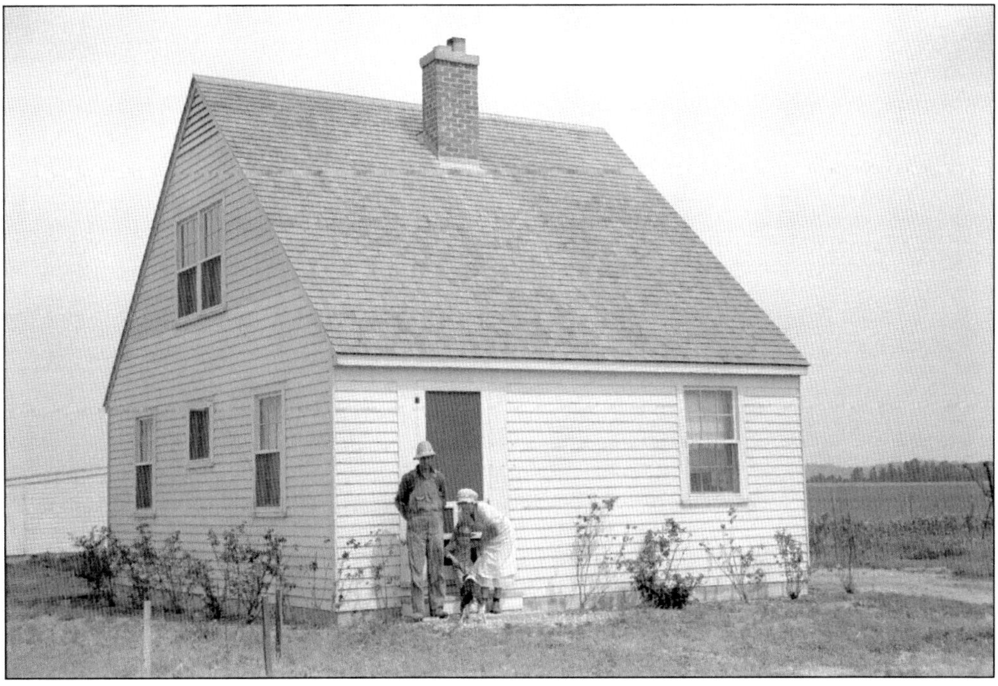

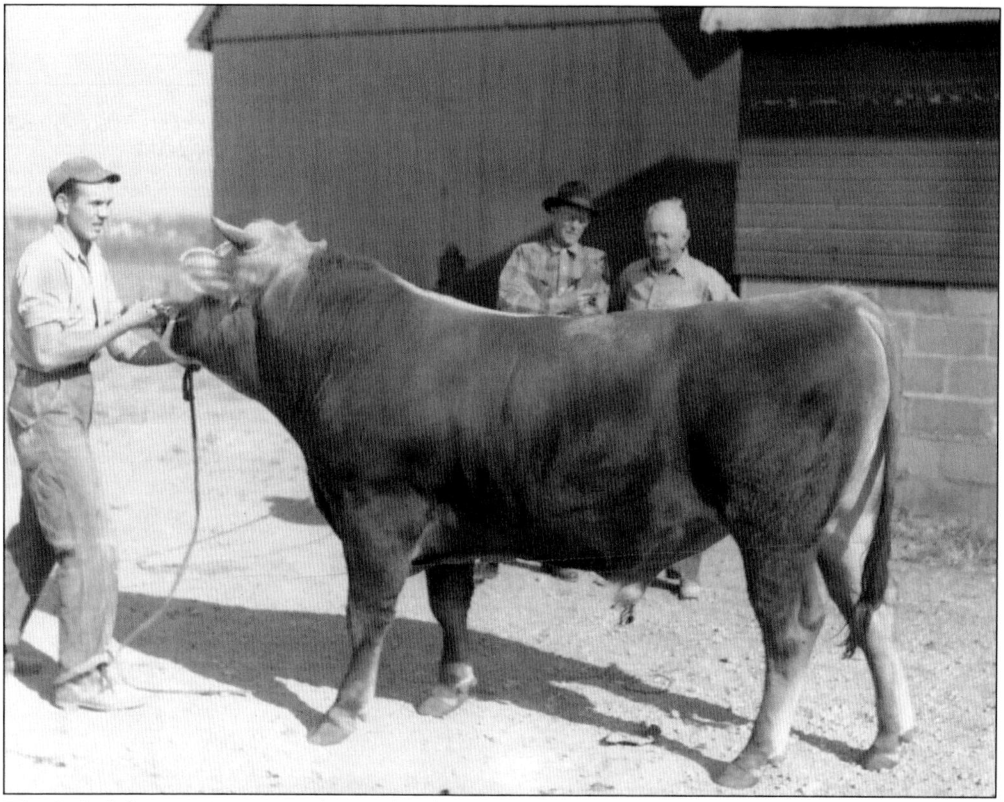

The Rehabilitation Program, also under the RA, offered help by granting small loans to enable farmers to replace working capital like equipment and livestock that had been wiped out by the hard times of the Depression. It also helped farmers lower their owed debts and become independent of relief rolls. According to Rexford Tugwell, "A loan, expert advice and some common sense between creditor and debtor enable these farmers to take their places again as self-supporting, self-respecting members of their communities." For example, the man above received livestock as his capital, and afterward, a government representative (below) met with him to explain details about managing his profits and losses. (Above, courtesy of the Palma family; below, courtesy of the Library of Congress.)

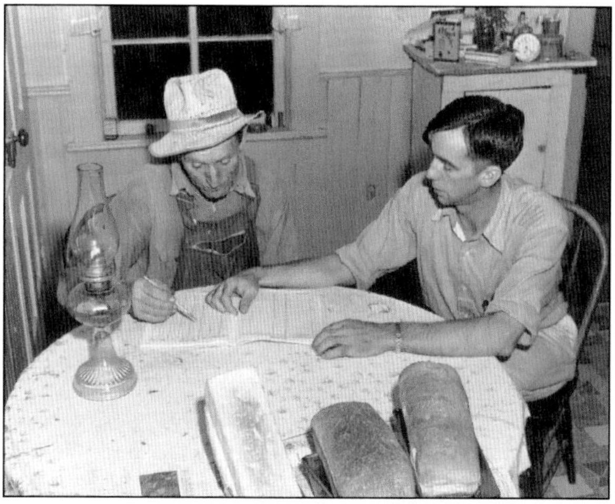

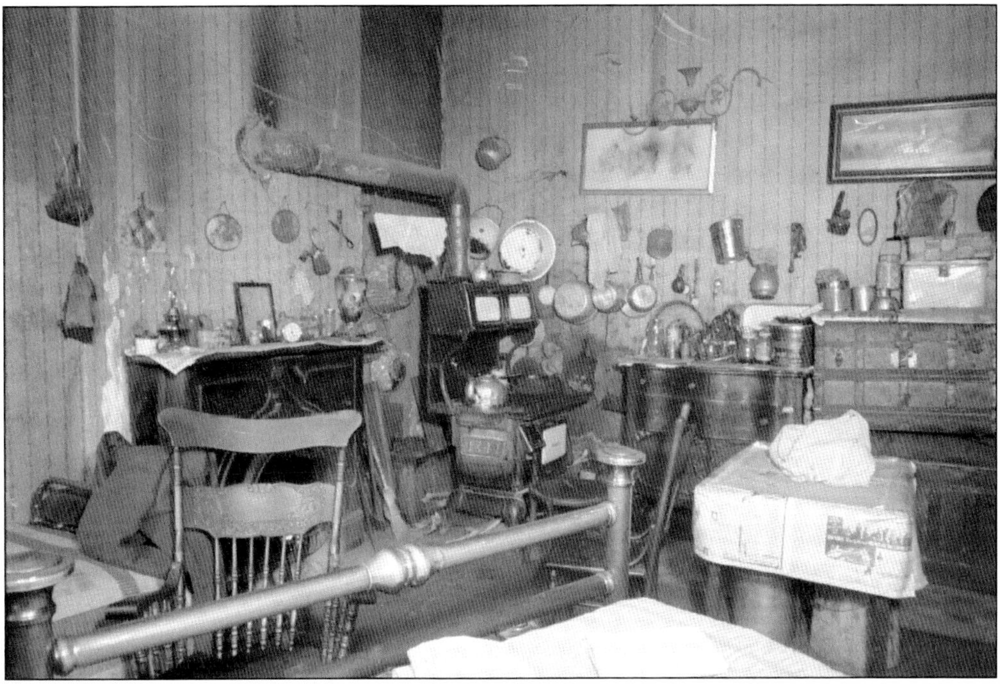

The Suburban Program was the fourth phase of the RA. As time went on, the poverty of inner cities and even of those with moderate income was documented by a group of assigned federal photographers working for the informal historical section of the Civil Service division. Photographic essays returned to Tugwell showed the shocking state of squalor and unsanitary living conditions (displayed above and below), which were more common than previously thought. Diseases such as rickets, due to a lack of vitamin D caused by not getting enough sun exposure, made dietary supplementation common. Also, in areas where people were forced to live very close together, tuberculosis had spread at inordinate rate. (Both, courtesy of the Library of Congress.)

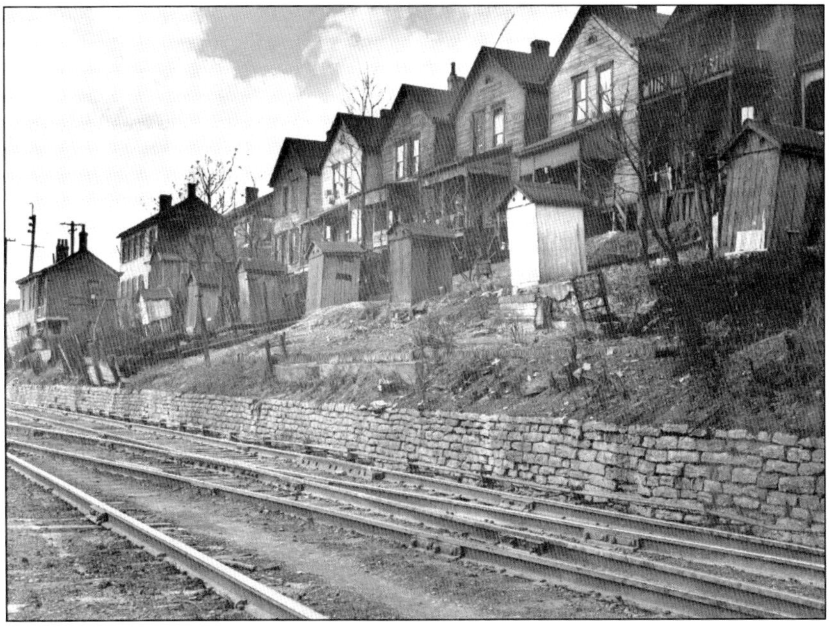

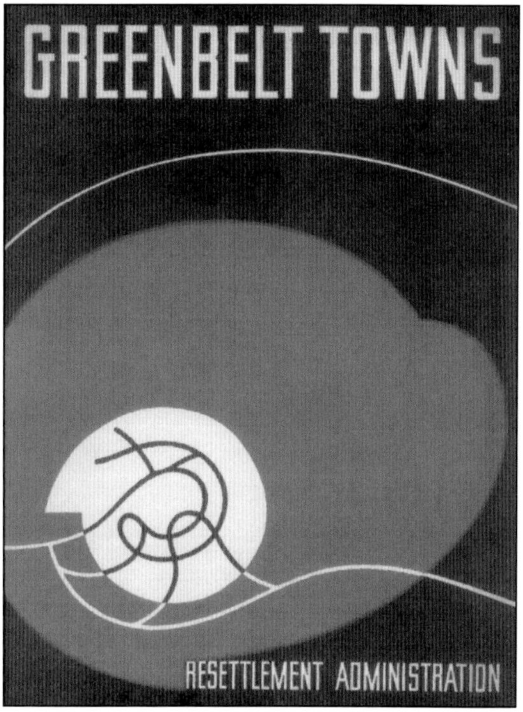

A number of advertisements like the ones seen here were planned to explain the amenities of greenbelt-town living. One section, the advertising art department, was assigned strictly to make brochures, posters, and the like even before towns were built. (Left, courtesy of the Greenhills Historical Society Collection; below, courtesy of the Library of Congress.)

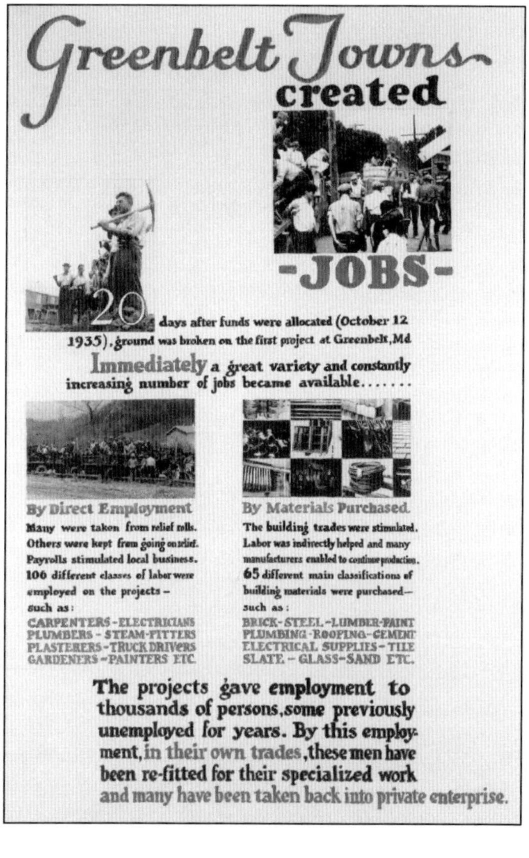

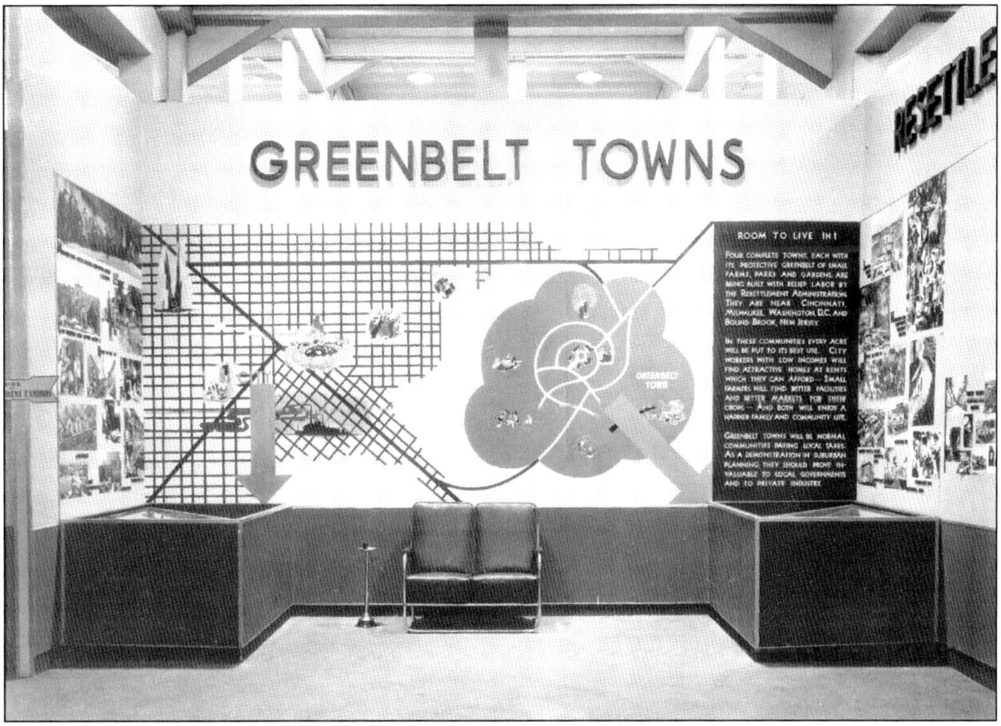

Displays of the greenbelt towns were present at the Great Lakes Exposition, which was held in Cleveland in the summers of 1936 and 1937. The fair brought more than seven million visitors and spanned more than 135 acres, opening in late June both summers and running for 100 days. A kind of miniature world's fair, its purpose was to hail the Great Lakes region's social and cultural progress in the past 100 years. The government had displays in the exposition touting the greenbelt towns (above and below). In the brochure for the exposition, it was made very clear that the government displays occupied space on the same basis as industrial and commercial exhibitors to ensure that the audience was aware of no favoritism. (Both, courtesy of the Library of Congress.)

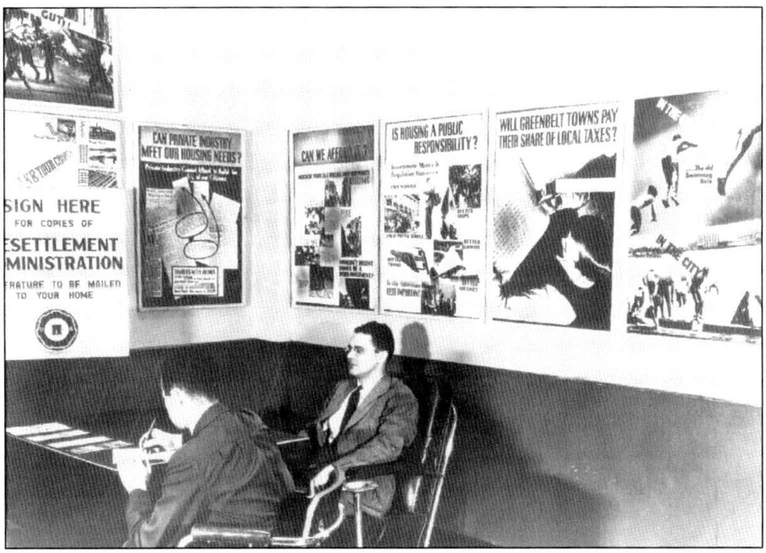

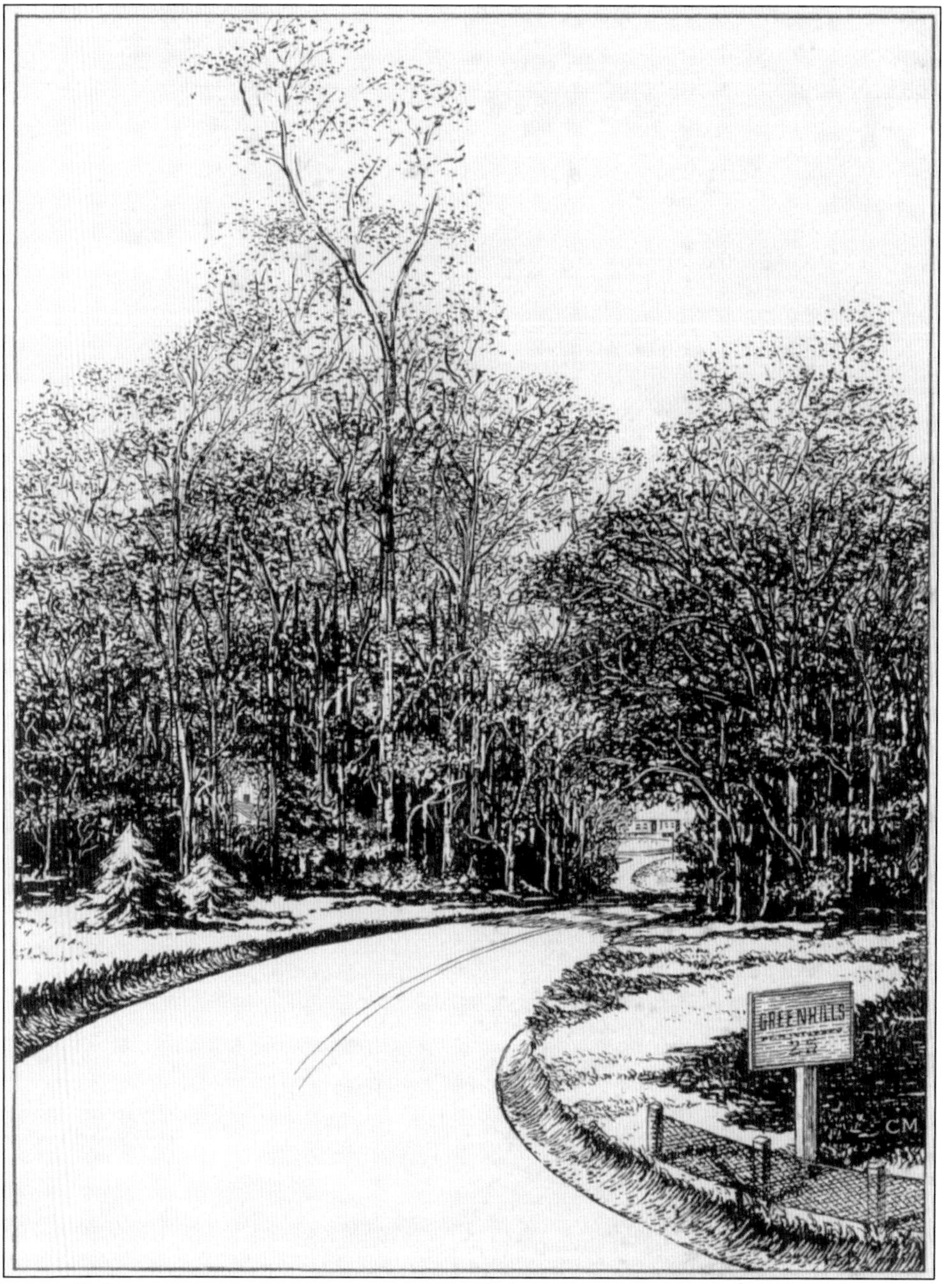

The greenbelt towns were an experiment in social engineering and agricultural economics, and Rexford Tugwell was as much an economist as he was a town planner. Greenbelt towns were to be a perfect mixture of functions, as the dynamic working of its parts supported the whole. Some people were destitute because of the stock market crash, but Tugwell surmised that others were destitute because of the poor planning of towns and structures. He believed that towns were not to be put together piecemeal, with disjointed parts. Instead, cities should be productive places for productive citizens. The greenbelt towns were to be the combination of the best of the city with the best of rural living. (Rendering by Greenhills artist Clement Mortashed, courtesy of the Greenhills Historical Society.)

Two

THE PLAN

Modern housing, if it is to be done at all, cannot be patchwork. It is not "reform" within the old pattern. It is either an entirely new method of providing an entirely new standard of urban environment, or nothing.

—Catherine Bauer, *Modern Housing*, 1934

The Greenbelt towns program, the building of complete communities in suburban areas near large cities, provided an opportunity to make a great variety and constantly increasing number of jobs. In addition to providing work for the unemployed, it presented an opportunity to demonstrate the advantages of large scale town and country planning.

—Letter to Dr. W.W. Alexander, administrator of the Farm Security Administration

The innovative Greenhills plan borrowed ideas from the most progressive town planning in the United States and Europe. It envisioned a town integrated with the surrounding countryside, allowing people to flourish in harmony with nature. The greenbelt town planners sought a large, single tract of land for their new community. For the ease of administration, it would have a single owner, preferably a public agency to which title could later be transferred. The planners would then devise a land use plan for the entire tract, which would be surrounded by an encircling greenbelt.

The town was planned for families of modest income, neither rich nor poor, who would pay affordable rent. Houses would be rented, not sold. In addition to providing a better place to live, the Greenhills planners hoped to create, according to greenbelt program director J.S. Lansill, a "better family and community life than [the residents] now enjoy, but which will not involve subjecting them to coercion or theoretical and untested discipline."

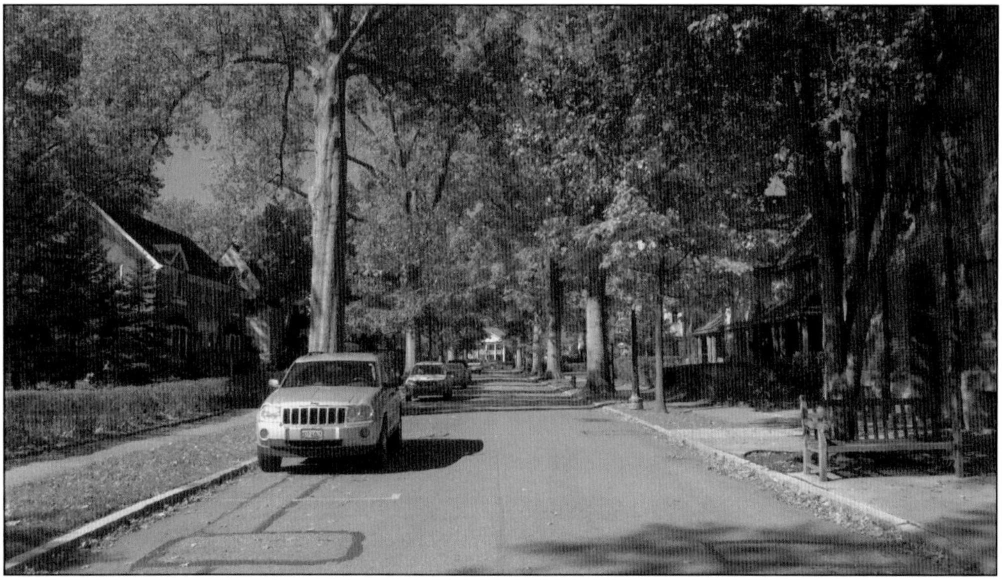

The Greenhills plan was influenced by planned communities in Europe and in America. A major influence was English Garden City planning, championed by Ebenezer Howard, which envisioned orderly, beautiful, self-sustaining villages surrounded by countryside. In Cincinnati, Howard's influence is visible in Mariemont, a planned suburb from the 1920s, an era when the success of the automobile encouraged experimentation with city plans. Oak Street, seen here today, featured gracious four-family residences under towering trees. (Courtesy of Margo M. Warminski.)

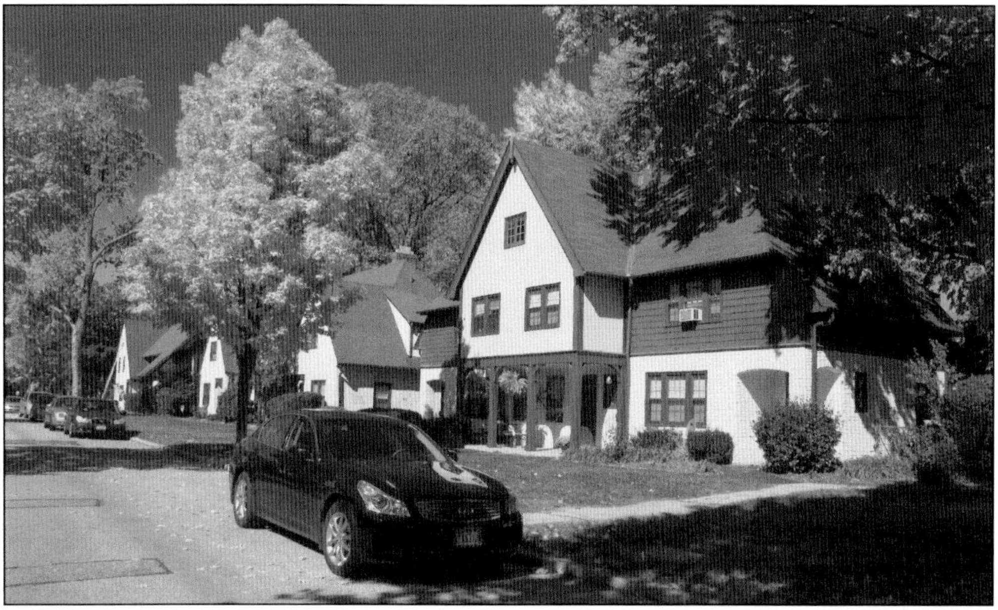

Mariemont planner John Nolen's thoughtful approach to urban design is evident on Maple Avenue, in the village's northwest corner. This Tudor Revival-style building, designed by the Kruckemeyer & Strong Group in 1929, was one of many picturesque, architect-designed townhouse groupings in Mariemont. The houses are identical in scale, setback, and materials, yet varied in detailing. A curved walkway serves each building, and there are no sidewalks. The rear yards are deep and include garages. (Courtesy of Margo M. Warminski.)

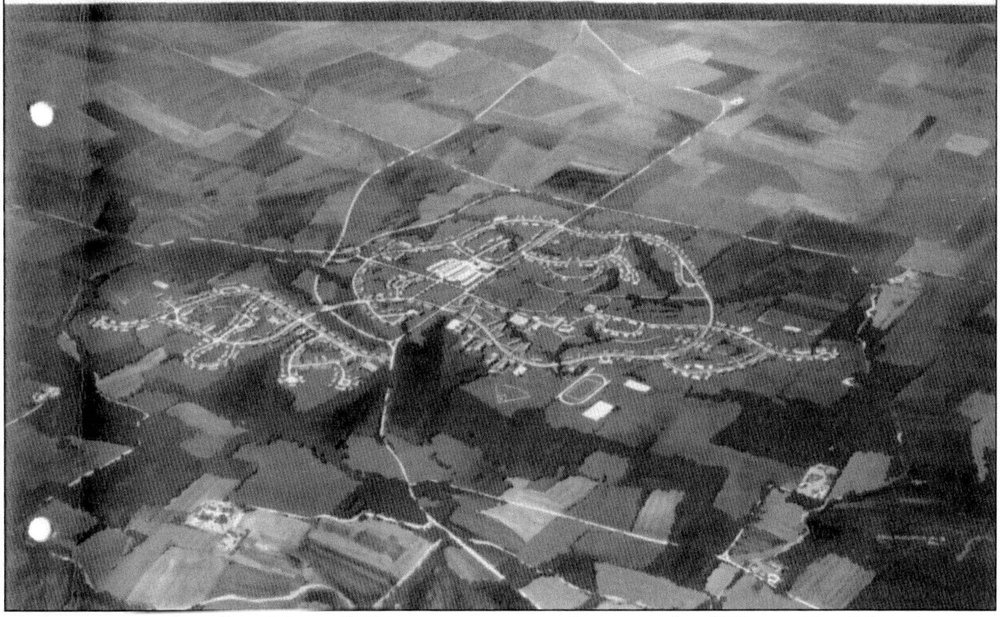

Early project studies placed Greenhills's town center on the west side of Winton Road, but the town center was eventually built on the east side to take advantage of the interesting terrain changes. This early proposal had a bypass road traveling westward in the middle of town, from Winton Road through what is now Palma Park. If built, it would have given Greenhills similar underpass features to those in the greenbelt town in Maryland. (Courtesy of the Village of Greenhills.)

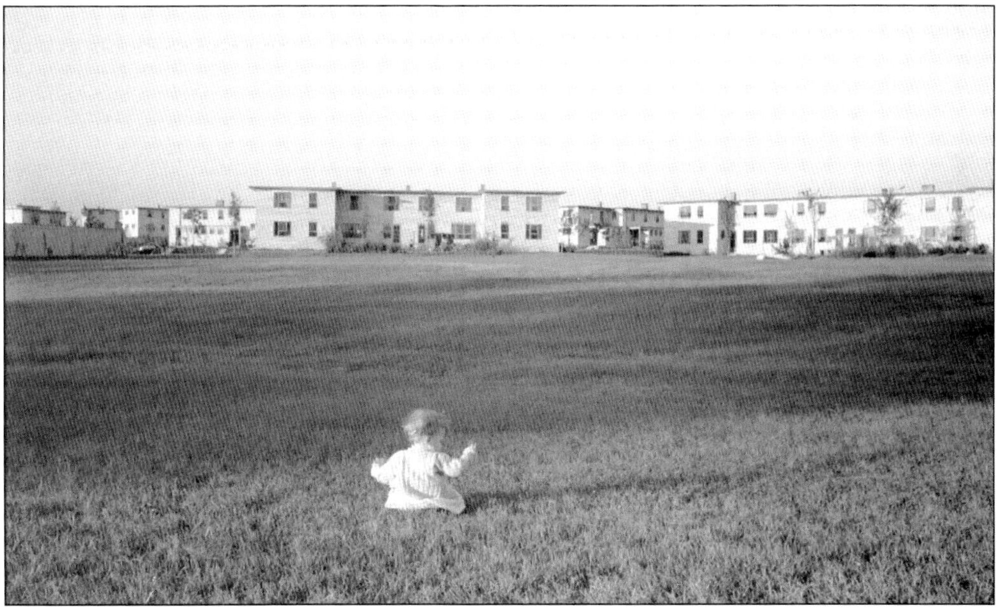

In a scene reminiscent of Andrew Wyeth's famous painting *Christina's World*, a toddler sits in an open field surrounded by newly built townhouses. While children were at play, moms and neighbors could easily keep a watchful eye on them from living room or kitchen windows. (Courtesy of the Library of Congress.)

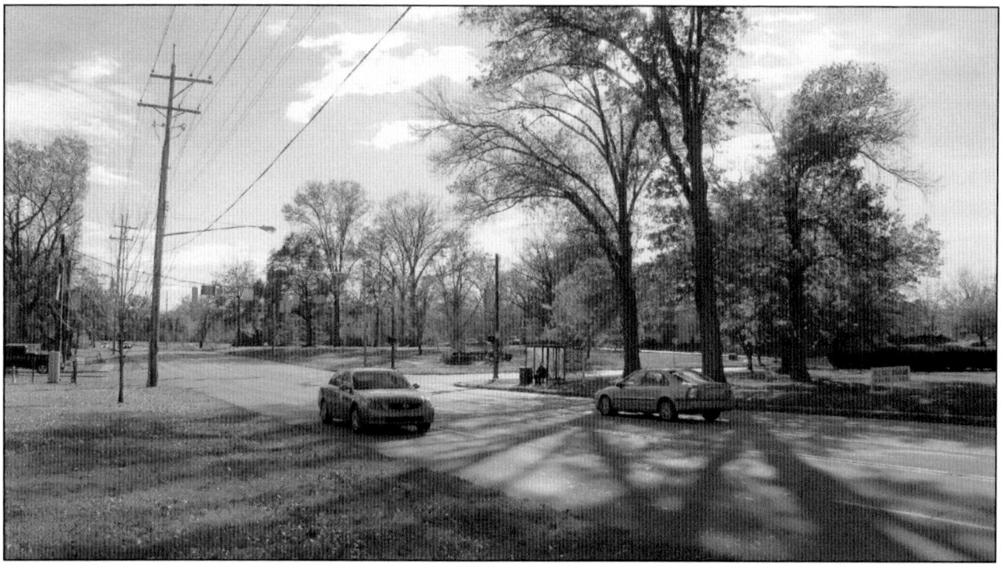

As cars became more popular, planners looked for new ways to manage traffic and improve safety. Winton Road, the main thoroughfare of Greenhills, was designed with only three access points. No driveways fronted Winton Road, eliminating the hazard of people backing into or pulling out of the busy road. Greenhills planners also proposed a pedestrian underpass below the road to separate people from cars, but it was dropped due to budget constraints and engineering challenges. (Courtesy of Paul Richardson.)

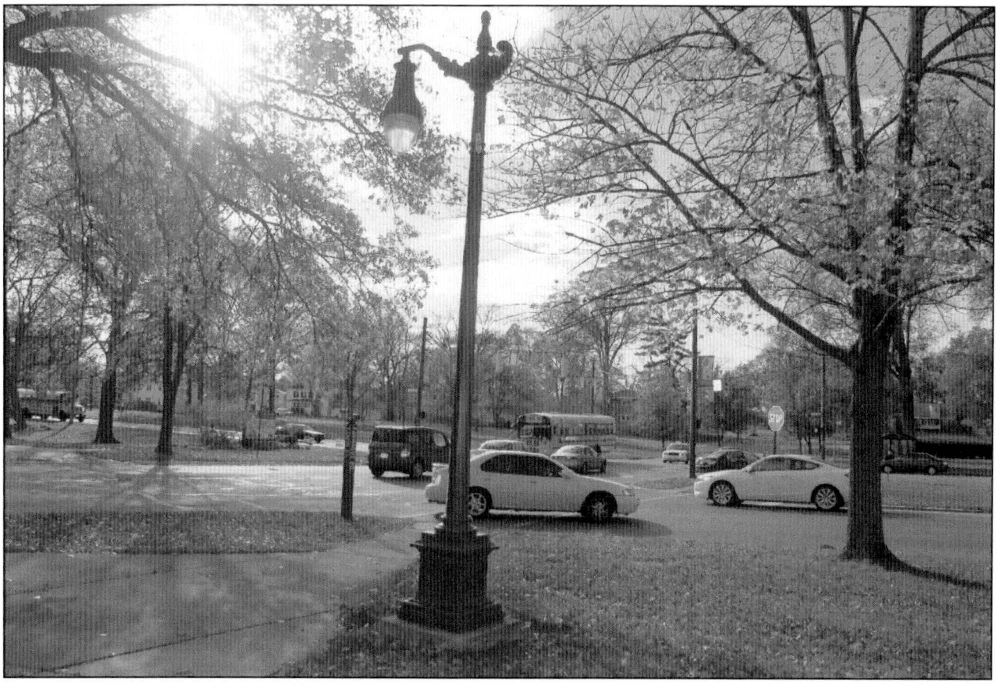

Looking west across Winton Road from Farragut Road, the ingenious street plan is on full display. Through traffic flows along Winton Road with few interruptions or obstacles while slower, local traffic to the village center follows Eswin Street to the right. Green space and trees line the road, creating a beautiful, peaceful vista for passing motorists. (Courtesy of Paul Richardson.)

The Greenhills village plan incorporated elements of the neighborhood unit idea of Clarence Perry, a New York City planner, sociologist, and author, which called for self-contained communities with homes, a centrally located elementary school, and local shops. Houses would be arranged, according to the RA, in "large parks with trees and playgrounds at the center." Arterial streets routed traffic around the community, and an internal street system discouraged through traffic. This plan, of Greenhills's A section (Andover, Ashby, Alcott, Avenell) puts Perry's ideas into practice with cul-de-sacs, greens, and walking paths. (Courtesy of the Library of Congress.)

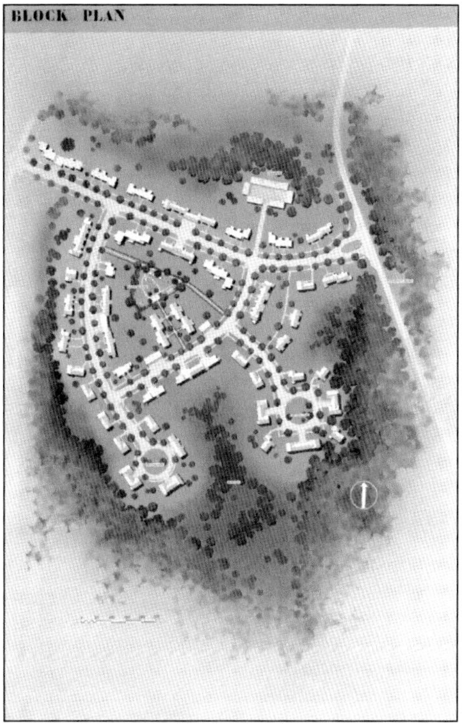

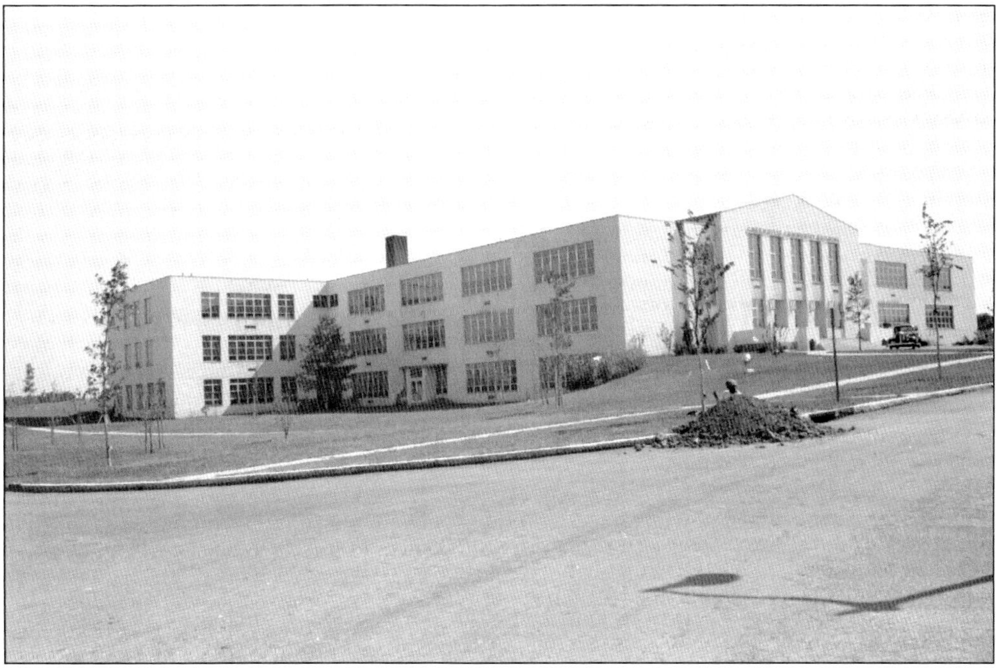

Greenhills's planners took full advantage of the undulating topography on the east side of Winton Road. The drop into a drainage creek became Ravine Park and, later, the challenge in the Greenhills golf course. The pool complex sat one step up as the land rose to the south. This steep grade allowed for the community building's prominent positioning, looking out over the level common while still featuring a lower walk-out floor. (Courtesy of the Library of Congress.)

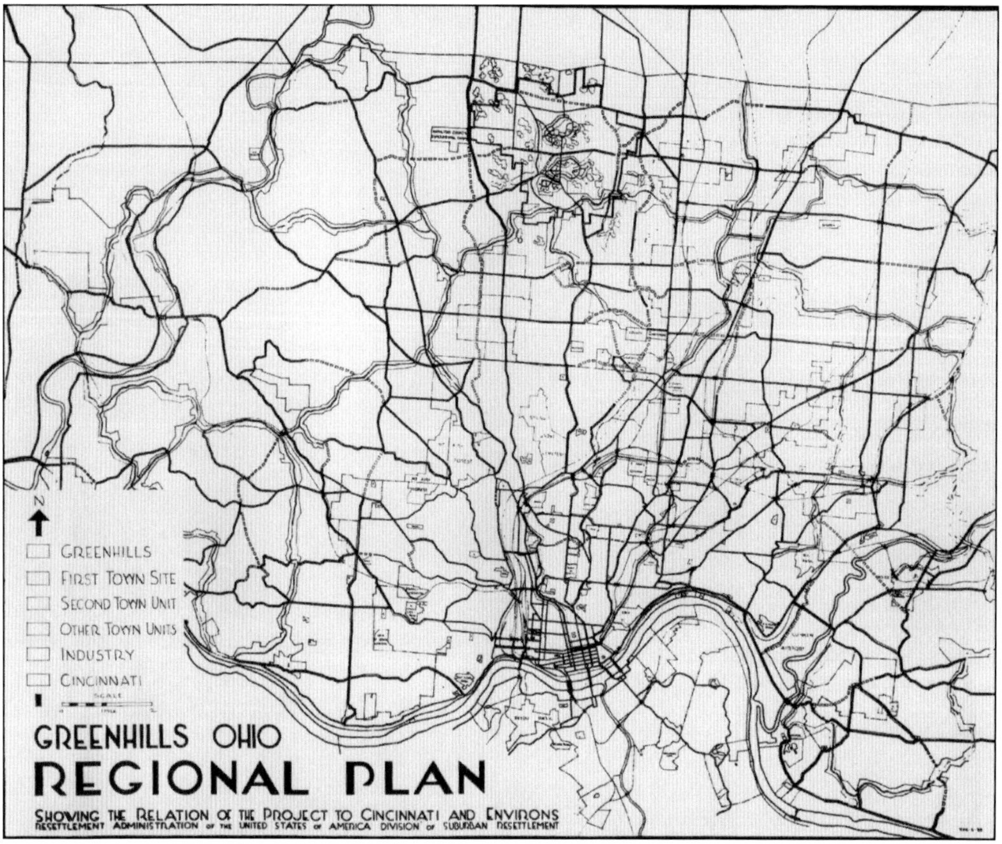

Many sites were considered for greenbelt towns. Greater Cincinnati was chosen because of its housing shortage, its strong, diversified economy, and its civic leadership. Greenhills planners worked closely with county commissioners and planners to make sure their plans meshed with those of local officials. Planners carefully chose sites to combine the best of city and country, as seen on this hand-drawn regional map. (Courtesy of the Library of Congress.)

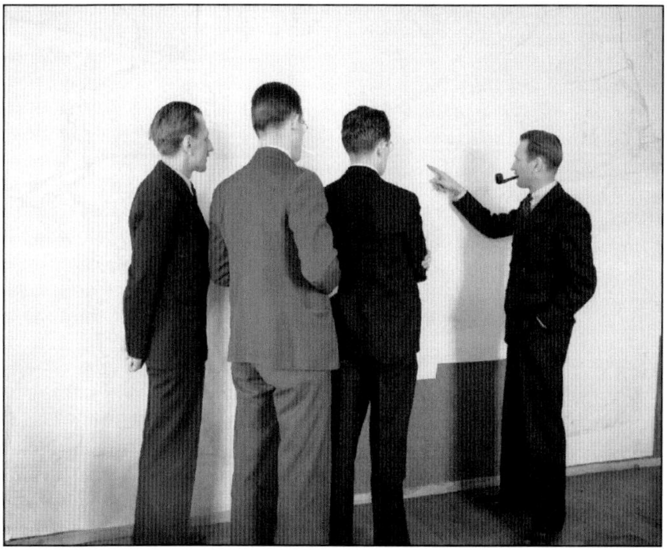

The all-star team of architects, engineers, and planners chosen to plan Greenhills included planner Justin Hartzog of the Department of the Interior, who previously worked with John Nolen on the plan of Mariemont. Also, Clarence Stein represented the RA and Hungarian-born architect Roland Wank worked represented the Tennessee Valley Authority. Here, engineers and architects study plans for the village. (Courtesy of the Library of Congress.)

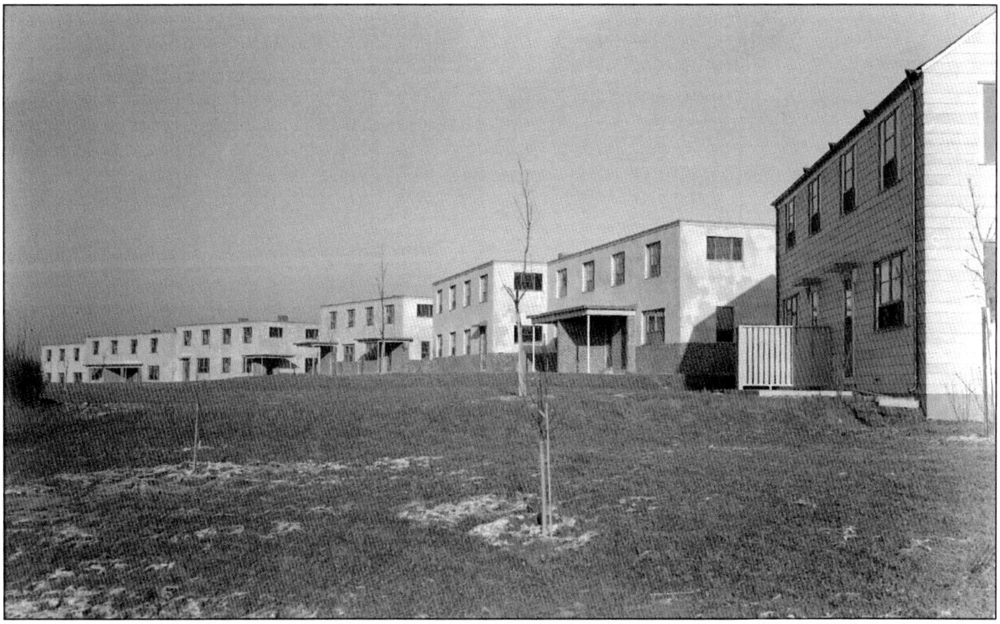

Years ahead of its time, the Greenhills plan included many features found in today's new urbanist communities, including underground utilities, neighborhood playgrounds, walkways, and a local business district incorporating mixed uses. Anticipating today's "green" architecture movement, airflow patterns were studied to site buildings for optimal cross-ventilation. Like the other greenbelt towns and urbanist towns of today, Greenhills was built more densely than typical suburban developments, with housing clustered to maximize open space. While close together, these frame townhouses shared ample green space for picnics, play space, and hanging laundry. (Courtesy of the Library of Congress.)

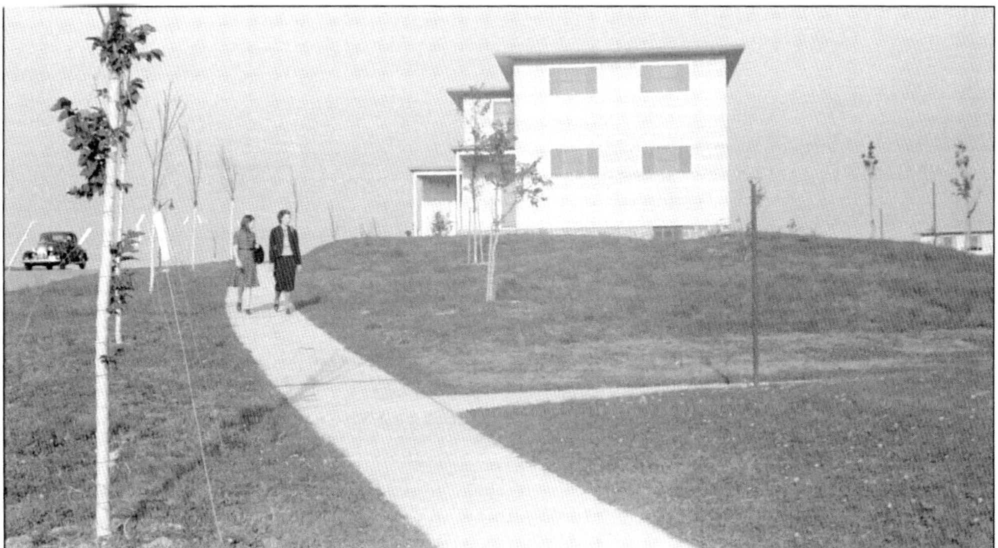

Two smartly dressed women walk on Cromwell Road through their new neighborhood. Greenhills's elegant planning is seen clearly in this post-construction view. The ground rises and falls with the natural topography, houses are carefully arranged to create a pleasing streetscape, and streets and a network of walking paths accommodate people and cars. (Courtesy of the Library of Congress.)

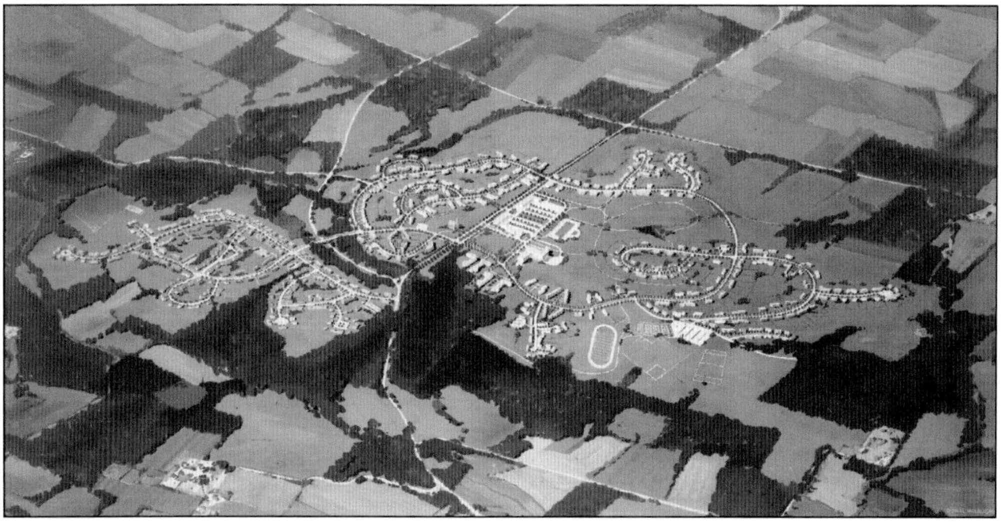

This aerial view shows how the new town was surrounded by woods and farm fields that would, according to the RA in 1938, "protect the community from being crowded by undesirable real estate and industrial developments." Nearby farmers could sell produce to village residents, families could cultivate plots of land set aside for gardens, and children could roam free in fields and forests. Houses looked out over fine stretches of green country. These ideas were not appealing to everyone, and some chose not to live in the new town because it was so far from the city. (Courtesy of the Library of Congress.)

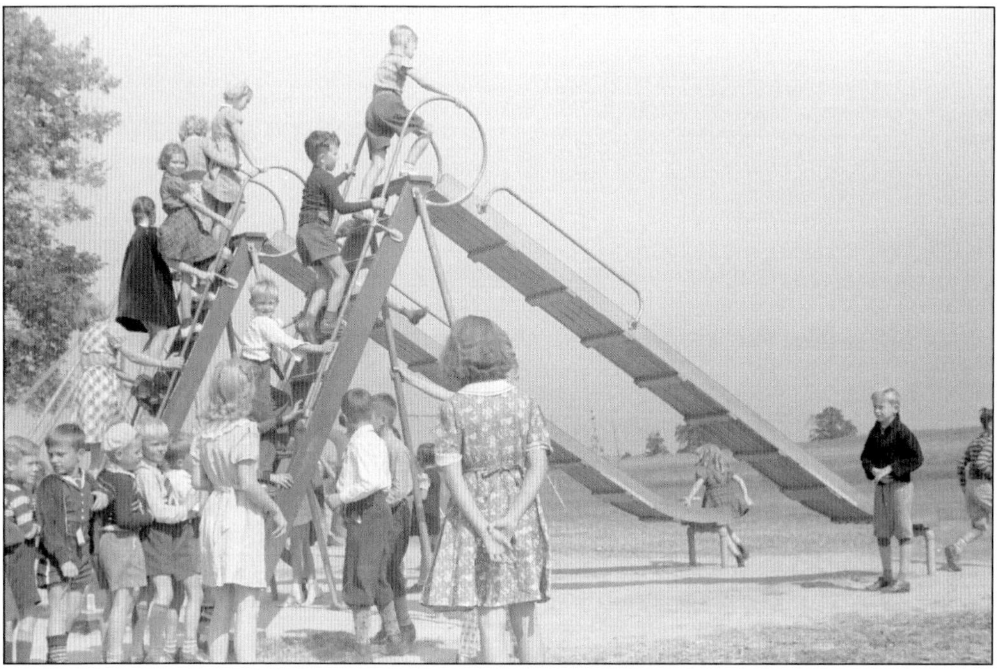

Public green spaces, both large central commons and small parks, were integral to Greenhills. The surrounding greenbelt also buffered the town from external development, limiting the incursion of unplanned development and chain stores that would compete with local businesses. The young girls and boys play on the slide in their neighborhood playground. (Courtesy of the Library of Congress.)

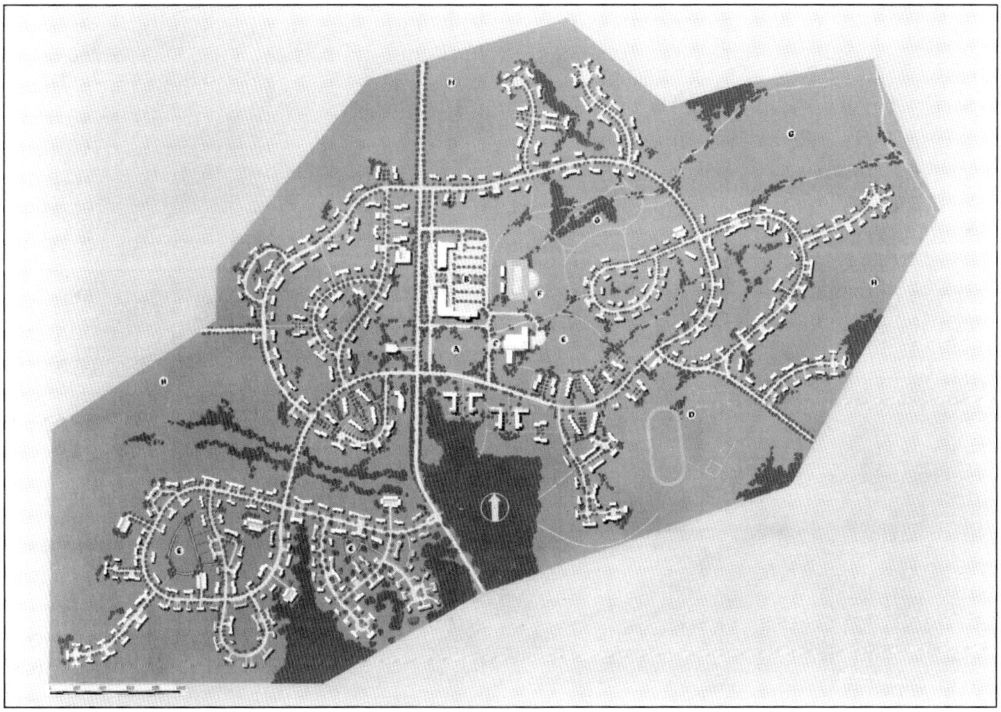

Typical of the New Deal greenbelt towns, the Greenhills plan set to balance private and communal life. Neighborhoods were quiet and green, but a variety of services were within easy walking distance. The plan reflected the influence of housing reformers and planners who believed that well-designed communities could promote civic engagement. According to Robert Fairbanks, suburban neighborhoods "should be arranged in a way to encourage a sense of community and interdependence," helping people become active, engaged citizens. This aerial view from January 1938 shows the public green spaces crossed by pathways at the center of each neighborhood. They were accessible but also safe and secluded. (Courtesy of the Library of Congress.)

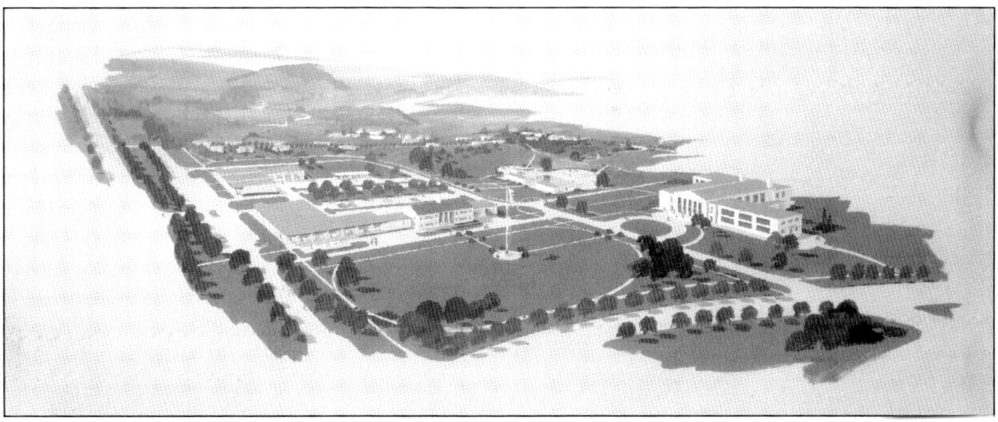

This detailed rendering depicts the village center with its public and commercial buildings. It combined churches, schools, shopping, recreational facilities, and government offices with lots of public green space. The community building fronted a broad lawn, the village's most important public space, that extended all the way to Winton Road. The modern shopping center, one of the first in the state, featured convenient front parking, a new idea in the 1930s. (Courtesy of the Library of Congress.)

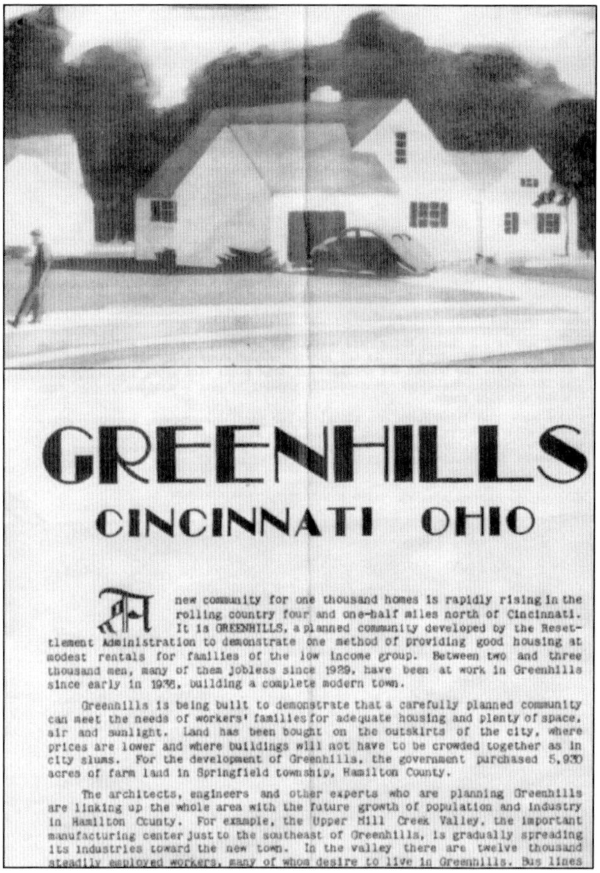

GREENHILLS

CINCINNATI OHIO

A new community for one thousand homes is rapidly rising in the rolling country four and one-half miles north of Cincinnati. It is GREENHILLS, a planned community developed by the Resettlement Administration to demonstrate one method of providing good housing at modest rentals for families of the low income group. Between two and three thousand men, many of them jobless since 1929, have been at work in Greenhills since early in 1936, building a complete modern town.

Greenhills is being built to demonstrate that a carefully planned community can meet the needs of workers' families for adequate housing and plenty of space, air and sunlight. Land has been bought on the outskirts of the city, where prices are lower and where buildings will not have to be crowded together as in city slums. For the development of Greenhills, the government purchased 5,930 acres of farm land in Springfield township, Hamilton County.

The architects, engineers and other experts who are planning Greenhills are linking up the whole area with the future growth of population and industry in Hamilton County. For example, the Upper Mill Creek Valley, the important manufacturing center just to the southeast of Greenhills, is gradually spreading its industries toward the new town. In the valley there are twelve thousand steadily employed workers, many of whom desire to live in Greenhills. Bus lines

To attract residents, the RA published an informative brochure touting the advantages of Greenhills. The cover featured an alluring image of one of the most desirable residences in the village, a single-family home beside the greenbelt, complete with a second American status symbol: a car in the driveway. (Courtesy of the Greenhills Historical Society.)

The first residents, including these strolling mothers and children, enjoyed a well-planned community with room for public and private space, adults and children, cars and pedestrians, towns and farms, and buildings and nature. (Courtesy of the Library of Congress.)

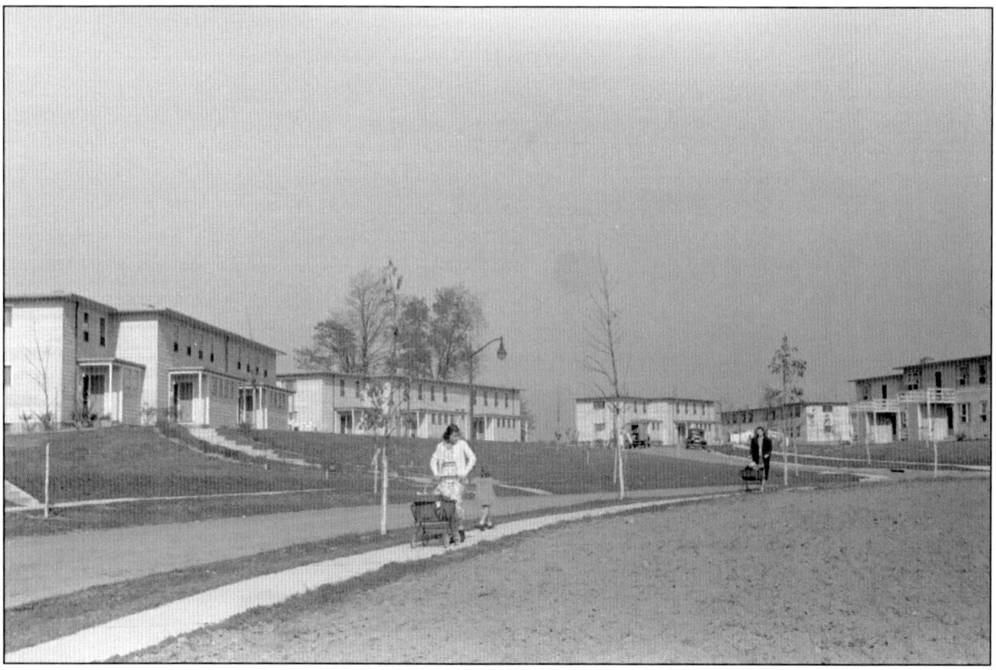

Three

The Greenbelt

To be a citizen in a democracy, a human being must be given a healthy start.
—Eleanor Roosevelt

The greenbelt feature was a pioneering design principle first introduced in 1898 by English town planner Ebenezer Howard (1850–1928). He envisioned the greenbelt as a permanent encompassing ring of open farmlands and protected natural landscape features in support of a central town core. This concept was fundamental to the design of the new greenbelt towns.

Two early communities recognized the importance of access to the natural environment through the use of smaller fixed park areas set throughout a town's interior. They were Frederick Law Olmsted's Riverside, Illinois, which was America's first planned community in 1869, and Radburn, New Jersey, which was developed in 1929. Radburn was founded specifically as a town for the motor age.

Howard had theorized that to achieve continuing health for residents, as well as sustainable growth for the town, the natural environment must constitute a larger part of a community's overall plan. An encircling greenbelt would establish a continuing food supply, and accessible parklands of vast acreage would maintain a protective incorporated town boundary, allowing for any necessary residential or industrial development in the future. Following Howard's model, the Greenhills greenbelt constituted the largest part of its development footprint with the use of small RA family farms. While satisfying the federal government's efforts to provide relief to struggling Depression-era farmers, the greenbelt lands provided a locally produced seasonal supply of fresh vegetables, fruit, meat, and dairy products, ensuring the health of the new town's citizens.

The greenbelt's set-aside open meadows and treed forests provided opportunities for physical recreation as well as calming mental respite from the busy social demands and pressures of living in the densely populated central areas. The greenbelt supported the government's social building-block goals for healthy living, which were improved nutrition, increased physical exercise, and an emerging focus on the positive psychological effects that a better environment, built through better design, could have on the mental and emotional well-being of its inhabitants. Greenhills residents would live better and more harmoniously with nature, with the greenbelt providing that vital connection.

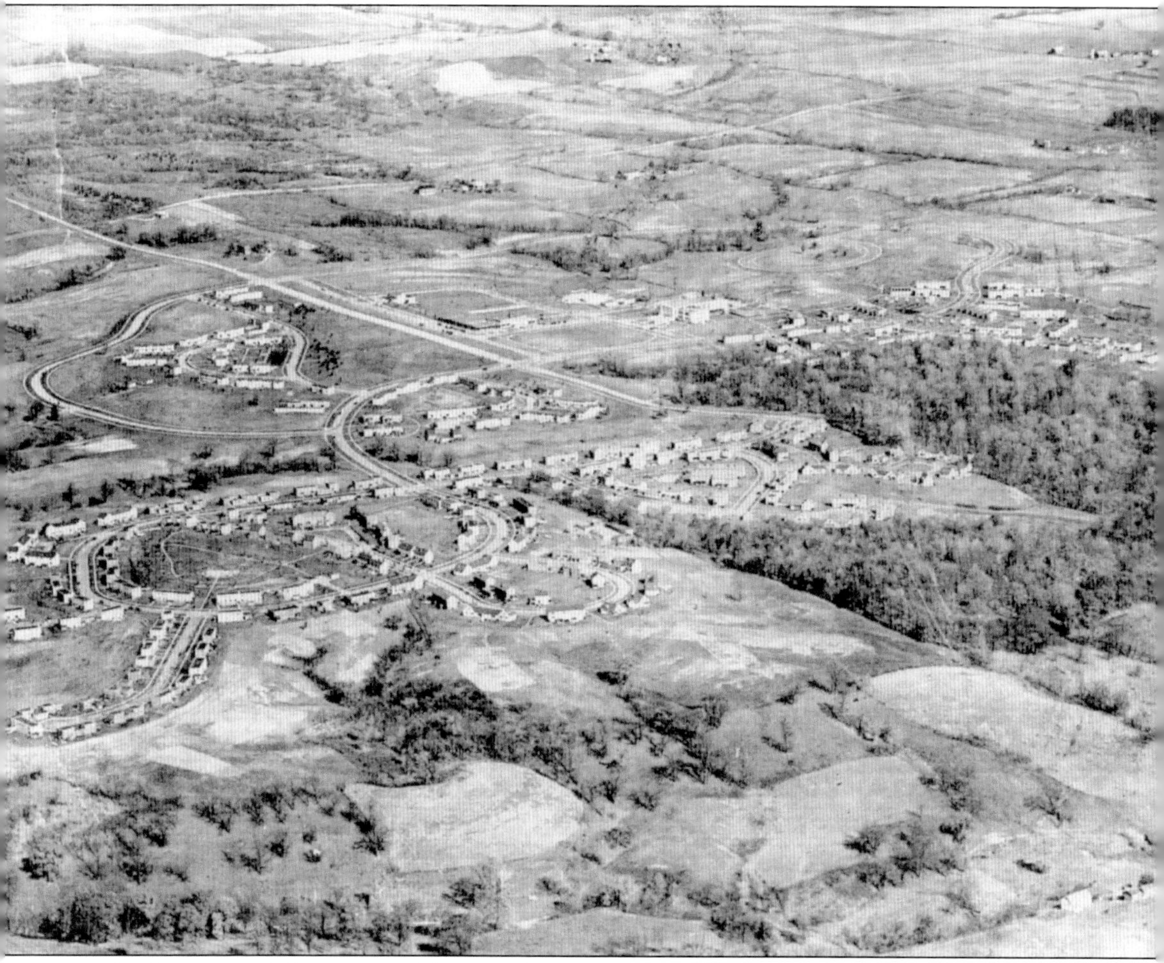

In December 1935, a group of 50 men from the roster of Cincinnati's US Employment Center, mostly locals from nearby Mount Healthy and College Hill, began clearing away brush and fence lines on what had been the Schumacher farm, just south of Cameron (now Sharon) Road. Over the next two years, the construction of Greenhills turned the surrounding countryside of open cornfields into a town. With a starting budget of $10 million for the entire Greenhills project, the federal government had been able to acquire 100 privately owned farms in Springfield Township, creating a contiguous 5,930-acre site just 15 miles north of downtown Cincinnati. The site's rolling fields and adjoining wooded ravines were subdivided, with more than 4,000 of those acres being set aside for the greenbelt area. Mostly populated with tenant farmsteads, the greenbelt lands were also used for erosion control and reforestation programs. The site's remaining acreage contained the new town and a county park. (Courtesy of the Lippmeier family.)

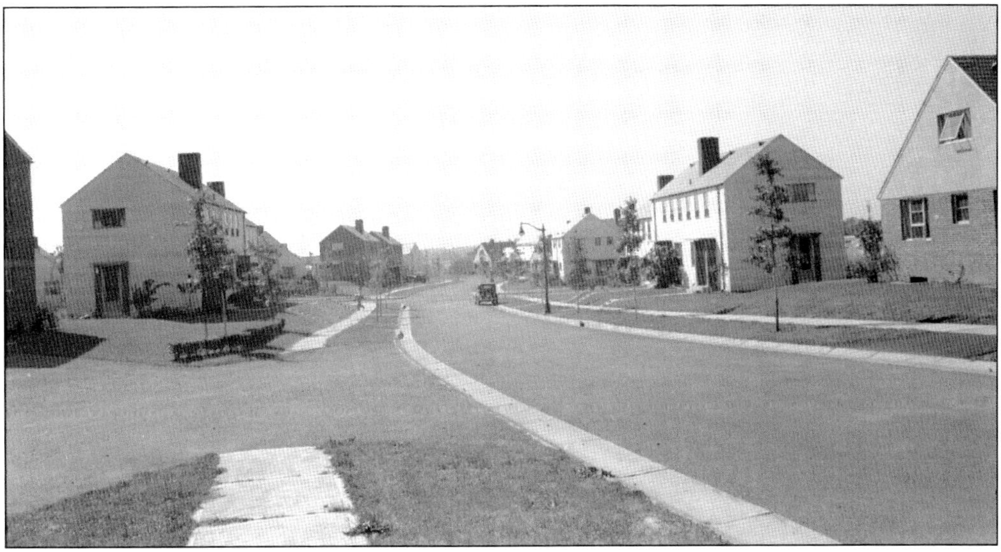

Almost 800 acres, or 1.2 square miles, were used to establish the incorporated town of Greenhills. A variety of homes were built along curving streets looping through neighborhood super blocks, each with its own centrally located pocket park. The photograph above shows Bachman Street looking toward Burnham Street. The town's core hugged the east side of Winton Road, which bisected the town as it ran northward up from Cincinnati. The early project proposal below illustrates how the inner edges of the surrounding greenbelt reached up to the backyards of the housing blocks. They provided access to recreation spaces and allotment gardens that were developed along the connecting primitive pathways running around the town's wilderness fringe. Beyond this, the greenbelt's farms and small woodlands dominated. (Above, courtesy of the Library of Congress; below, courtesy of Dan Derner.)

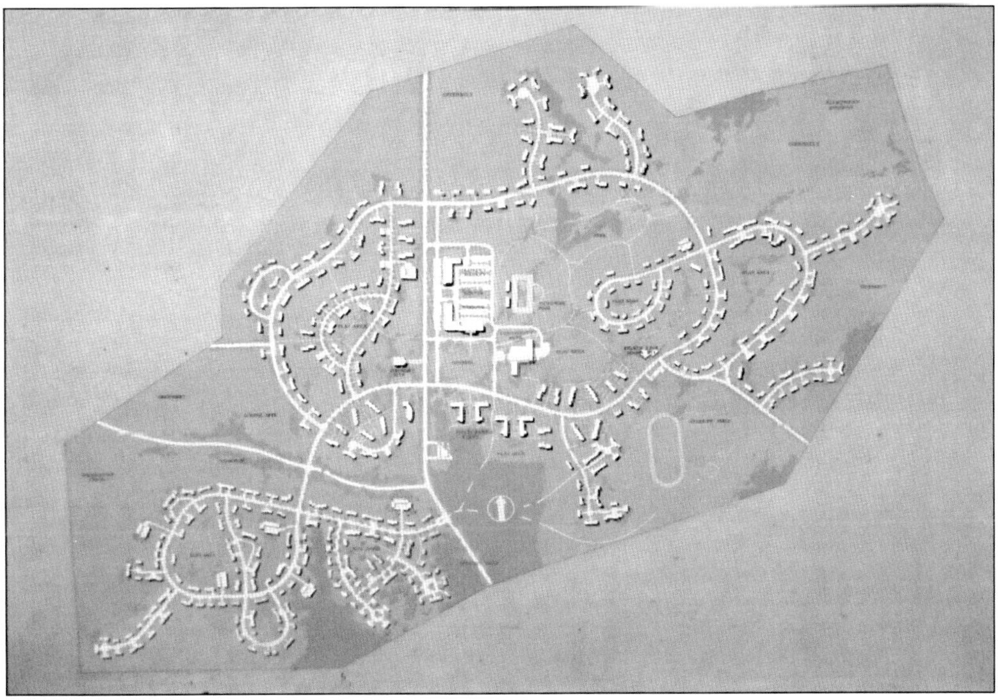

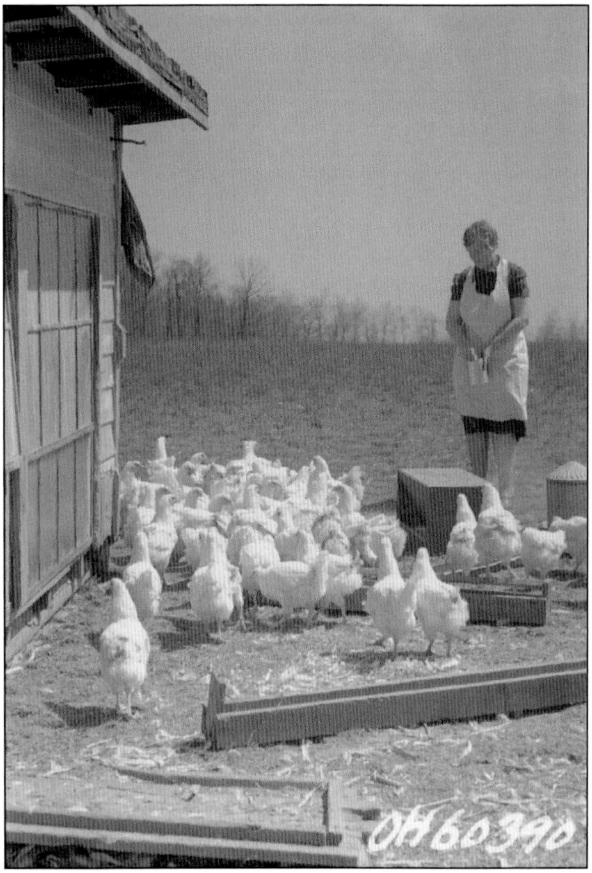

Greenhills was built on farmland depleted from generations of over-farming. The worst and smallest farms lay to the tract's southern edge, planners placed the new town and the proposed county park there. To the north, 48 farms, totaling 3,400 acres, were reorganized into 68 new tenant farmsteads under the government's control. Ranging in size from 40 acres to 204 acres, 37 of those farms were large enough to support full-time farming. The rest required a second source of family income. The largest farms were reserved for dairy production to serve Greenhills and the surrounding county. Tenant farms met strict requirements for crop types, field rotation, and fertilization. Subsidies to not produce certain crops helped to stabilize regional agricultural prices. New prefabricated farm structures like the chicken coop below, the introduction of mechanized equipment, and farm loan programs ensured success. (Both, courtesy of the Library of Congress.)

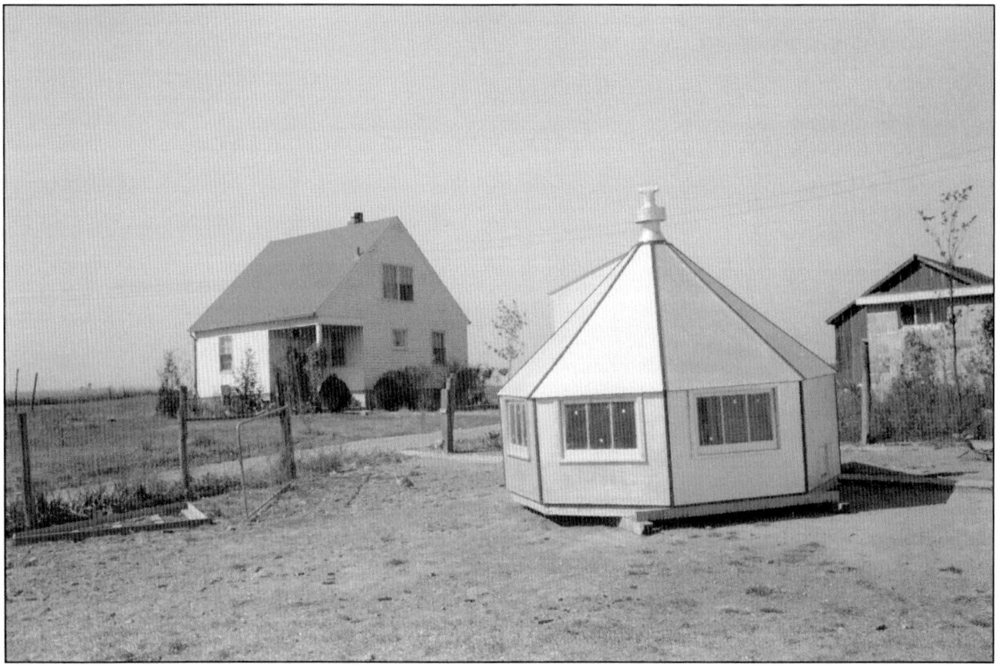

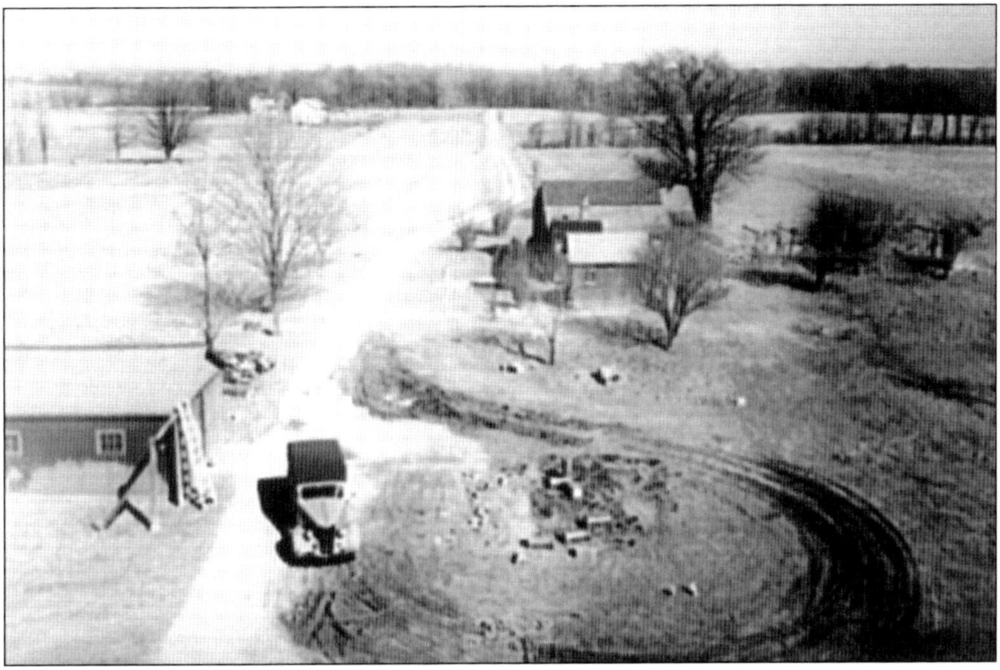

Taken in 1935 from the top of a barn, the photograph above shows farmland purchased for the Greenhills project, looking east to Winton Road, which runs perpendicularly in the distance. A stand of future greenbelt forest is in the background. The construction of Greenhills (below) commenced less than a year later. Note the same farm trees from above, now boxed for protection during the building phase. This townhome grouping—1, 2, 3, and 4 Belknap Place—got a redbrick veneer and faced a small interior roundabout's park when they were finished. Yards were shaded from the start by the trees that were thoughtfully preserved. Neighbors in the distance, along Burley Circle and Andover Road, had to wait a decade for the saplings planted along streets, in backyards, and in the adjoining pocket parks to mature. (Both, courtesy of the Library of Congress.)

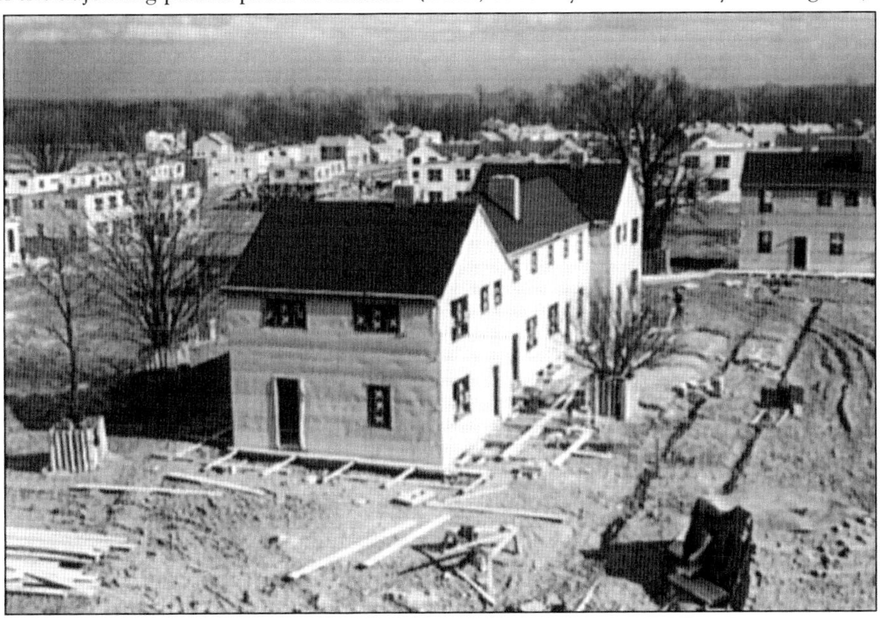

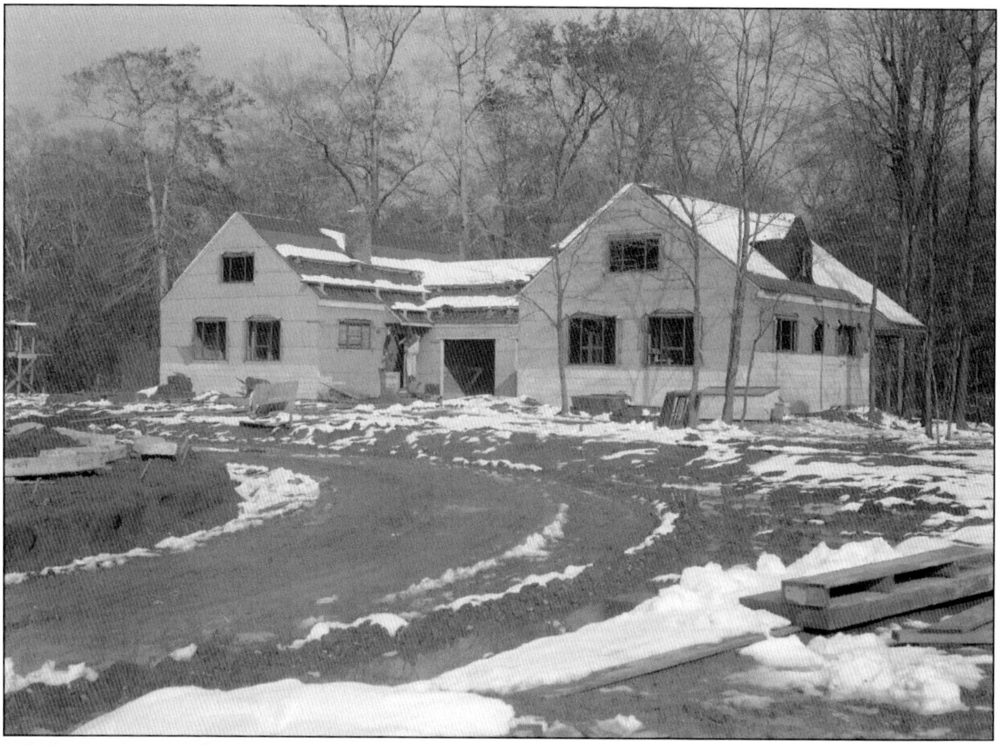

While the Greenhills project site was mostly bare farm fields, a significant stand of mature forest cut across the southern edge of the proposed town. This wooded area, with ridge tops that quickly fell into gullies and creek beds, had been an untillable wasteland to farmers, but it became a coveted asset of Greenhills architects. Planners hugged the first neighborhoods snuggly to this greenbelt feature, taking care to preserve trees surrounding the individual building sites. Above, a duplex home under construction—6 and 8 Alcott Lane—gets its cement lap siding applied. Below, only two years later, the same duplex sits prominently, illustrating the forethought of maintaining the mature greenbelt canopy. Many of the A, B, and F neighborhoods also enjoyed this southern border of forested wilds just beyond their back doors. (Both, courtesy of the Library of Congress.)

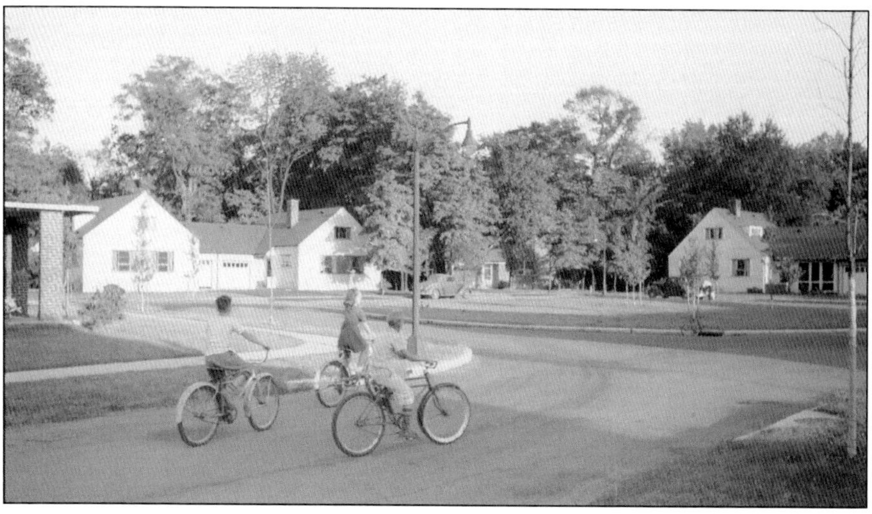

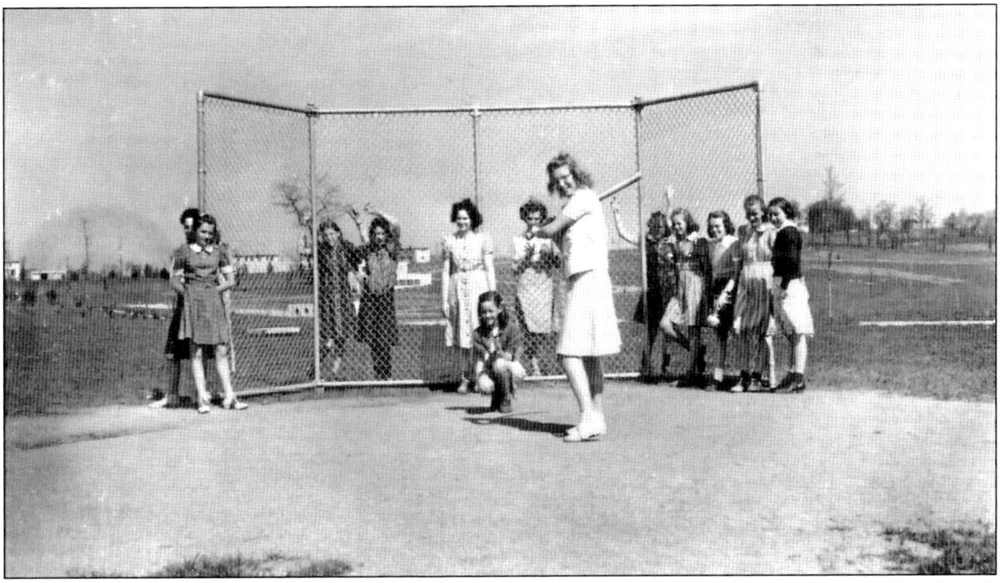

The inner edges of the greenbelt provided ample space for recreation. Easy access from neighborhoods meant that children could be let loose to play safely in parklands, meadows, and woods. Ball fields were also located across the community along this edge, but many would be lost to later infill constructions. This ball field behind the community building remains. Recently, it enjoyed the bonus of renovation with funding assistance from the Cincinnati Reds, the local National League baseball team. (Courtesy of the Greenhills Alumni Association.)

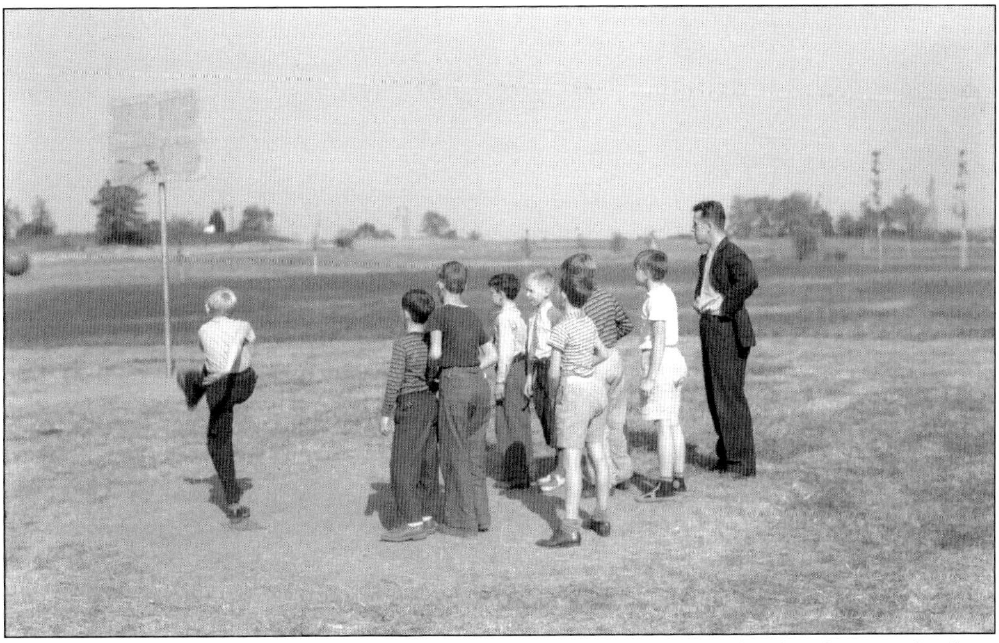

The open lands of the surrounding Resettlement Program farms made it hard to distinguish where the country ended and the yet-undeveloped town neighborhoods started. These young basketball players behind the community building are oblivious to the farms in the distance, which would soon fall to the development boom of the 1950s, when new, single-family neighborhoods—the I, J, and H sections—were built to the north and east. (Courtesy of the Library of Congress.)

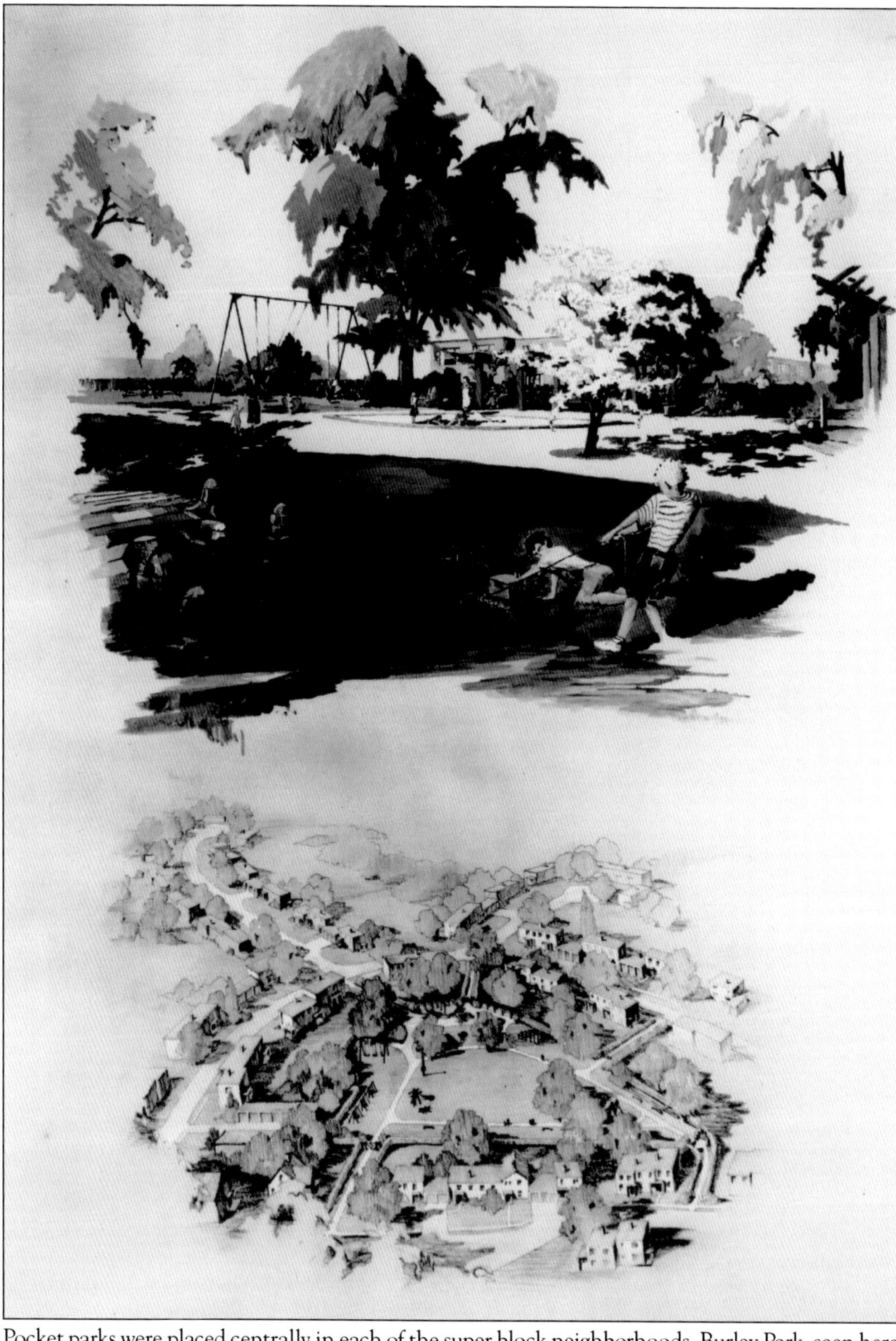

Pocket parks were placed centrally in each of the super block neighborhoods. Burley Park, seen here in early design renderings, was the largest, with a play area and open recreation fields, all encircled by interconnecting walkways dotted with benches. (Courtesy of the Library of Congress.)

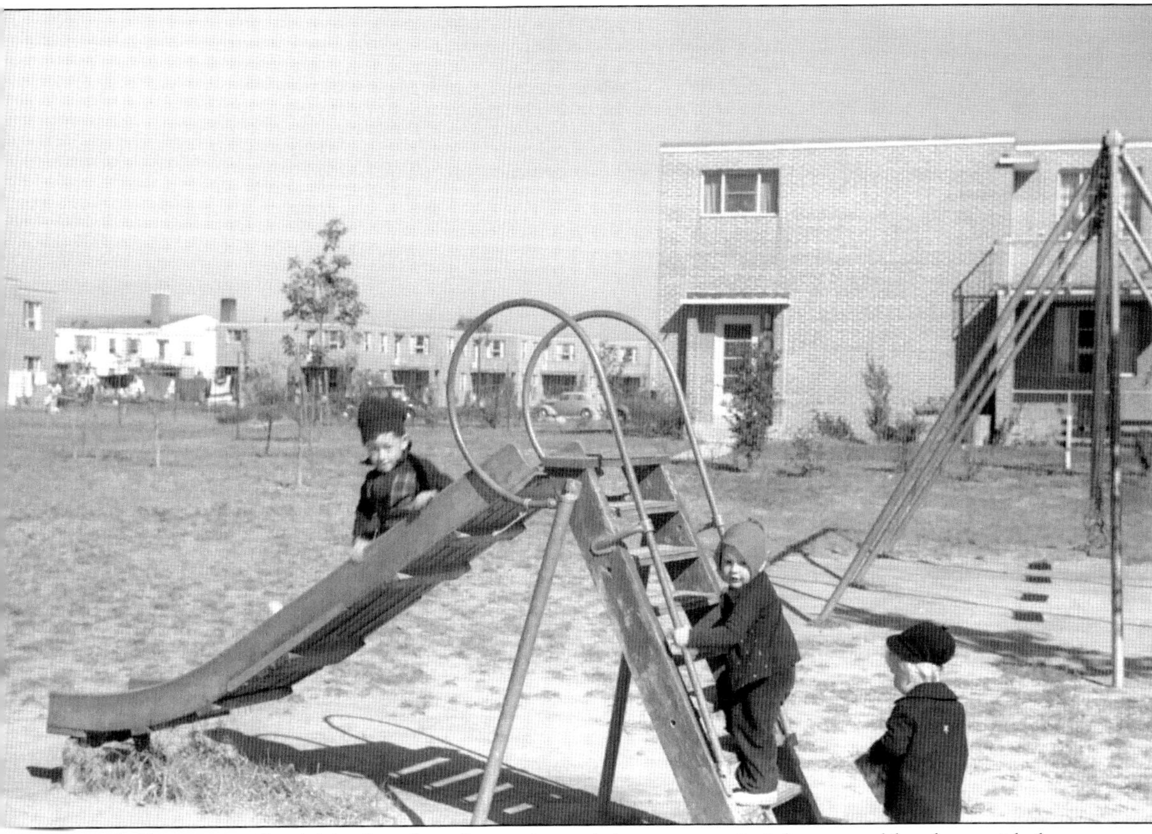

Greenhills's six small neighborhood pocket parks and the community's larger parklands provided easy access to recreation, picnicking, and gardening spaces. Ravine Park, adjacent to the pool, sloped gently down to a small creek. An amphitheater with hillside seating was proposed there, but it never materialized. Early allotment and wartime victory garden spaces lined the terrain that would later become the nine-hole community golf course. The second-largest community park, Palma Park, would be developed and straddled between the A and B neighborhoods to the south and the C and D neighborhoods to the north. Mostly flat, it would include tennis courts and multiple ball fields. Here, children play in the Foxworth Lane pocket park, safely tucked in off the small cul-de-sac. Each winter, the town's service department folded up the slides and swings in the parks so they could all be refurbished and stored away until spring. (Courtesy of the Library of Congress.)

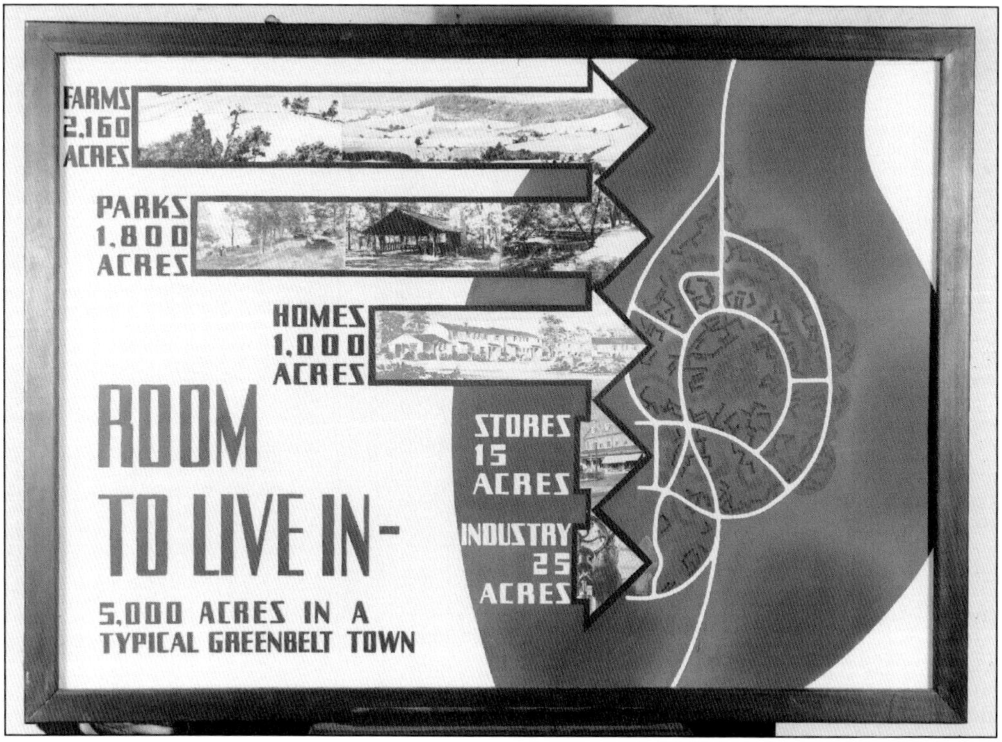

Above, an RA poster emphasizes the importance of the parks to each greenbelt town. More land was dedicated to parklands than the living, working, and shopping areas combined. That fact did not escape Jerry Stegman (third from right) and his friends, seen below in 1947. This kids' camp was built in the Chalmers Lane pocket park and provided hours of enjoyment while allowing developing minds to play at being "town designers" themselves. "We would go down on Damon Road where they were building the Cape Cods, and take the scrap wood and bent nails that had been thrown away. That's what we used to build our camp. However, someone complained about the mess, and then it was all gone," explained Stegman. (Above, courtesy of the Library of Congress; below, courtesy of Jerry Stegman.)

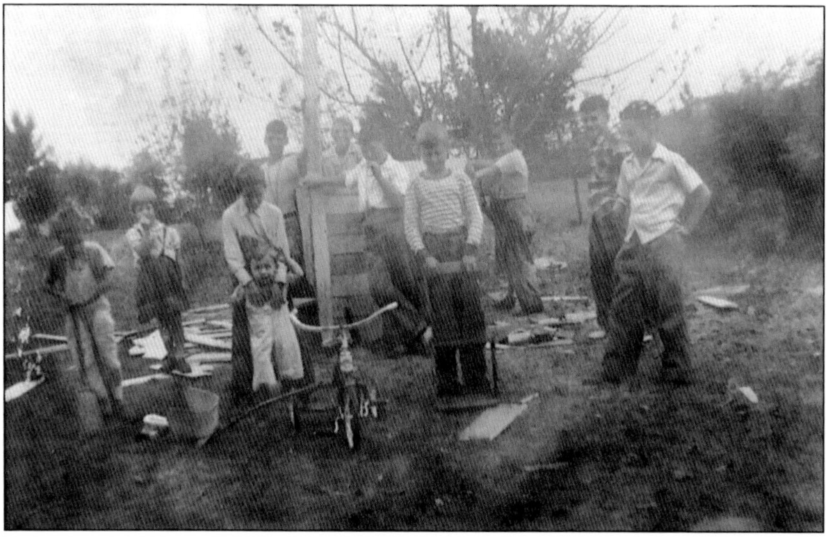

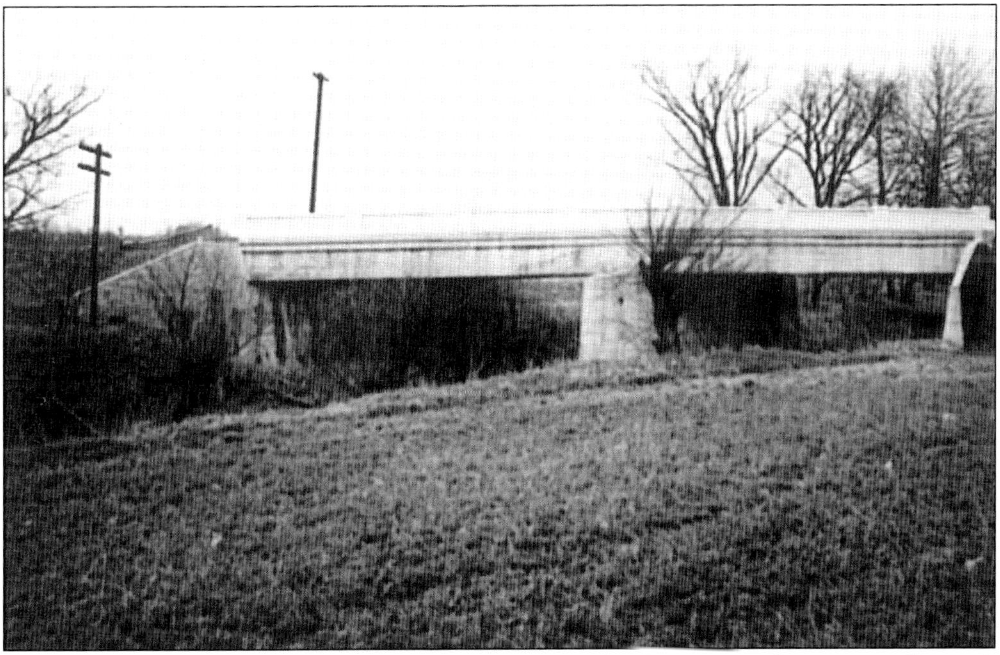

The Hamilton County Park District opened its first park, Sharon Woods, in 1932. The park district leased 905 acres of the greenbelt of Greenhills from the federal government in 1939 and called it Greenhills Park. This created the second park in Hamilton County, and Greenhills Park was later renamed Winton Woods. The new public park was going to have its own professional golf course and recreational facilities, but World War II put the project on hold. By the end of the war, another federal project, the creation of a major flood control reservoir, had presented itself on the farmlands encircling Greenhills. Above, the Winton Road Bridge spans Mill Creek, flowing within the proposed park areas. (Courtesy of the Lippmeier family.)

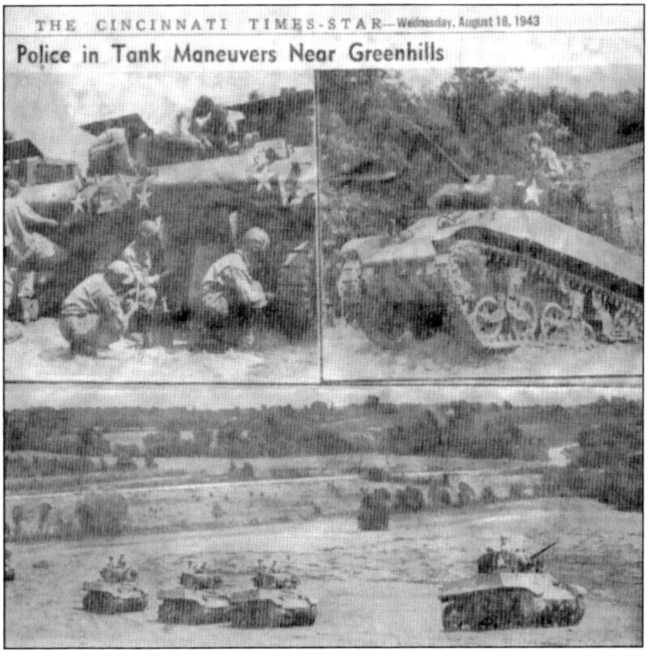

Here, the 737th Military Police Battalion trains in tank driving in 1943 on the park grounds. (Courtesy of the *Cincinnati Times Star*.)

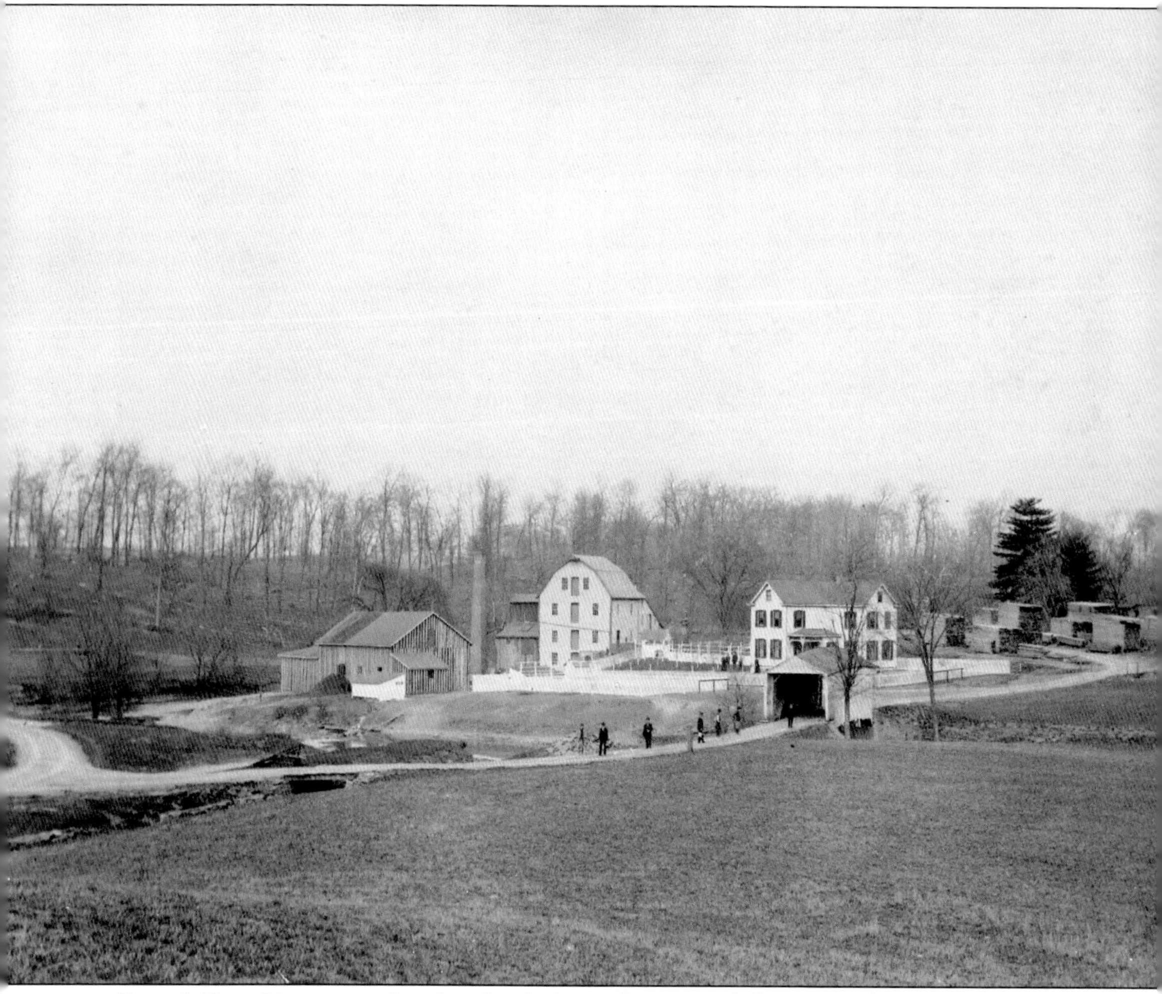

Greenhills and its surrounding farmlands drained into wooded ravines, which emptied into Mill Creek. This creek flowed eastward from Mount Healthy, crossing under the Winton Road Bridge and snaking through Greenhills's southern greenbelt area. It eventually drained into the Ohio River just west of the city, in Cincinnati's industrial bottomlands. Mill Creek got its name from the sawmill built on its banks in 1825 by Jediah Hill, pictured here, in nearby Mount Healthy. This working complex also gave Mill Road and Covered Bridge Road their names. Converted to a gristmill in 1898 due to decreasing timber resources, the mill continued to produce coarse flour and feed for area farmers, including Greenhills's original tenant farmers, up until its purchase by the Army Corps of Engineers in 1950. Today, the creek and its tributaries still flow eastward toward Greenhills, now emptying into the West Fork Lake Flood Control Reservoir, known as Winton Woods Lake. The mill's covered bridge, rebuilt twice, is listed in the National Register of Historic Places. (Courtesy of the Library of Congress.)

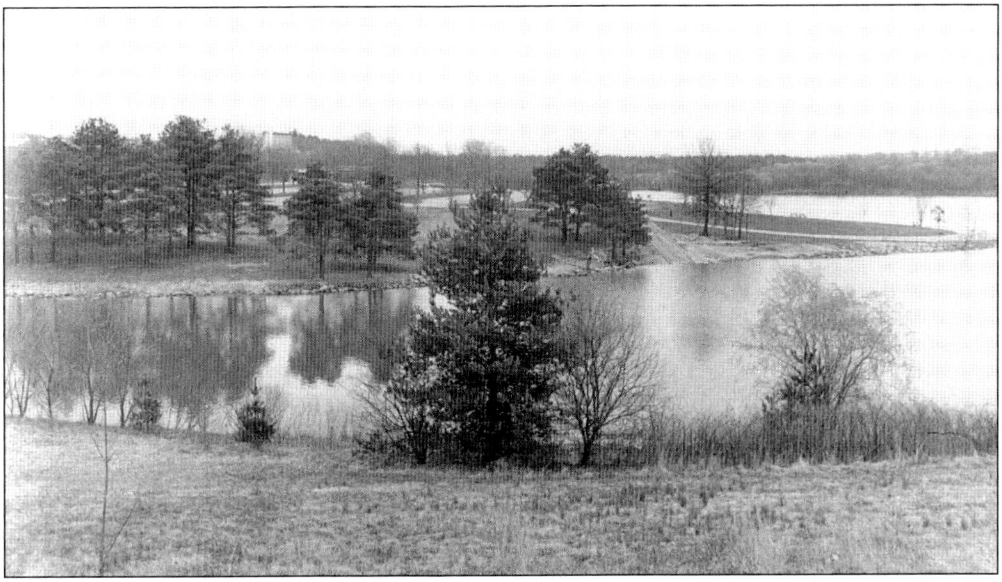

In January 1937, Greenhills was in its final construction phase when the Ohio River flooded to unprecedented heights. Before the floodwaters receded, Cincinnati's industrial basin was devastated by exploding oil tank fires. Previous floods had caused Pres. Franklin D. Roosevelt to sign legislation ordering the Army Corps of Engineers to begin constructing protection for the Ohio and other major rivers. A barrier dam soon protected Cincinnati's bottomlands from Ohio river surges. It was not until 1951, with the construction of the West Fork Mill Creek Reservoir in Greenhills's southern greenbelt, that the city's industrial basin was guarded from additional flooding coming down the countryside via the Mill Creek. The reservoir (above), held by an earthen dam 1,100 feet long and 100 feet high (below), created a 183-acre lake that became the recreational center of the new Winton Woods Park. (Above, courtesy of the Lippmeier family, below, courtesy of Deborah J. Tilford-Mills.)

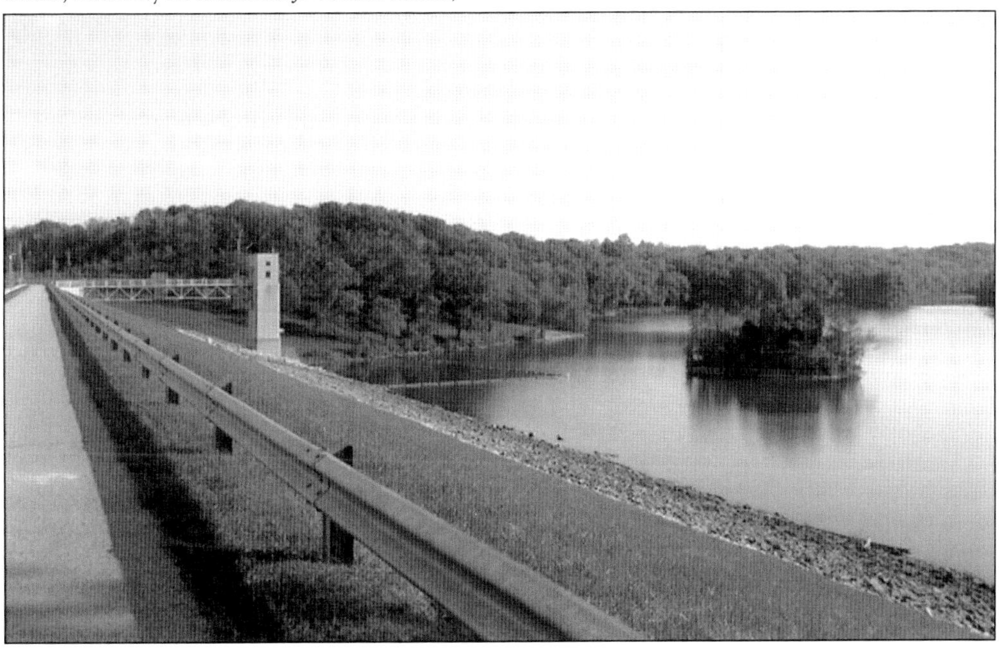

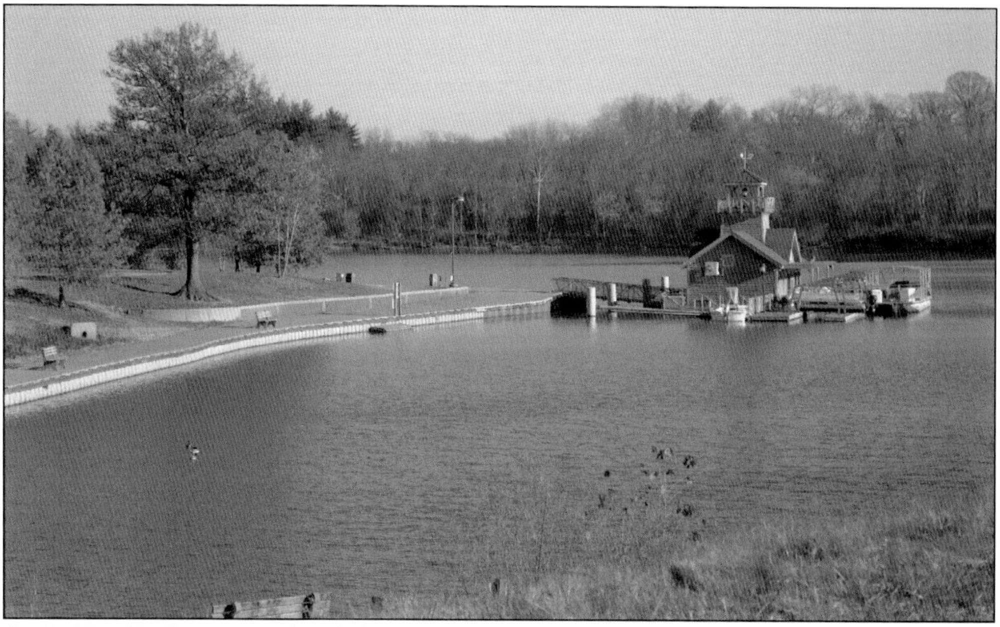

As the New Deal programs closed, the federal government divested itself of the Greenhills project, and the greenbelt was gradually split apart. In 1949, the federal government transferred 1,000 acres of greenbelt to the Army Corps of Engineers for the reservoir project. Those lands were then leased to the county's park district for recreational use. With boating and fishing facilities developed, in addition to the camping, archery, and golfing features already in place, Winton Woods became the county's second-largest public park. The rural tenant farms of the greenbelt did not fare as well when the government sold the majority of the Greenhills greenbelt, the 3,400-acre northern tract, to private developers, who then created the competing city of Forest Park. In addition to losing their farming income, many farmers were evicted from their homes for the construction of the new city. (Above, courtesy of Paul Richardson; below, courtesy of the Library of Congress.)

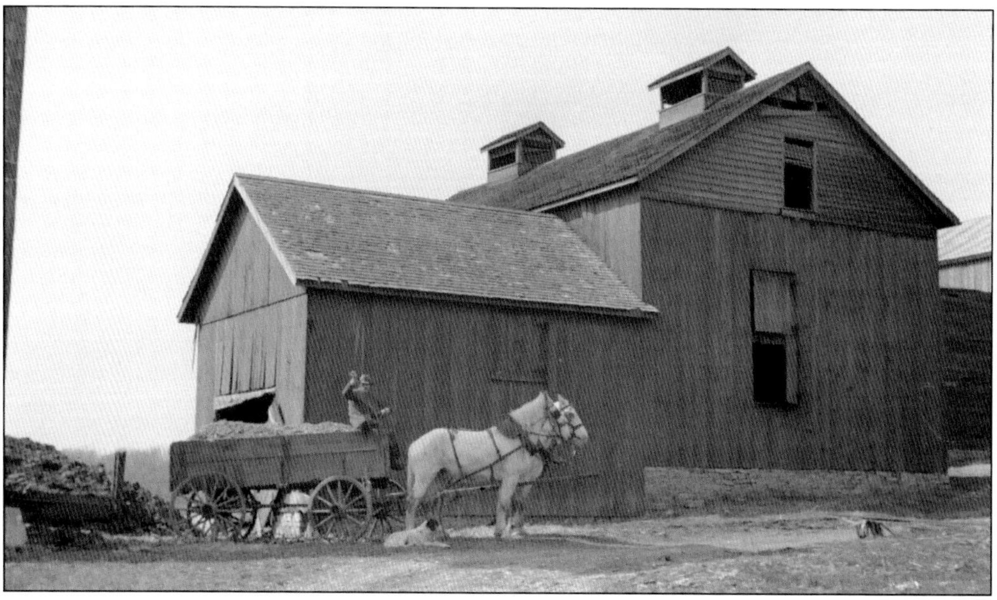

Four

The Buildings

Each material has its specific characteristics which we must understand if we want to use it . . . This is no less true of steel and concrete [than of wood, brick, and stone]. We must remember that everything depends on how we use a material, not on the material itself . . . New Materials are not necessarily superior. Each material is only what we make of it . . . We must be as familiar with the functions of our buildings as with our materials. We must learn what a building can be, what it should be, and also what it must not be . . . And just as we acquaint ourselves with materials, just as we must understand functions, so we must become familiar with the psychological and spiritual factors of our day. No cultural activity is possible otherwise; for we are dependent on the spirit of our time.

—Ludwig Mies van der Rohe, from his inaugural address at the Illinois Institute of Technology, 1938

When contemplating the site for Greenhills, the federal government had carefully surveyed the bucolic countryside just north of Cincinnati. Considerations regarding typography, seasonal wind, rain, sunlight patterns, existing vistas, and natural features played important parts in the design of the town's residential housing units and the community's public buildings. The configuration and placement of buildings along streets and aside parks and the greenbelt were artfully orchestrated to take advantage of the natural elements, adding to the daily enjoyment and service to the new town's inhabitants.

Only a few of the buildings standing in 1935 remained to be integrated into the new greenbelt town, with many of them utilized for field offices or materials storage during the town's construction. The design of Greenhills's new buildings incorporated features of the past and future. The comfortably familiar Colonial Revival style; the sleek, curving Moderne style; and the emerging austere International style of architecture stood side by side. This gave the town a sense of having been developed over time rather than just having been plopped down anew. The broad range of architectural styles first played upon the pleasing and accepted village attributes of quaint English garden cities. Over time, they strategically incorporated many of the progressive features already being used in Europe's most successful new housing developments.

Concrete block, redbrick, stucco, and the innovative Transite, a fireproof cement lap siding, were the palette of materials available to establish a building's type and character. A kit of standardized steel metal windows, in awning, hopper, and fixed panel styles, combined with lighted exterior doors, pipe railing systems, unique light fixtures, and roofing options to bring variety to the neighborhood while still creating a unified spirit.

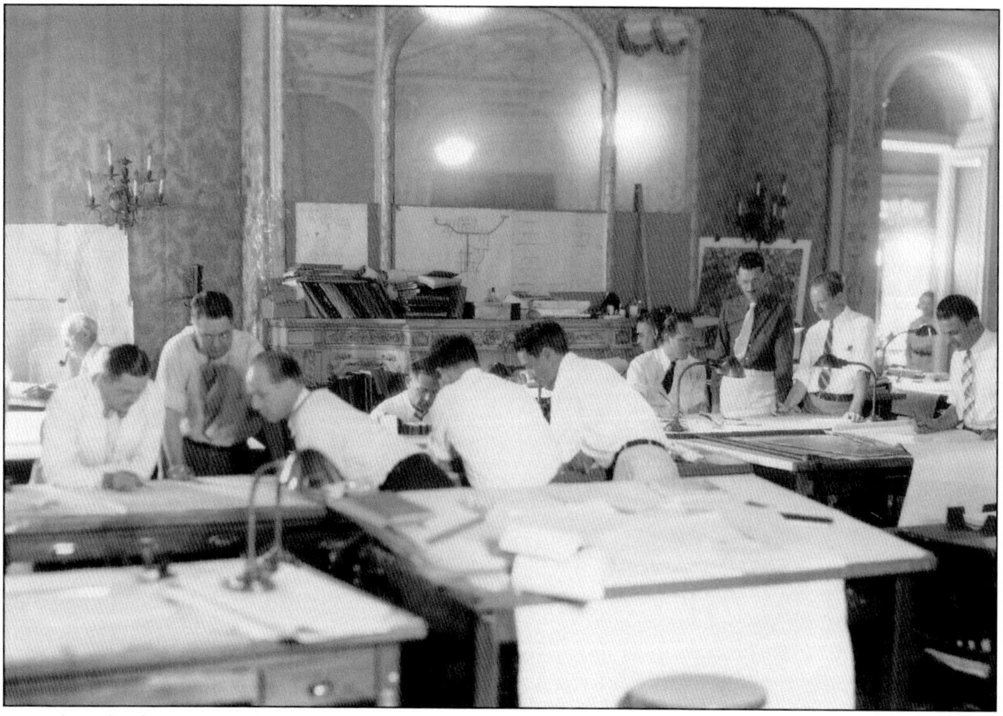

It took only three years for the Greenhills project to go from the Resettlement Administration's drafting boards in Washington, DC, (above) to the beautiful modern town whose first residents moved in on April 1, 1938. The country's best architects, planners, landscape designers, and civil engineers came together, creating three unified teams to design the greenbelt towns. Each town had its own unique plan and buildings presenting an integrated, inseparable whole. The buildings and the envisioned life that would be lived within them became just as dependent on the good design of the individual structures as they were on their particular placement upon the land. Detailed surveys and topographical studies of the sites combined with architectural drawings, models (below), and building materials carefully selected for durability and aesthetics to create the best possible outcome. (Both, courtesy of the Library of Congress.)

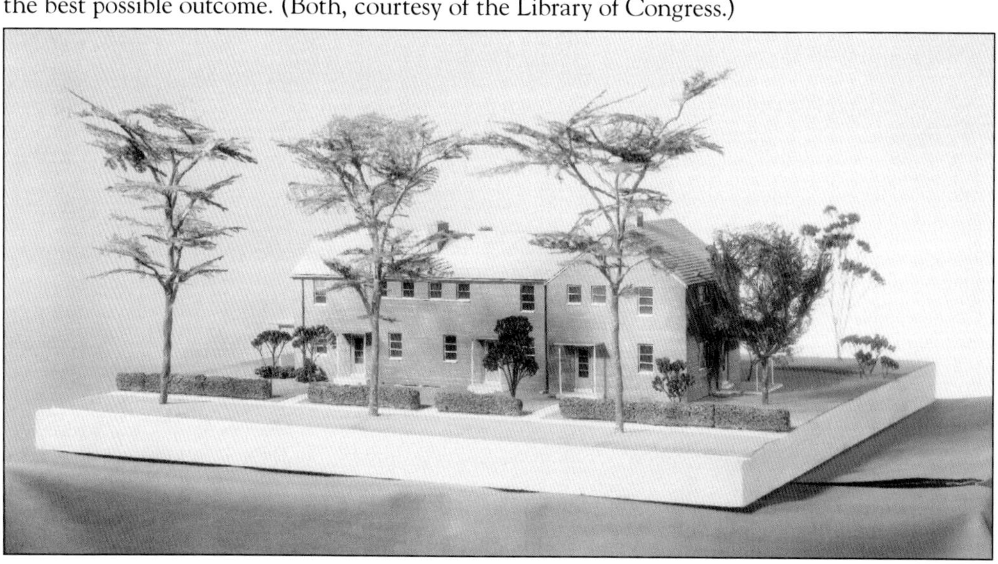

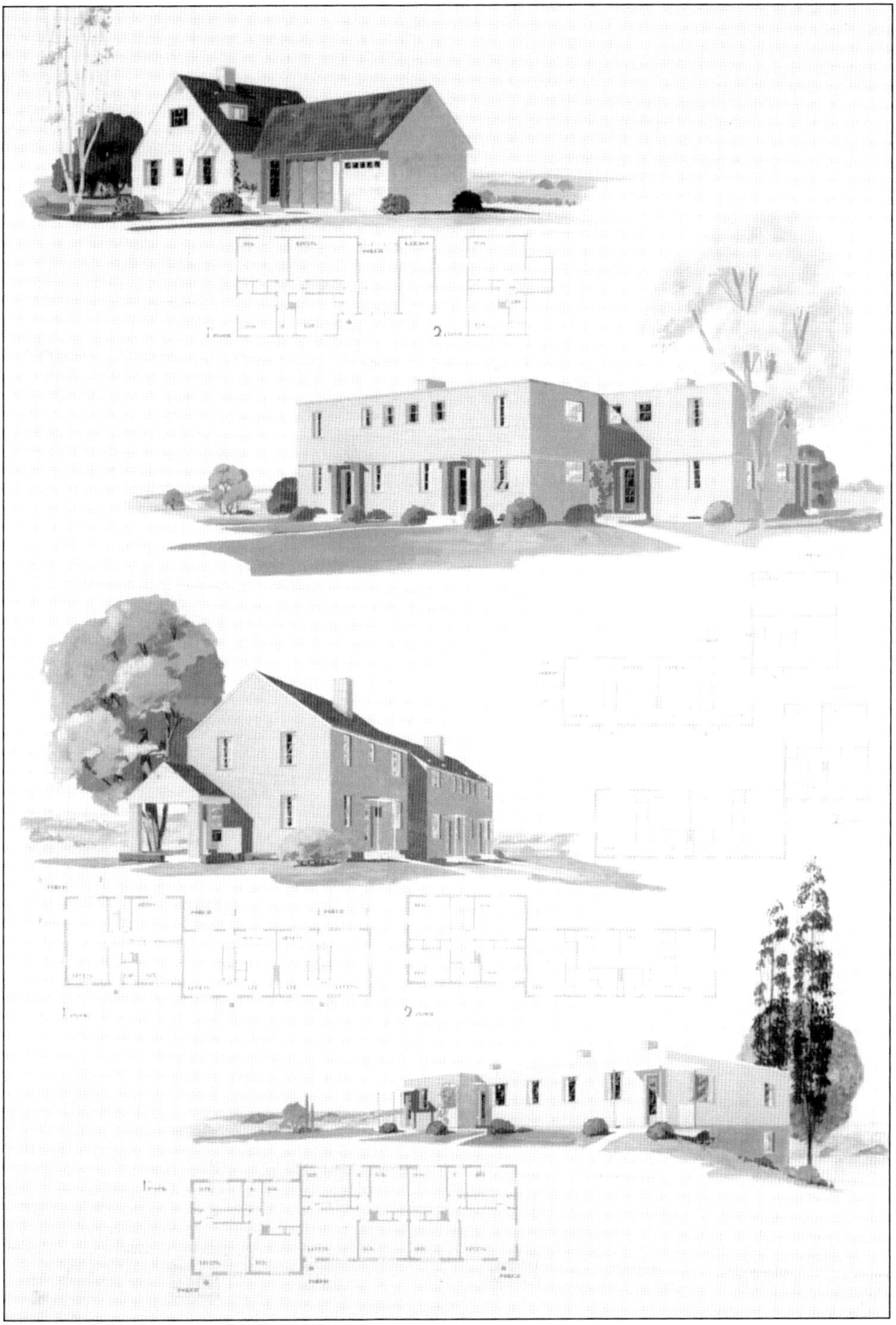

Homes in Greenhills offered something for every family size or personal preference of architectural style. Traditional single-family and townhome groupings intermingled seamlessly with the more streamlined, modern, flat-roofed units that predominated the new town project. (Courtesy of the Library of Congress.)

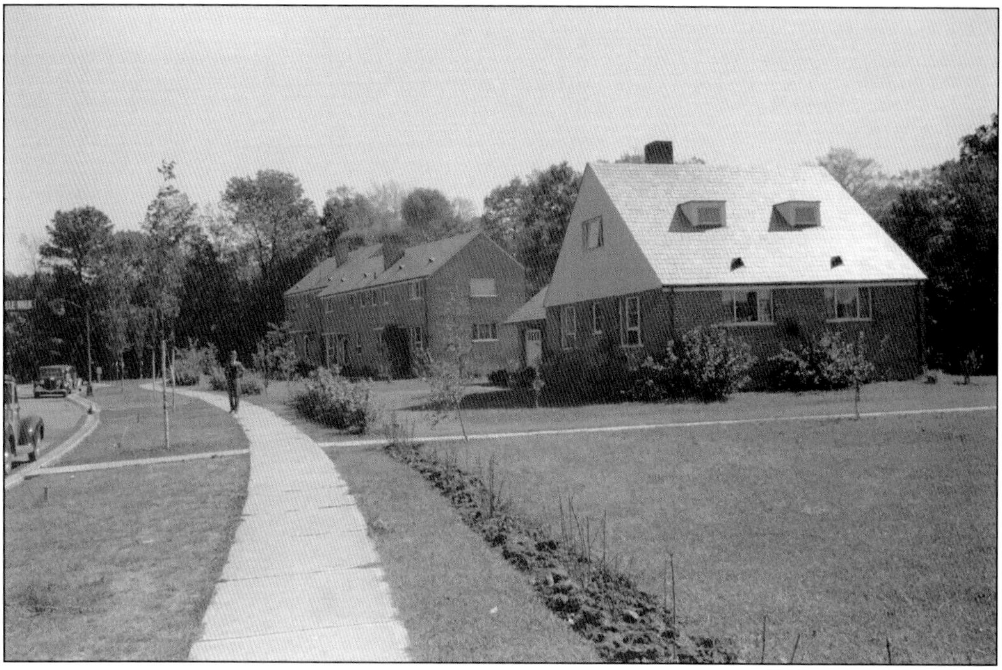

Architects carefully started construction with the project's more traditional houses and townhome groupings. The RA's decision to build the project outside Cincinnati had met local opposition. To calm fears about the project's purpose, construction began in the A and B neighborhoods, with homes that brought to mind the region's beloved English Tudor and cottage styles. Seen here is the entrance into Greenhills on Andover Road. (Courtesy of the Library of Congress.)

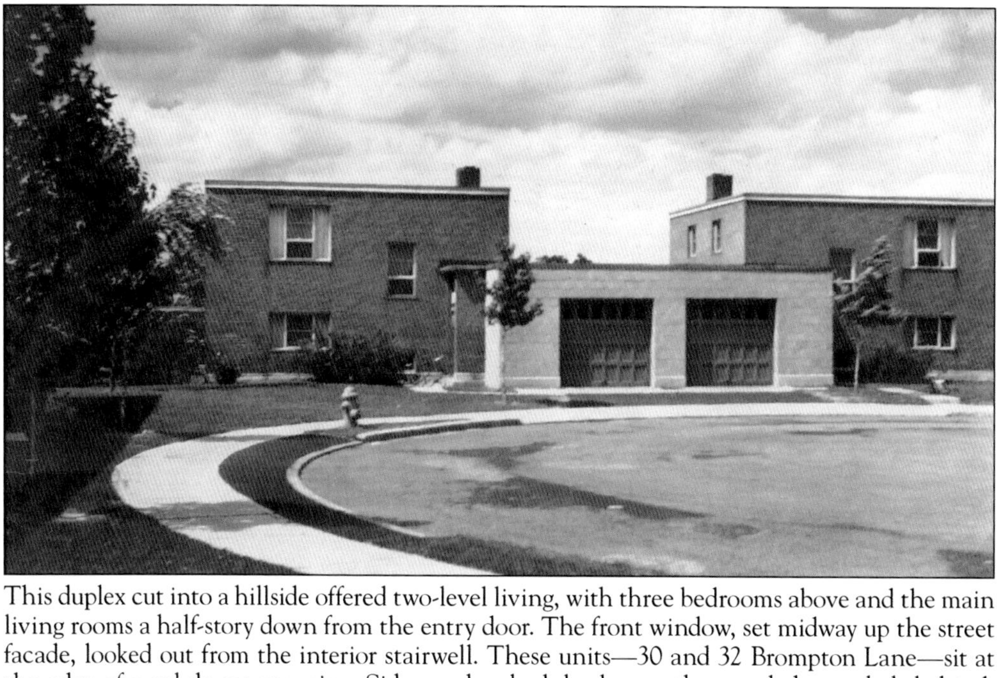

This duplex cut into a hillside offered two-level living, with three bedrooms above and the main living rooms a half-story down from the entry door. The front window, set midway up the street facade, looked out from the interior stairwell. These units—30 and 32 Brompton Lane—sit at the edge of a cul-de-sac grouping. Side porches look back over the wooded greenbelt behind. (Courtesy of the Palma family.)

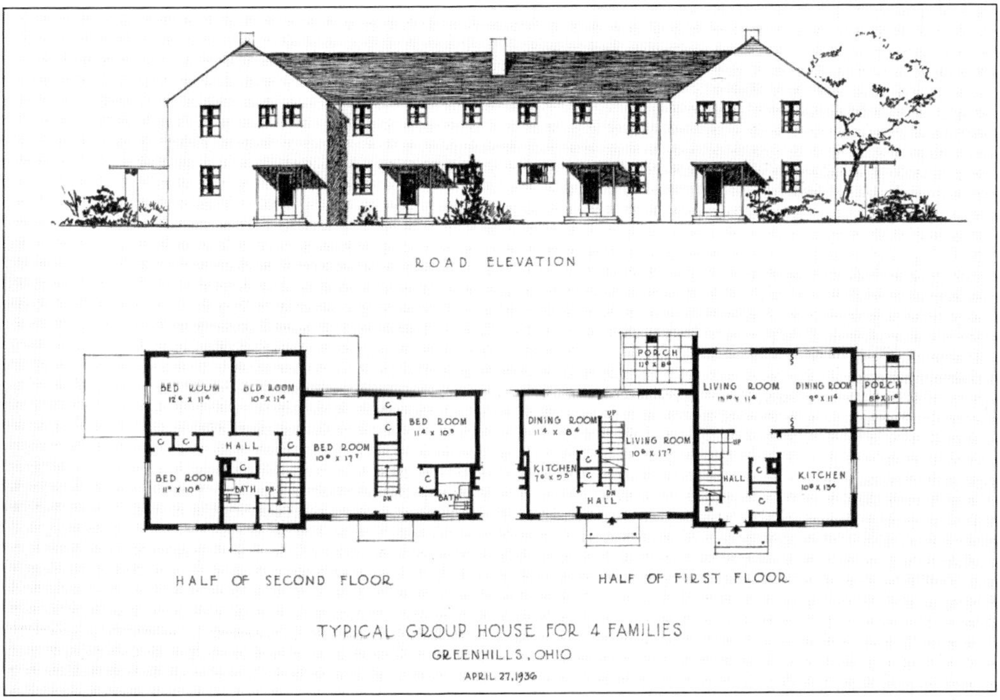

Architects developed floor plans and elevation drawings for all the different housing styles. These were then reproduced with a roofline changed from pitched to flat or exterior veneers manipulated with combinations of lap siding, brick, or stucco. This allowed the designers to create a variety of looks from the same floor plan, keeping streetscapes free from the repetitive monotony that plagued older Cincinnati neighborhoods. Note that the plan above is a mix of two- and three-bedroom units, giving the architects freedom to vary even the family mix within buildings. The plan below, being built on Avenell Lane, became a five-unit dwelling with a mix of brick and cement lap sided units and heavier brick wall porch supports. Groupings of two- and three-bedroom units were also built in the same neighborhood, some fully bricked. (Above, courtesy of the Library of Congress; below, courtesy of the Village of Greenhills.)

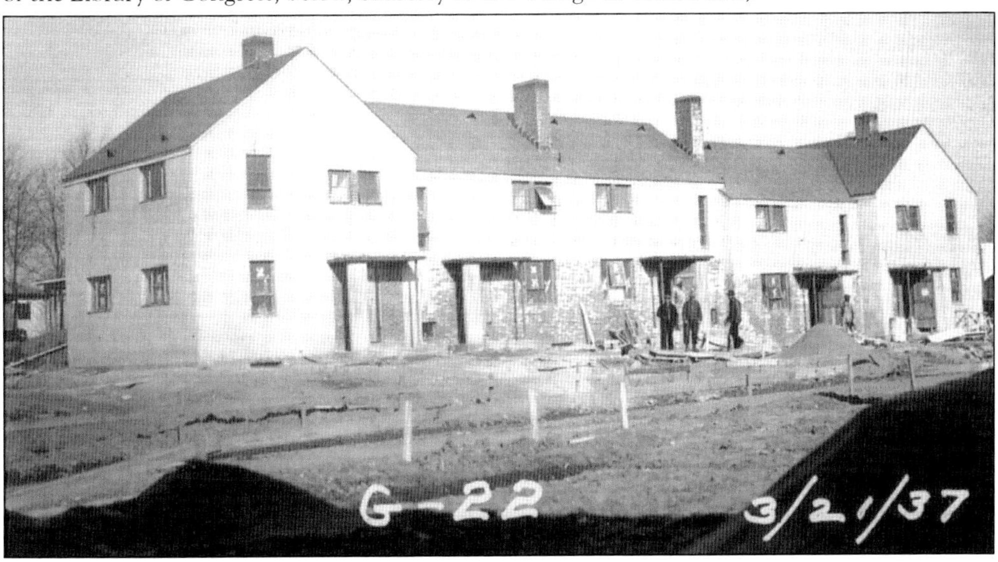

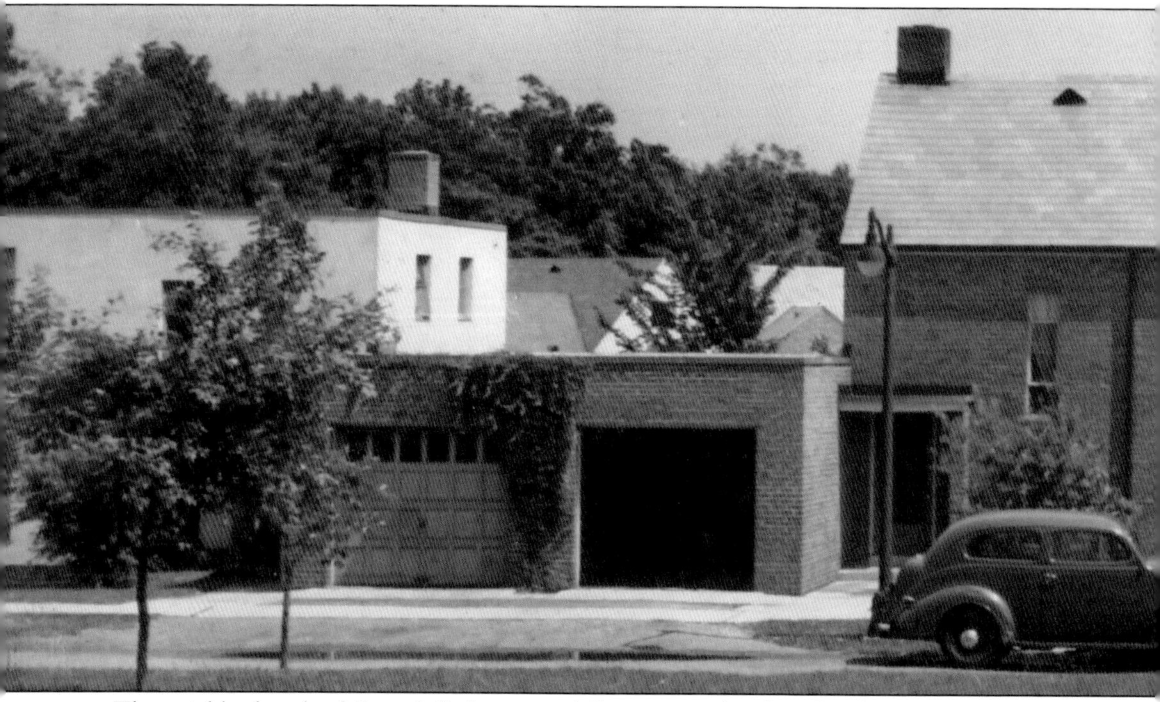

The neighborhoods of Greenhills have carefully integrated styles of architecture, creating both visual interest and a sense of timelessness. Traditional Colonial Revival townhomes with brick facades and slate-shingled pitched roofs sit bookended by more modern homes with stucco exteriors that corner up and over crisply into flat roofs. Above, the fronts of 14, 16, 18, and 20 Ashby Street include garages undulating forward, setting a rhythmic pattern to the streetscape. The image

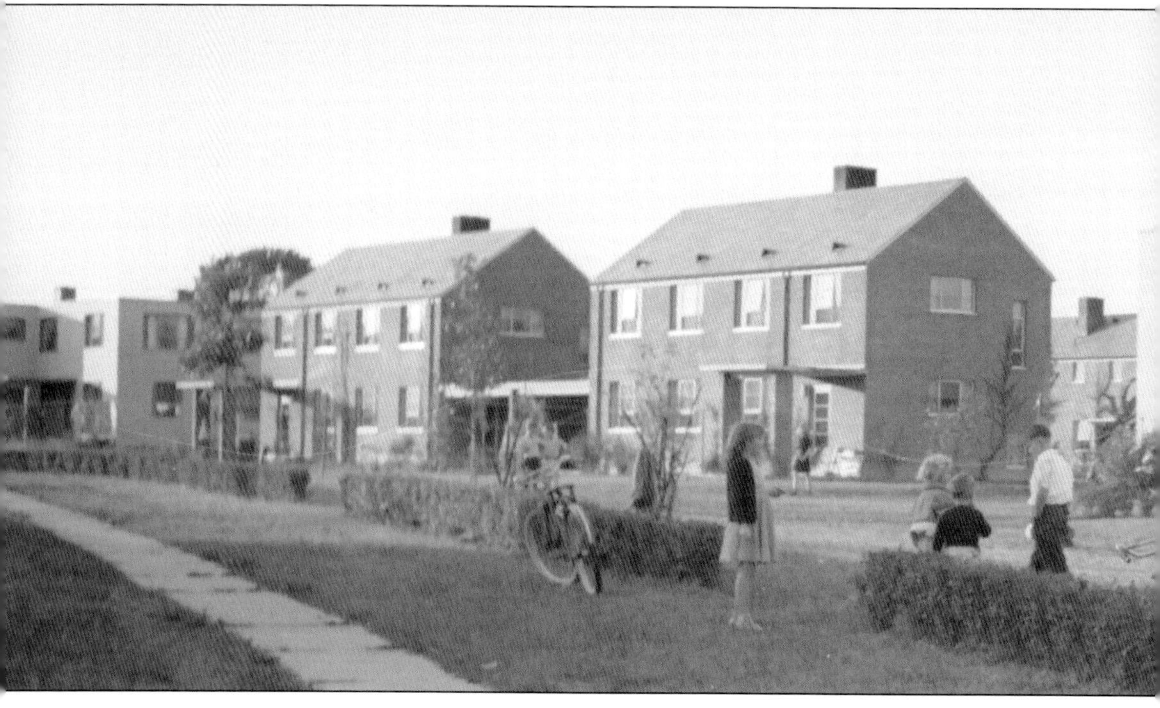

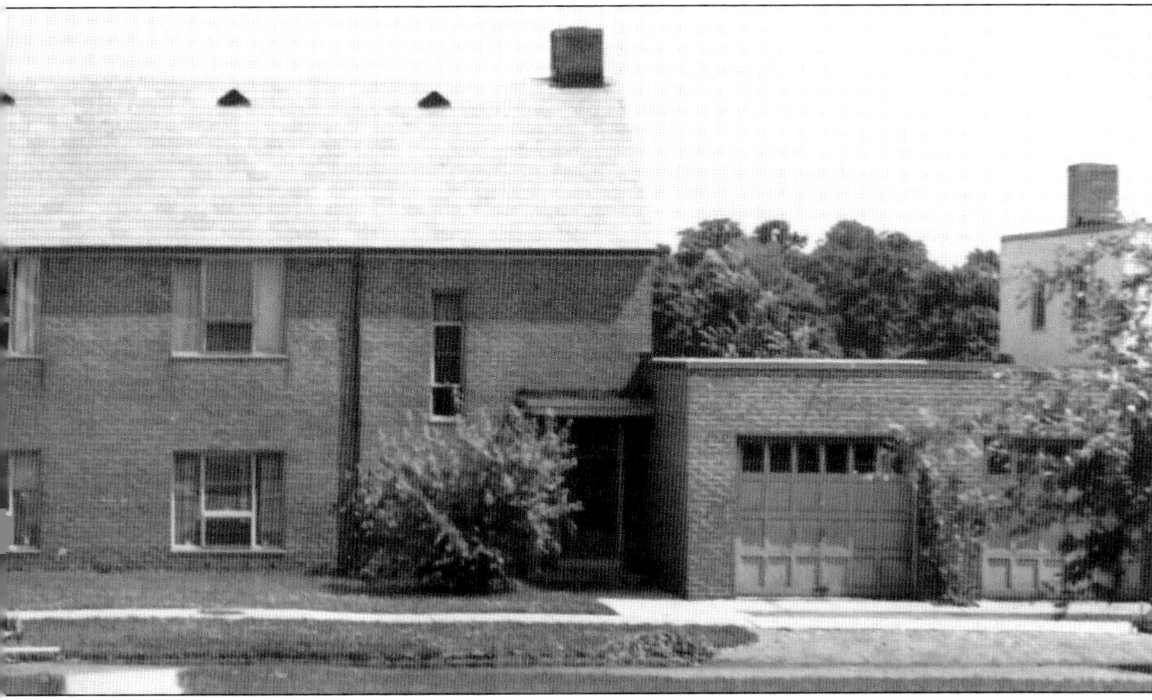

below includes 13, 15, and 17 Ashby Street and shows the backs of homes. Their covered porches stepped out towards the pocket park tucked beyond the super block's interior pathway, seen at left. Even though buildings were made of different materials in different architectural styles, the flat roofs of the porches and garages unified the elements. (Above, courtesy of the Lippmeier family; below, courtesy of the Library of Congress.)

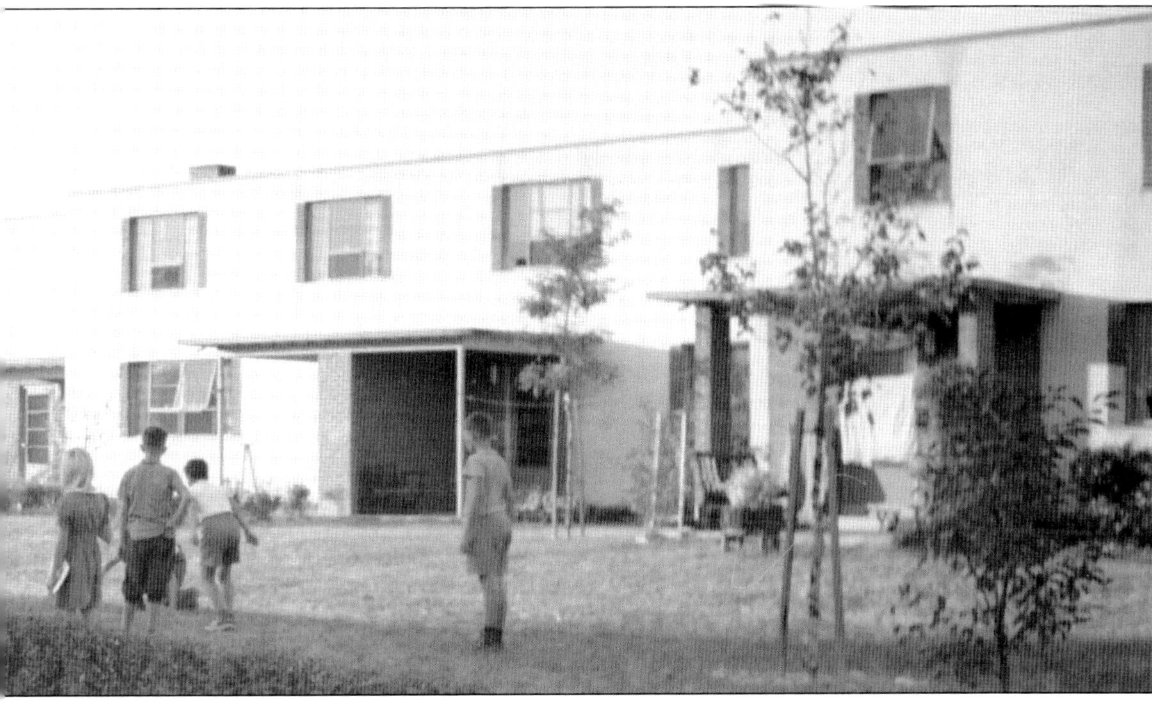

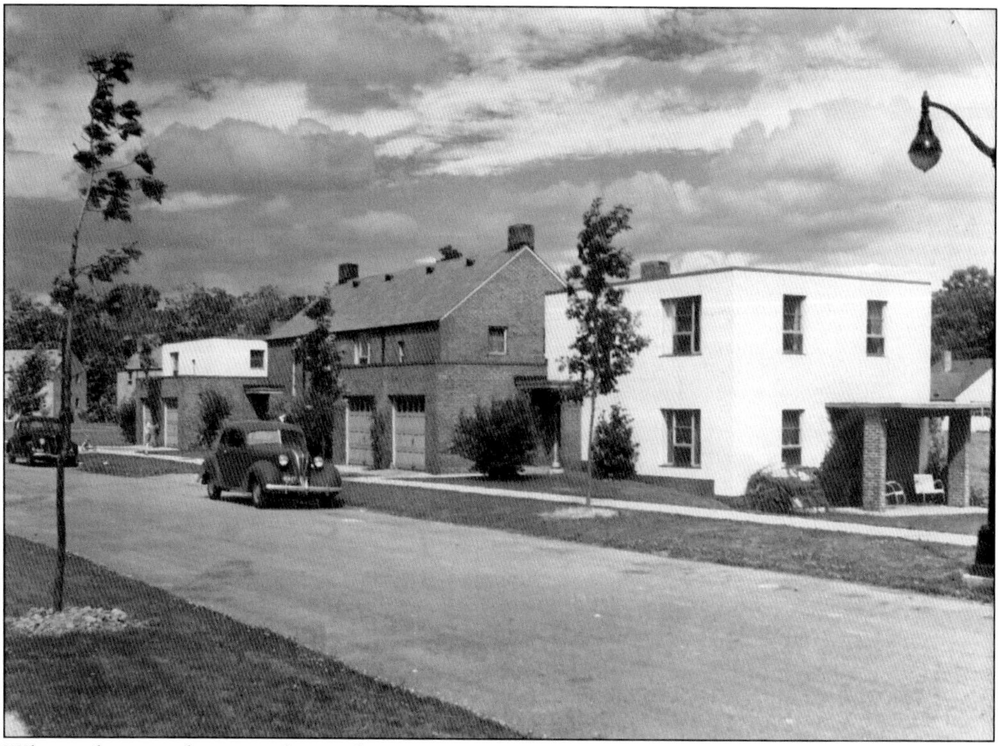

When taking applications for residency, the government determined that only 70 percent of the families coming to the new town owned an automobile. This worked out well in the early years, as not every Greenhills home had an attached garage bay. For those that did, the garage was constructed of cinder block, creating a fire separation from the adjoining homes. (Courtesy of the Library of Congress.)

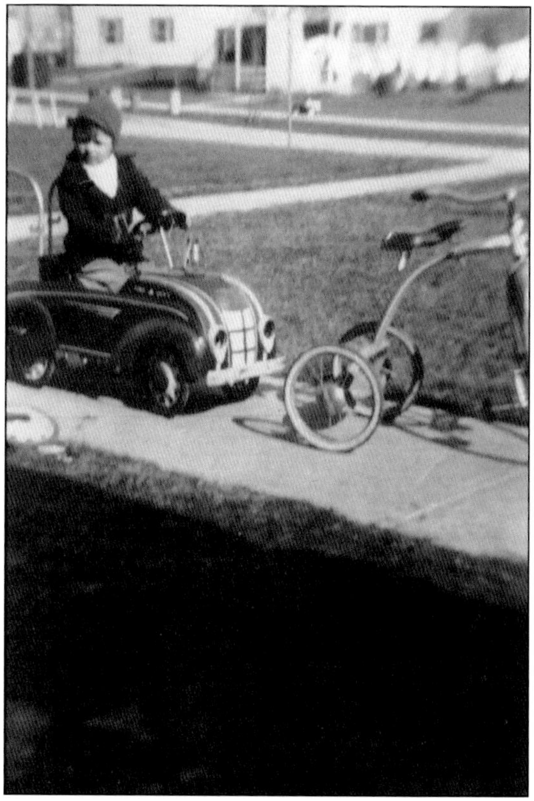

Compounds of ganged garages were also created and scattered strategically throughout neighborhoods. In the 1960s, these compounds, suffering for maintenance, were demolished to create space for new apartment buildings. This loss of parking continues to be an issue for present-day Greenhills residents like Jerry Stegman, seen starting his driver's education on Dewitt Street in 1941. After serving in the Marines, Stegman returned to Greenhills with his new wife, Rose, to reoccupy the original family townhouse, where they still live today. (Courtesy of Jerry Stegman.)

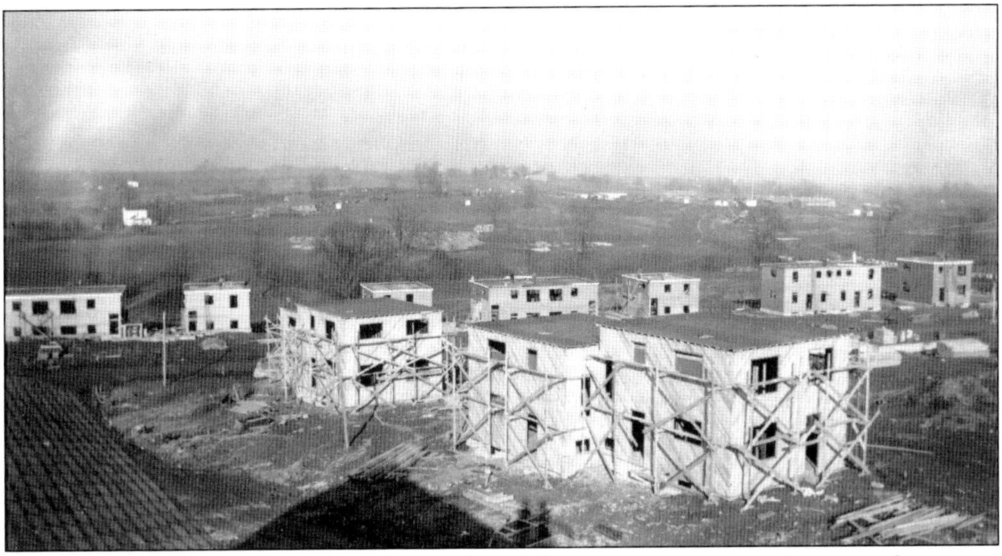

No matter the style, all the residential units shared the same construction. A concrete basement, block-laid crawlspace, or slab foundation supported living areas that were created from site-constructed wood framing. Homes were designed in combinations of 10- and 12-foot-wide room bays with 8-foot ceiling heights, which were uniform in order to keep wooden materials consistent across the project. (Courtesy of the Library of Congress.)

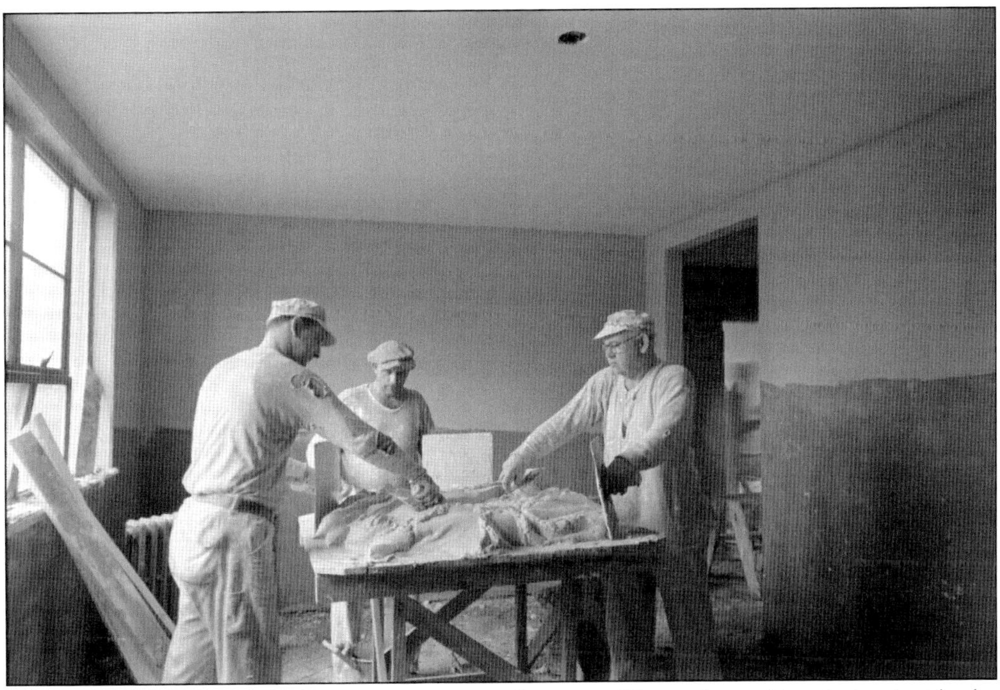

The interior finishes of the housing units were the same. The rock wool insulation inside the wall and attic cavities kept interiors comfortable while providing fireproofing, as well as sound dampening, between attached living units. The introduction of gypsum board panels, in lieu of old-fashioned wooden lath strips, streamlined the first step of the hand-plastered wall system. (Courtesy of the Library of Congress.)

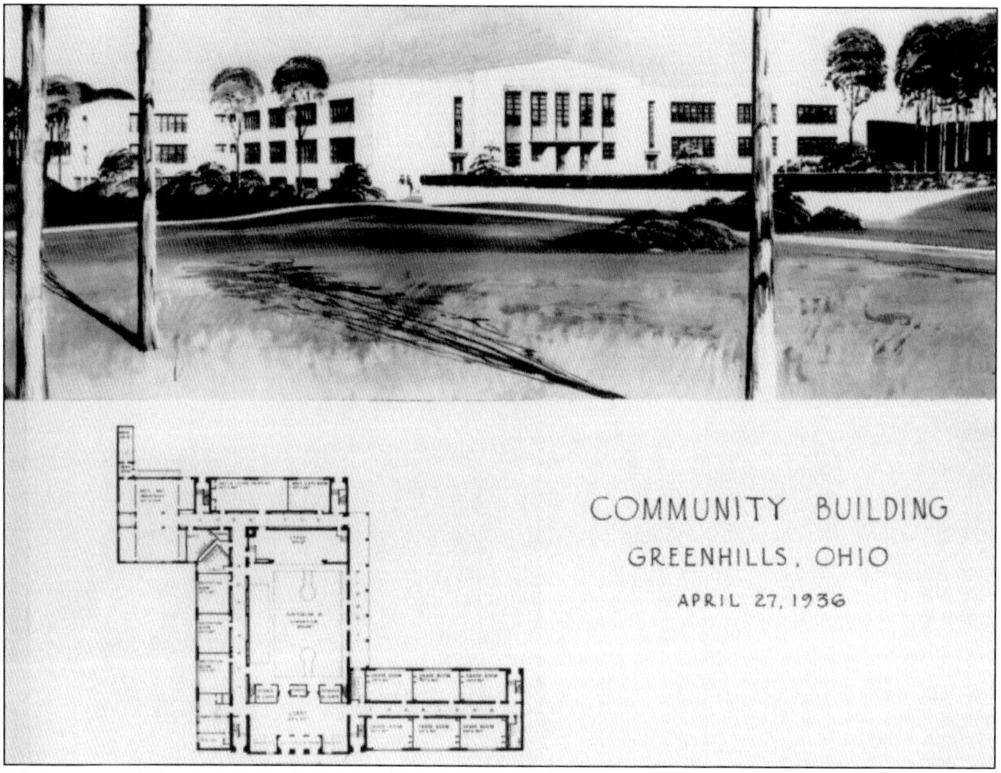

The proposed floor plan for the Greenhills Community Building (above), drawn pointing upwards to the east, shows how designers placed the auditorium in the center as the hinge between the elementary school wing to the right and the high school classrooms to the left and top. The auditorium's large south-facing glass block windows (below) allowed the sun's harsher midday rays to either warm the large space in winter or be assimilated comfortably into the high ceiling's upper holding space in summer. Classroom windows facing east, west, and north received softer natural lighting during the progression of the school day. The building's placement created two side lawn areas facing north and south, which were perfect for outdoor classroom gatherings. A formal front yard facing the town's common contained the grand staircase and a long, curving concourse driveway. A backyard, which contained parking next to the building and a collection of playground equipment and ball fields beyond, swept eastward, bounded by apartment buildings and future homes. (Both, courtesy of the Library of Congress.)

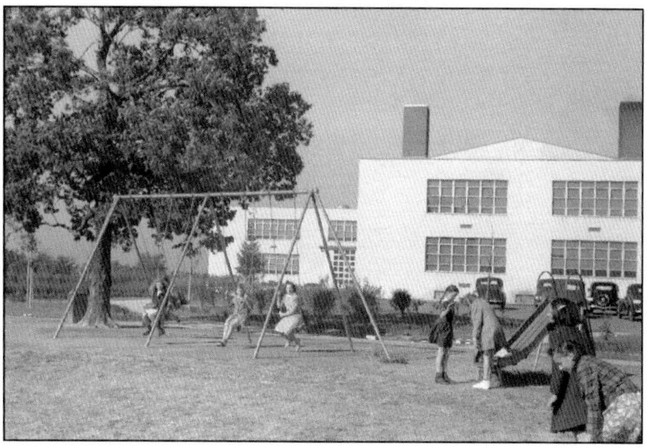

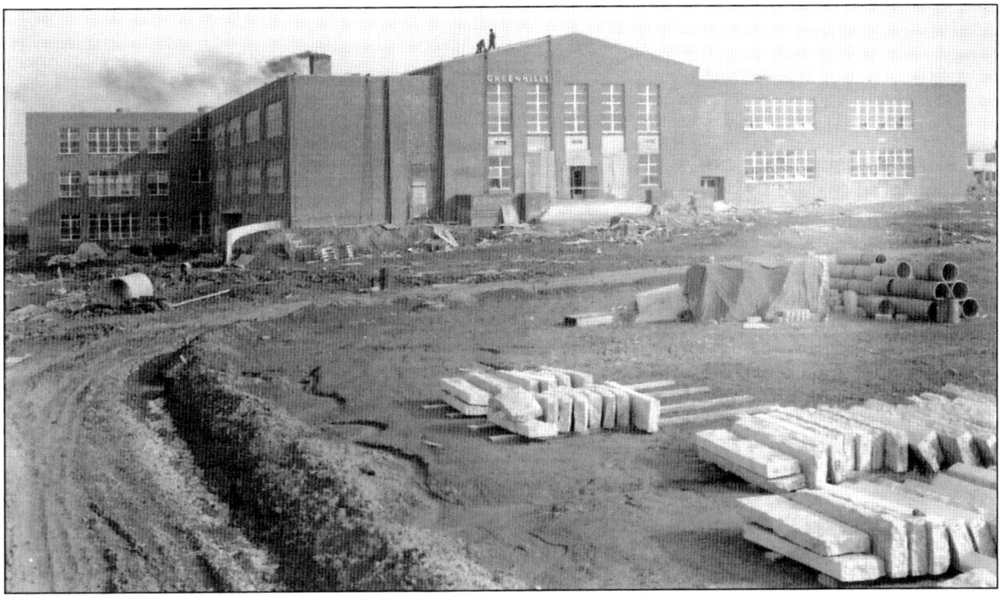

The Greenhills Community Building's true structure, with redbrick veneer applied over a system of steel framing and reinforced concrete block construction, is seen here. The exterior was painted white to keep with the International style of architecture and to further strengthen the building's visual presence as the dominant and sacred community center. Granite street curbing blocks sit stacked on what became the town's common. (Courtesy of the Library of Congress.)

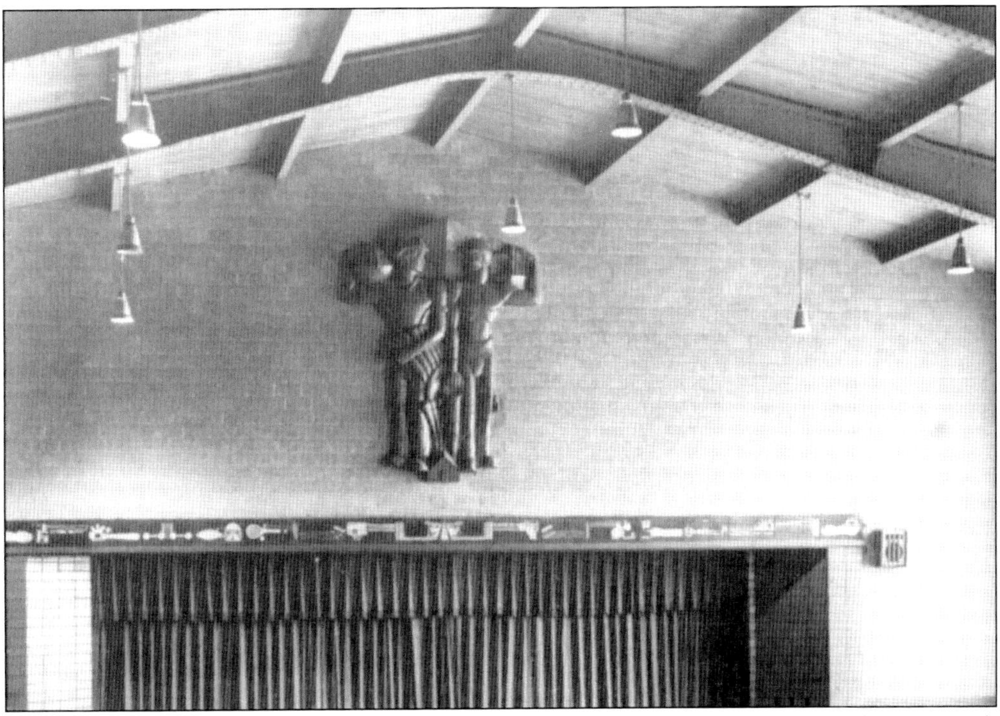

Reminiscent of an inverted ship's hull, the auditorium's huge steel beams supported an exposed-wood ceiling that along with velvet fabric drapes worked to acoustically dampen the noises of civic or athletic events held in the room. (Courtesy of the Library of Congress.)

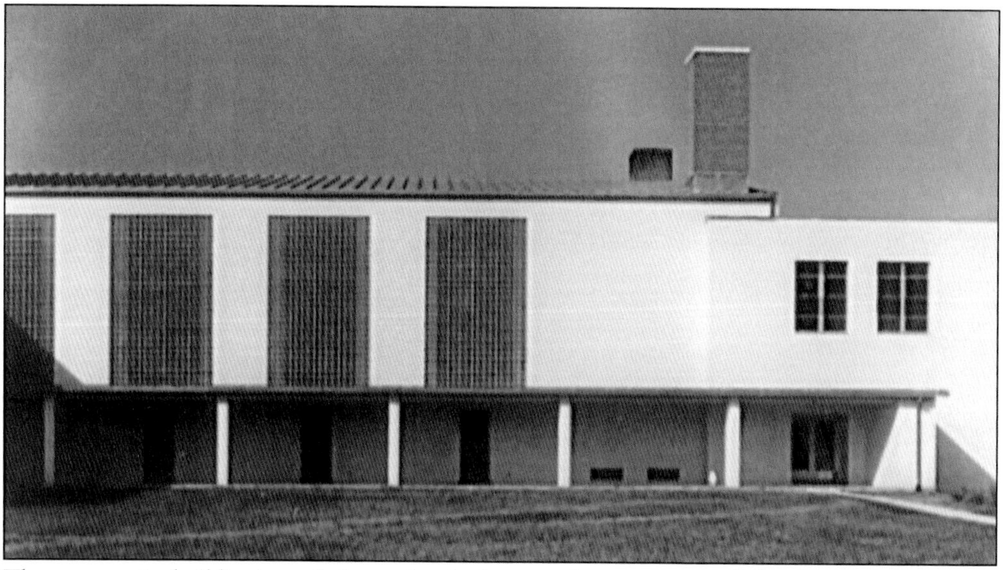

The community building's south-facing facade shows its four monumental glass block windows. Just visible inside, velvet window curtains provided light control, acoustical dampening, and during winter's coldest days, thermal insulation. Aligning below each of these windows was an entry door opening directly into the auditorium from the side porch. These glass block windows are now closed off with solid infill, and the loss of the curtains causes sound to reverberate throughout the auditorium. (Courtesy of the Library of Congress.)

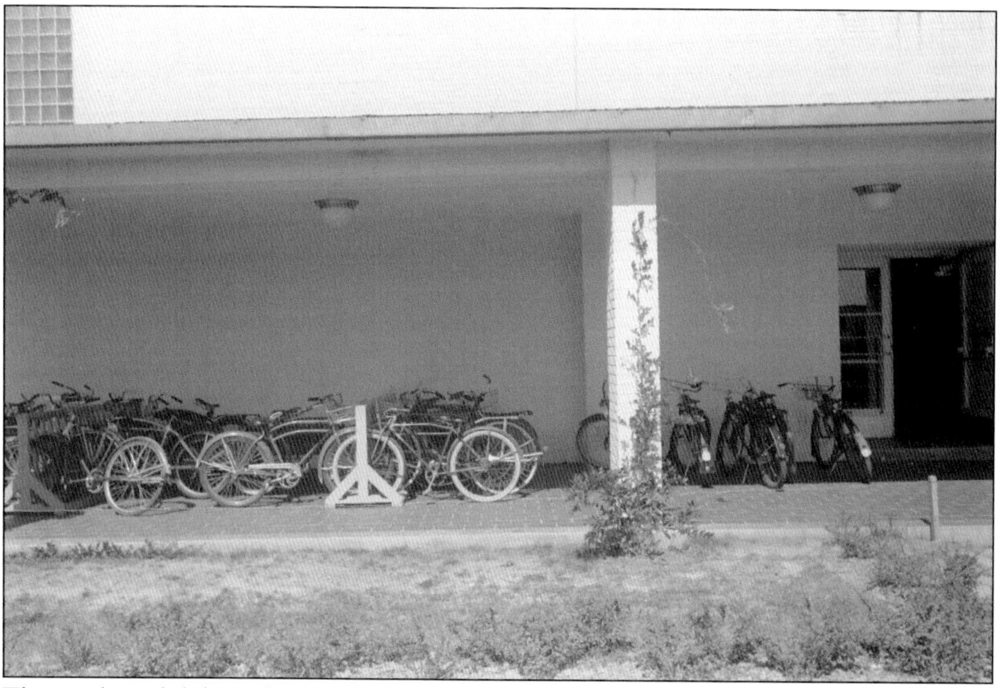

The porch, with bike racks installed, provided a place for children to park bicycles during the school day. At night, the baby carriages and wagons of families having walked to attend community events held in the building would find a place protected from the weather. Today, this side porch stands fully enclosed with expanded classrooms. (Courtesy of the Library of Congress.)

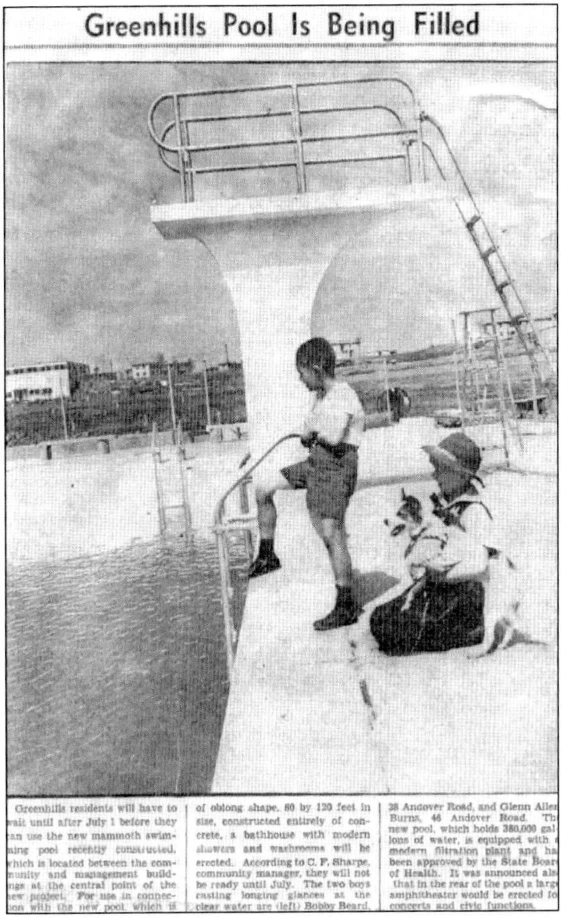
Greenhills Pool Is Being Filled

Greenhills residents will have to ait until after July 1 before they an use the new mammoth swimming pool recently constructed, hich is located between the community and management buildngs at the central point of the ew project. For use in connecion with the new pool, which is of oblong shape, 80 by 120 feet in size, constructed entirely of concrete, a bathhouse with modern showers and washrooms will be erected. According to C. F. Sharpe, community manager, they will not be ready until July. The two boys casting longing glances at the clear water are (left) Bobby Beard, 28 Andover Road, and Glenn Allen Burns, 46 Andover Road. Th new pool, which holds 380,000 gallons of water, is equipped with modern filtration plant and ha been approved by the State Boar of Health. It was announced als that in the rear of the pool a larg amphitheater would be erected fo concerts and civic functions.

Many a student sat in the Greenhills Community Building overlooking the Greenhills pool and longed for school to be out and summer fun to begin. In the image at right, the pool fills with 380,000 gallons of water for the first time, becoming a second home to residents during Cincinnati's sweltering summer days. Complete with three diving boards, a slide, and a separate baby wading area, the pool also offered swimming lessons and lifeguard safety, important features to families who likely never had access to a pool or a swimming hole before. The bathhouse (below) faces the community building, with nautical porthole windows floating above the entry porch and its changing room wings spread wide. (Right, courtesy of the Paul family, *Cincinnati Times Star*, 1938; below, courtesy of the Library of Congress.)

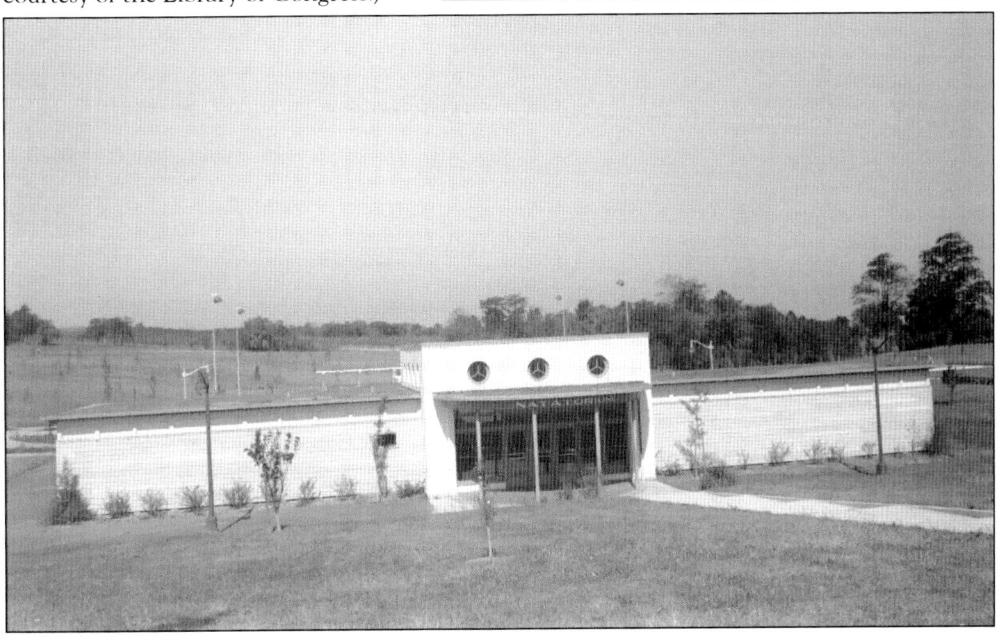

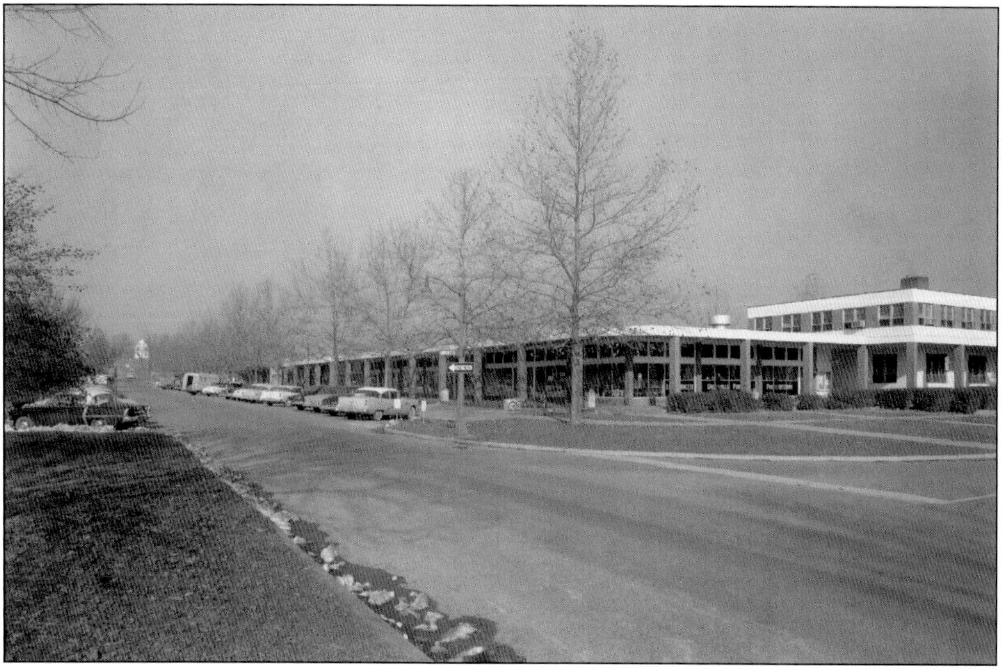

The community building and swimming complex was placed safely back from Winton Road traffic. However, Greenhills's retail area was pulled up closer to attract the road's passing potential customers. Sited on the secondary Eswin Street, seen here, which ran parallel with Winton Road, it provided a calmer vehicular "front yard," allowing for the safe backing up of cars and pedestrian crossings. (Courtesy of the Lippmeier family.)

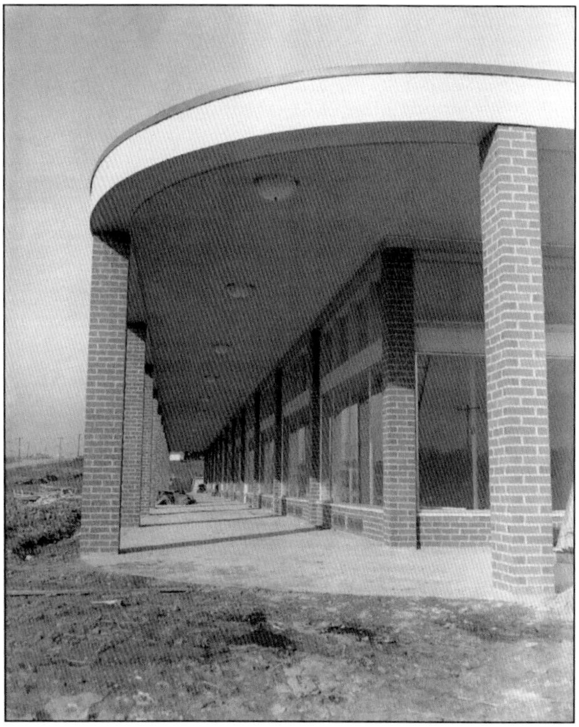

Sitting below the Winton Road elevation, this storefront and its bright white signage band at the roof edge fell in line with the vision of passing motorists. One of Ohio's earliest examples of strip mall design, Greenhills's modern retail complex ran very long and linear with Winton Road, and its signature curving soffit line turned back towards the adjoining two-story municipal building. (Courtesy of the Library of Congress.)

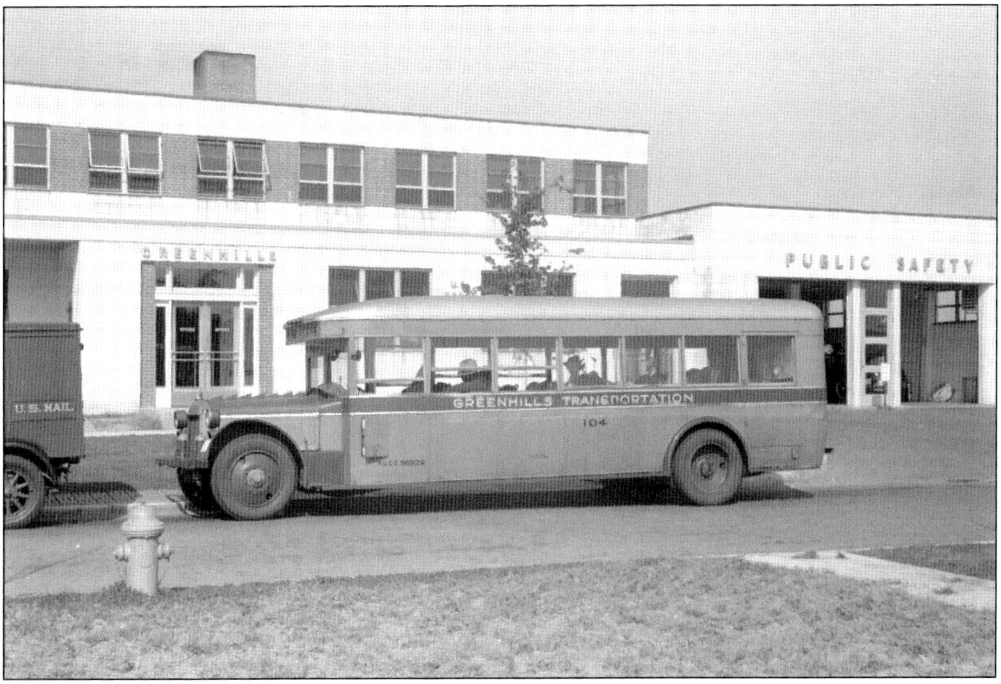

Greenhills's municipal building looks south out over the town's central common. The building housed the town's management offices, police and fire services, and a post office. A second story included the offices of doctors, dentists, and businesses. The lower walkout level contained a municipal service garage and two rarely used jail cells. Here, Greenhills's public bus and the mail truck sit ready to roll. (Courtesy of the Library of Congress.)

On June 30, 1938, the *Greenhills News Bulletin* reported the arrival of the "new Combination pumper and hose and ladder truck, and the installation of the automatic fire alarm system that blankets the community with its protection." Fire alarm call boxes like the one seen here were placed on street poles across the community. Citizens created the all-volunteer fire department that is still in operation today. (Courtesy of the Library of Congress.)

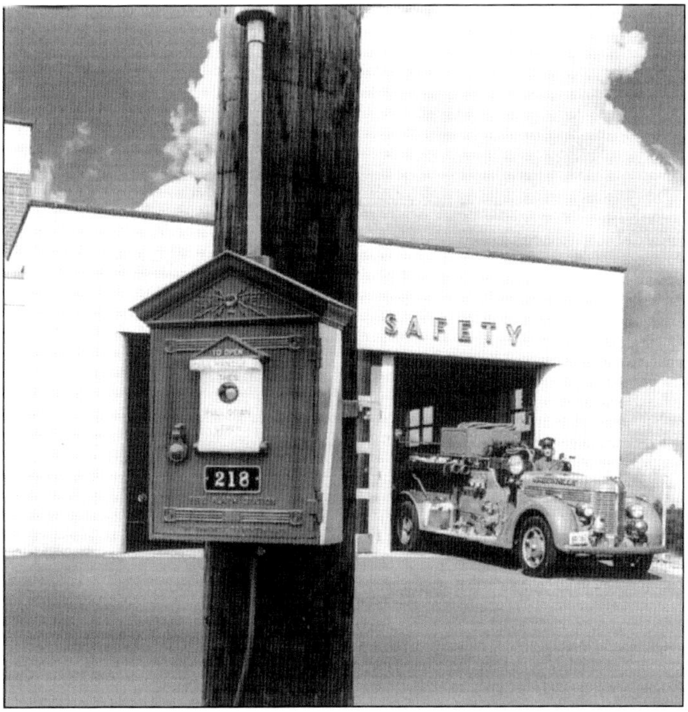

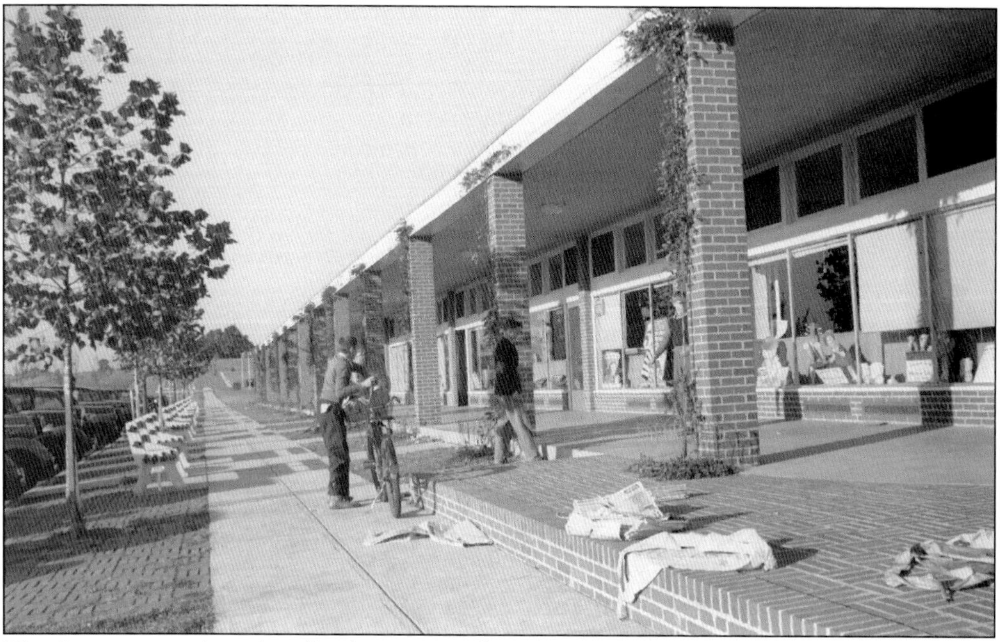

The shopping arcade with redbrick support columns created a rhythmic pattern across the front of the buildings that was mimicked back at the windowed storefronts. Window bays with operable transom windows allowed for the cooling ventilation of the retail spaces in summer. The arcade protected pedestrians from sun, rain, and snow. (Courtesy of the Library of Congress.)

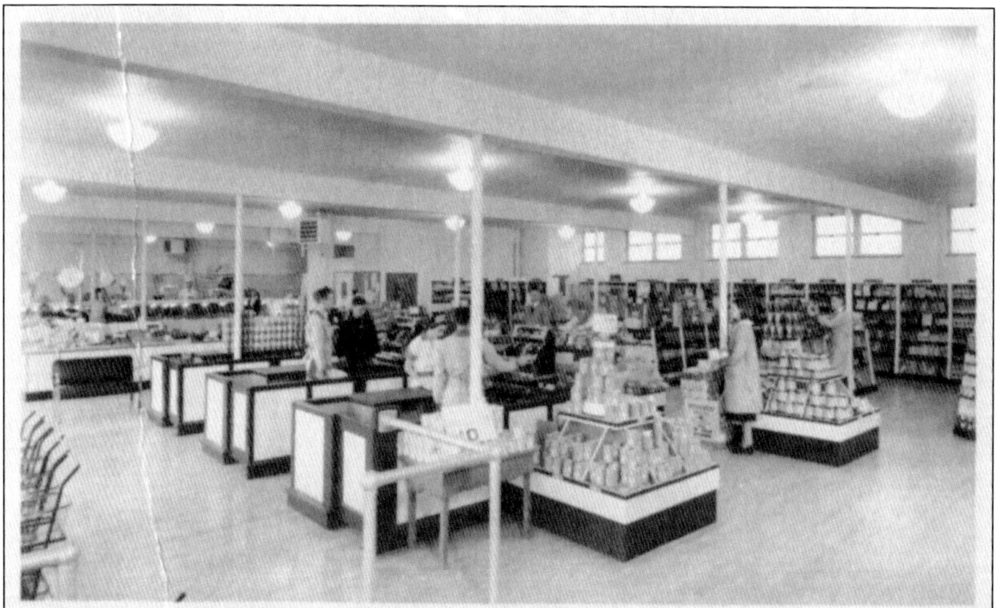

The retail strip was designed in structural bays. Solid walls between large bay groupings provided strength, keeping the building from moving in high winds. The intermediate lines of steel support columns and ceiling beams held up the roof and gave flexibility to the floor plans. Larger spaces, like the cooperative grocery seen here, could be subdivided into future smaller retail venues by simply constructing walls along the column lines. (Courtesy of the Greenhills Alumni Association.)

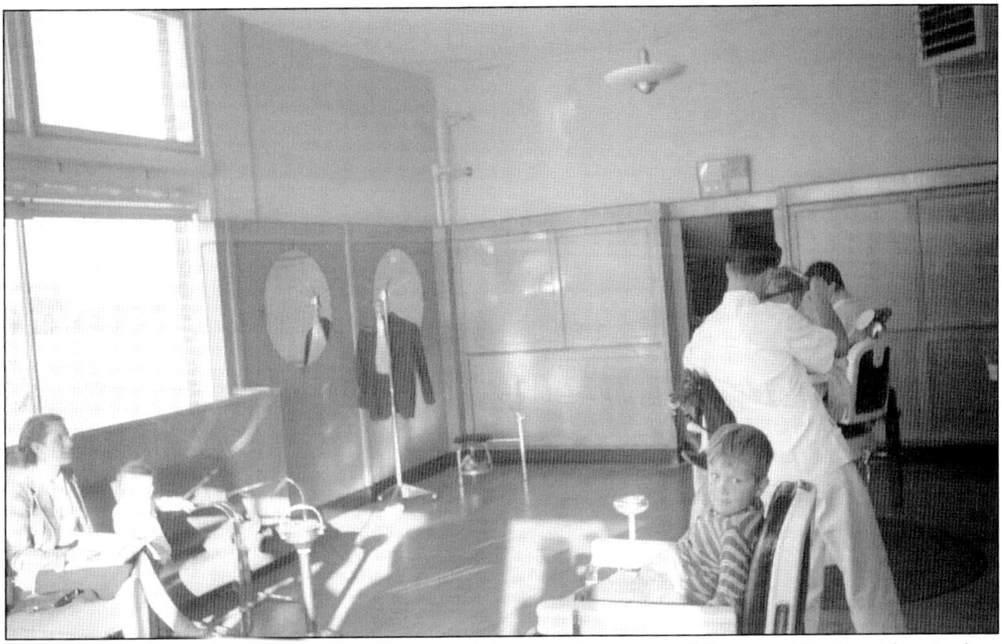

In 1938, the Greenhills barbershop occupied the strip's end retail bay, and had a side window looking northward out over the concrete steps that took pedestrians down to the shopping center's lower level shops and back parking lot. Barber Frank Krieger, seen here, gave many a little boy his first haircut as mom watched anxiously. (Courtesy of the Library of Congress.)

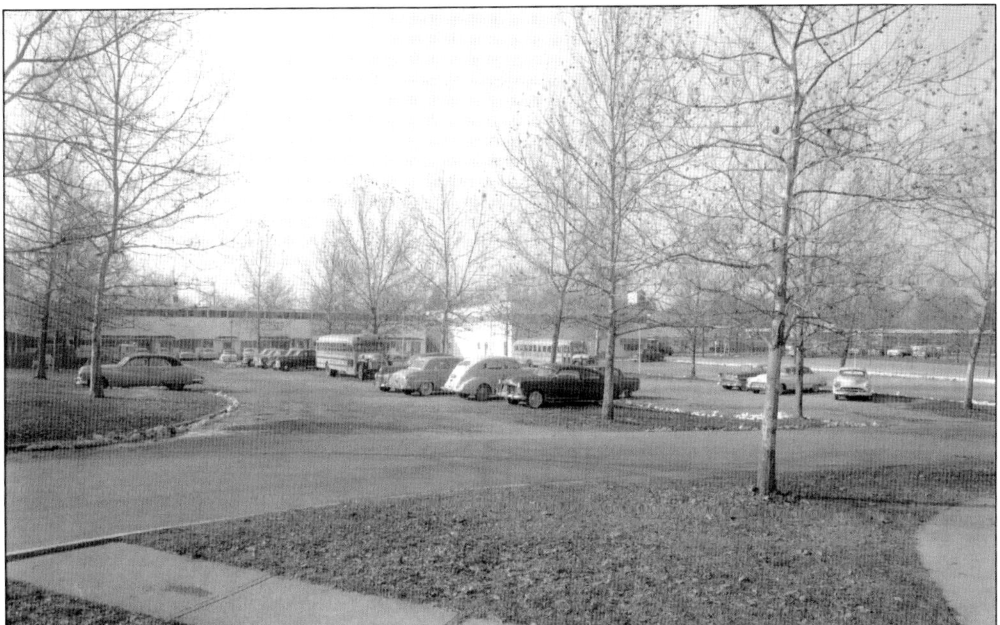

The backside of the strip mall opened out to a vast parking lot that served the lower level's retail stores and the swimming pool to the east. A new large building (center) containing a grocery store above and a bowling alley below became the midpoint for more mirrored retail development northward. Greenhills's original shopping and municipal buildings flank to the left. (Courtesy of the Lippmeier family.)

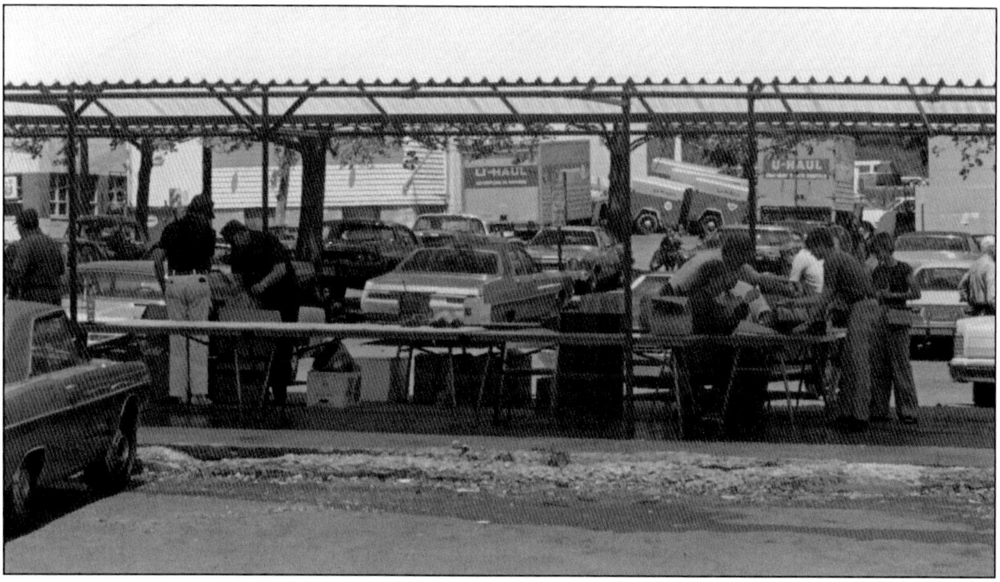

The farmers' market sat on a raised pad in the middle of the lower back parking lot. The open-sided building had steel piping supporting a simple roof. Designed as a sheltered retail space for the greenbelt's farmers, the market quickly found other uses. On July 27, 1938, the Federal Music Project held an open-air band concert for the first residents, who had only moved in four months earlier. The announcement read, "This will be held at the farmers market back of the Mercantile Center. You may enjoy this concert from your automobiles for which parking space will be available. If you don't have a car, we suggest that you bring a pillow." Below, in 1976, the Kiwanis restored the market. The local Kiwanis club, established in 1954, championed Greenhills's inclusion in the National Register of Historic Places in 1989. (Both, courtesy of the Lippmeier family.)

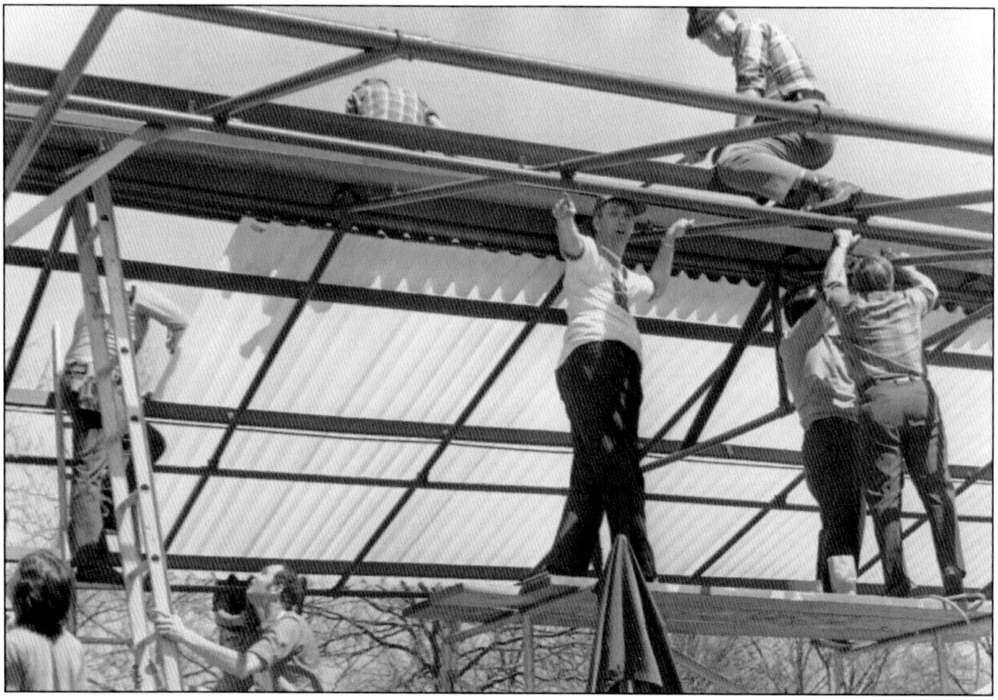

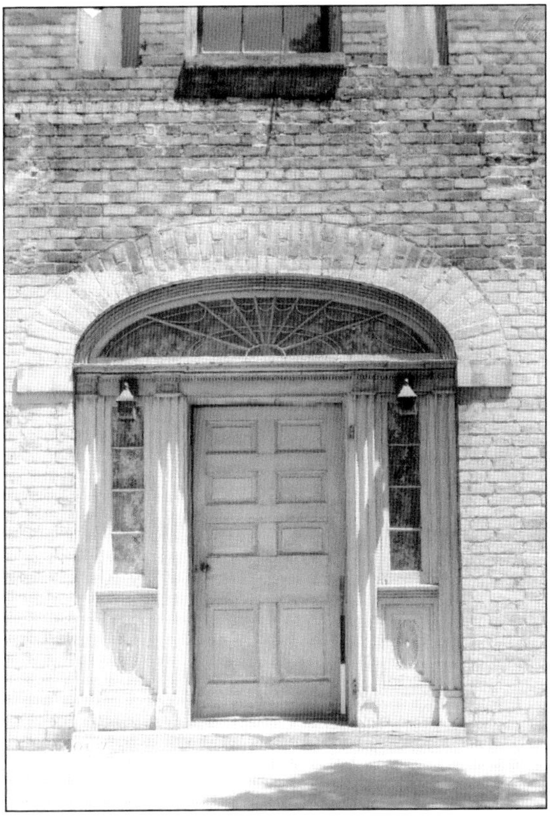

Sitting at Greenhills's highest point, the 1816 James Whallon House is constructed of bricks fired on-site. It is the oldest structure standing in Greenhills and is listed in the National Register of Historic Places. The house reportedly hid visitors along the Underground Railroad and was the victim of Morgan's Raiders, the Civil War–era thieves. Over the decades, the Whallon farmlands were subdivided. In January 1936, George and Willard Marquardt, father and son respectively, were the first to receive federal checks when the house and its adjoining lands were sold to become the site for the new town of Greenhills. Noting the house's regional significance, the Resettlement Administration had a historical survey completed. The house was sold to a local veterans' group and later to the Greenhills community, which restored it. The house is currently rented out as office space. (Both, courtesy of the Library of Congress.)

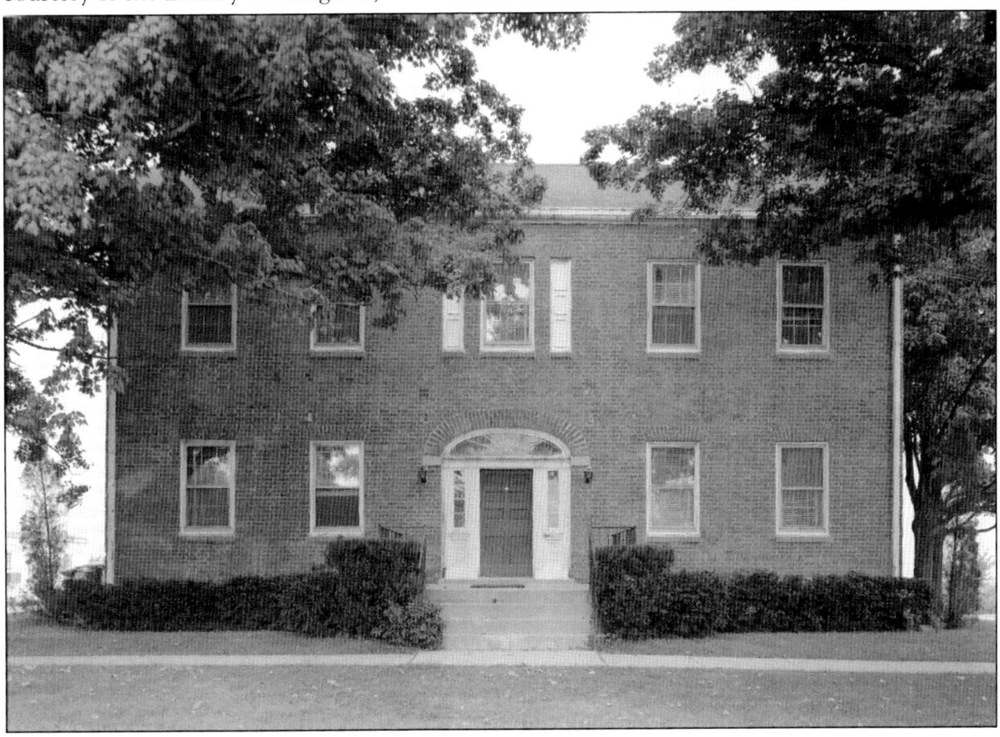

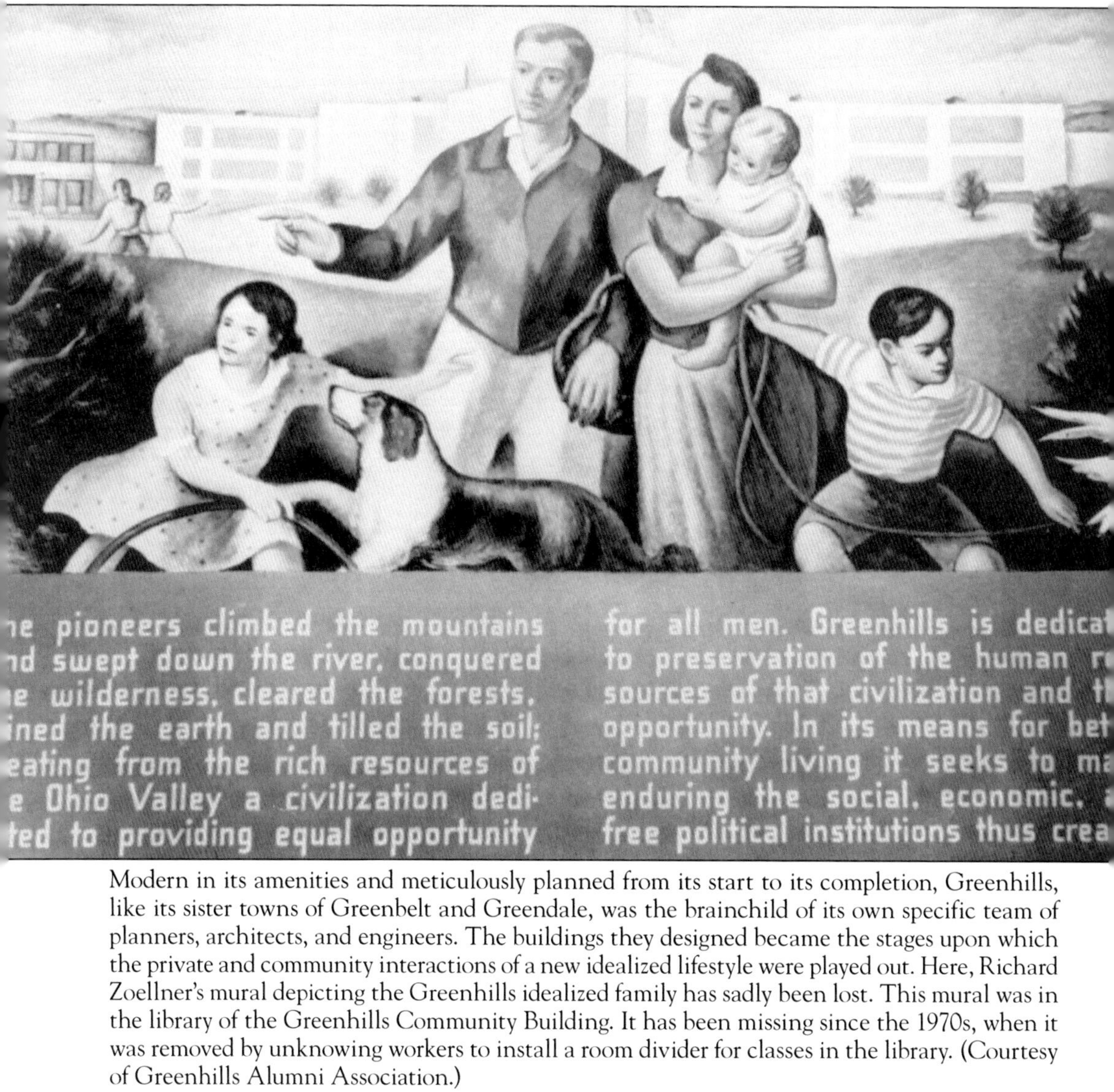

Modern in its amenities and meticulously planned from its start to its completion, Greenhills, like its sister towns of Greenbelt and Greendale, was the brainchild of its own specific team of planners, architects, and engineers. The buildings they designed became the stages upon which the private and community interactions of a new idealized lifestyle were played out. Here, Richard Zoellner's mural depicting the Greenhills idealized family has sadly been lost. This mural was in the library of the Greenhills Community Building. It has been missing since the 1970s, when it was removed by unknowing workers to install a room divider for classes in the library. (Courtesy of Greenhills Alumni Association.)

Five

Family Life

It was almost like a miracle. The fact that we were moving into a brand new place. It had never been lived in . . . It was like heaven for the kids. They had a sandbox, swings and slides.

—Irene Connerman

Many experts planned family life in Greenhills long before the first families began to unpack their belongings on April 1, 1938. There were 26 families in residence when the first neighborhood meeting was held in the construction shed. The next month, with 48 families in residence, a meeting was held in the community building to form civic committees in various areas, including transportation, recreation, churches, and newspaper distribution.

By the end of 1938, Greenhills's 676 units were 90 percent occupied and all farm units occupied. In late June, the golden moment arrived. The July 4, 1938, edition of the *Greenhills News Bulletin* stated, "The serenity of a rural village has settled today on Greenhills, suburban housing development of the Farm Security Administration, U.S. Department of Agriculture, with the departure of an army of workmen that completed 25 months of construction activity on June 30. Five hundred men lay down their tools for the last time on the project Thursday afternoon. Today the shouts of children splashing and diving in the new swimming pool take the place of the roar of tractors and graders and the sound of hammer and saw . . . On that same day, 40 more families arrived to swell the population to approximately 900 persons."

When families arrived, they found a complete town of modern homes set in wide, landscaped open spaces of parks and playgrounds and bounded by tree-lined winding streets. A new food store opened a week later in the new Greenhills Shopping Center. Amenities eventually included a barbershop, a beauty parlor, a gasoline service station, and a general merchandise store complete with a drug department and a lunchroom. The beautiful Greenhills Community Building offered a K–12 school, an adult vocational school, a place for community activities, and even religious services. One of the last jobs completed was the community swimming pool, considered the finest in the Cincinnati area.

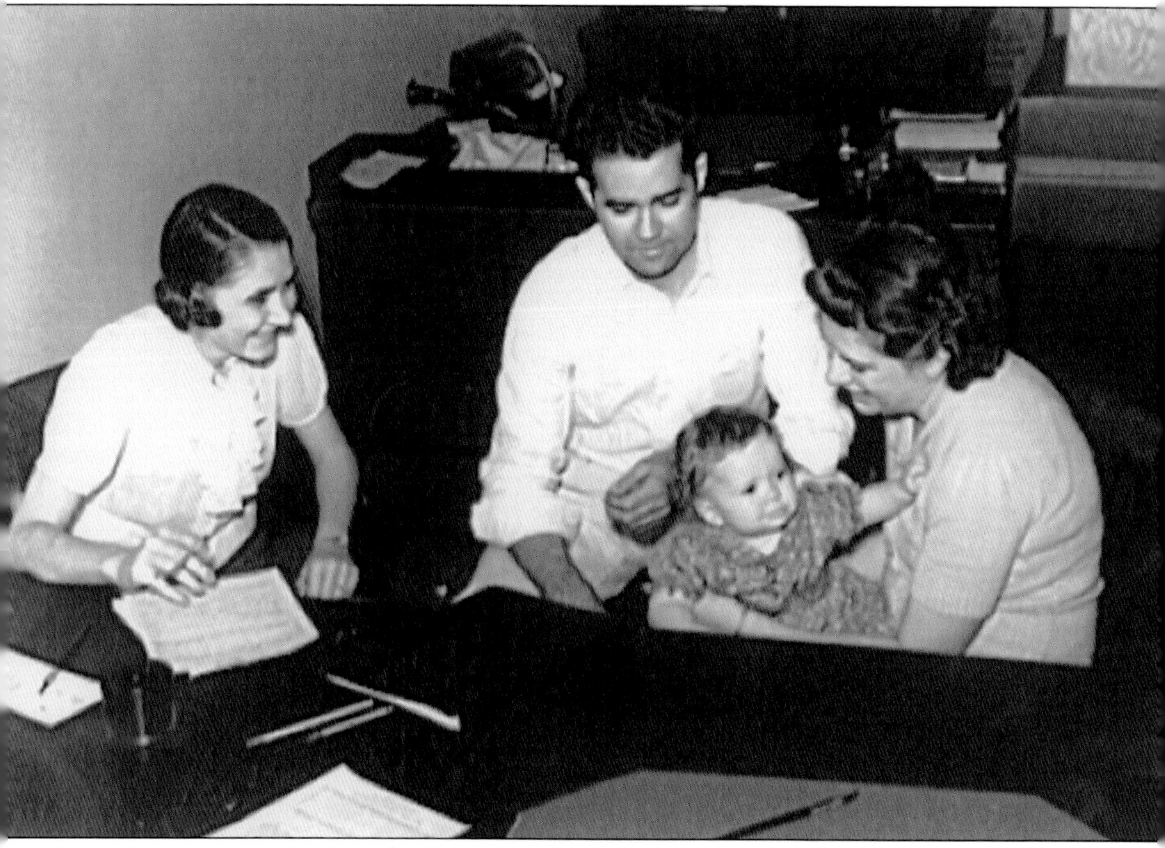

Prospective tenants went through a lengthy process that began with a 17-page application that included all family particulars: size, income, goals, and health. After the initial review, the family selection committee investigated extensively. They checked all references and past and present employers, landlords, and friends. The committee then made a home visit to make sure good housekeeping standards were in practice and that all family members were enthusiastic about the chance to help create a new community. They also checked the family's attitude toward each other, friction, harmony, or dominance of one member over another. Initially, there were quotas established to make sure there was a large distribution of occupations among tenants. Guidelines required women with children under 14 years old to be homemakers and not employed outside the home. (Courtesy of the Library of Congress.)

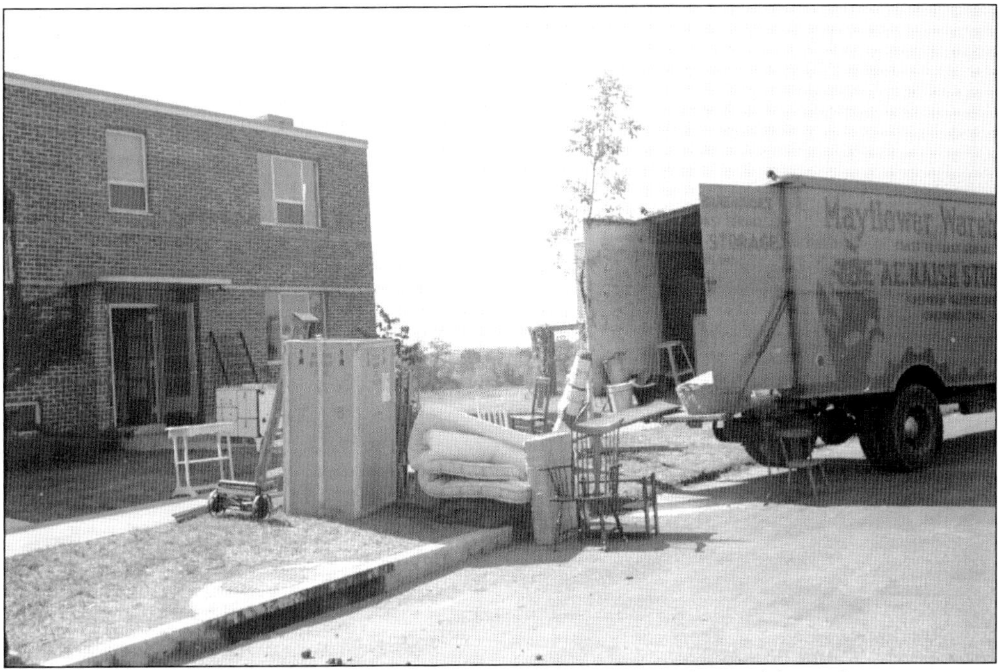

Who the first family to move into Greenhills was became a matter of great debate after a newspaper article featuring the Paul family named them the "first pioneers." The *Greenhills News Bulletin* printed a letter stating that, in fact, the W.H. Jones family of 17 Avenell Lane had all their furniture in their apartment on March 31 but were not allowed to spend the night. On April 1, the official day of opening, James Blackwood of 30 Andover Road arrived at 7:30 a.m., Fergus Sullivan's furniture arrived at 8:30 a.m., and the Robert Paul family arrived at 11:00 a.m. (Both, courtesy of the Library of Congress.)

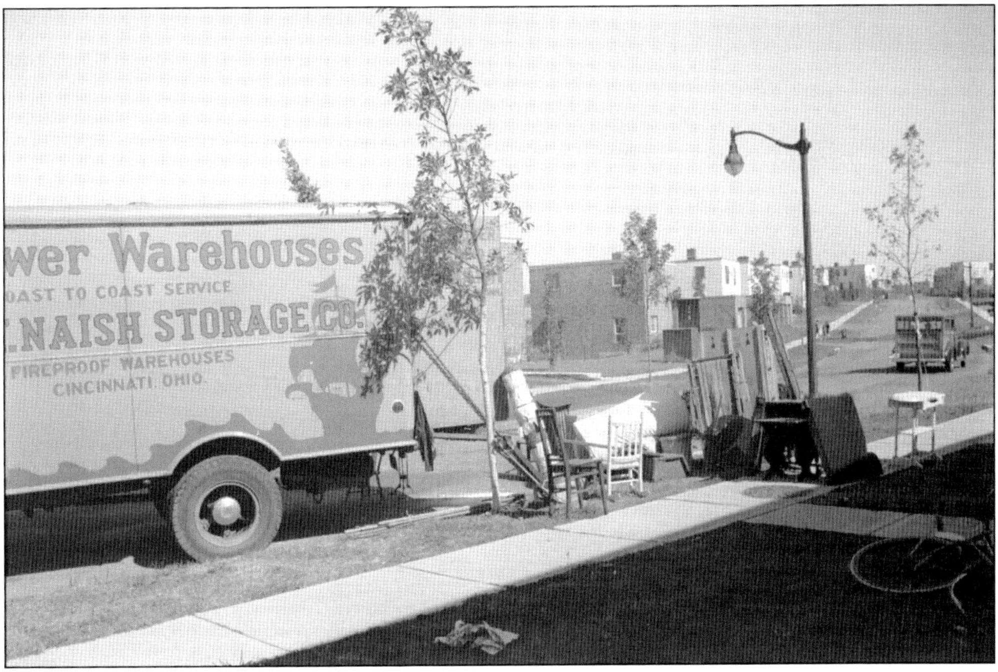

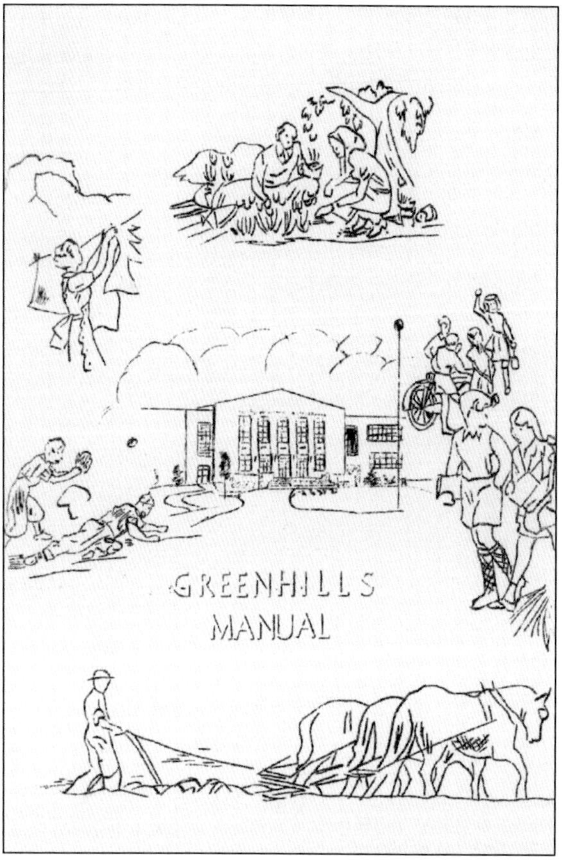

Each new resident received a book with specific instructions about living in Greenhills and how to be a good neighbor. These instructions were confusing in some regards, especially concerning the hanging of laundry, which was not permitted on Sundays. The clotheslines were to be taken down on Saturday by 3:00 p.m. No flowers were to be planted in yards; only up against the house. Bicycles were not to be ridden on sidewalks, and nails were not to be driven into walls. In spite of these restrictions, the new residents were delighted with the hardwood floors, the clean, large rooms, and the modern kitchens. (Left, courtesy of the Greenhills Historical Society; below, courtesy of the Library of Congress.)

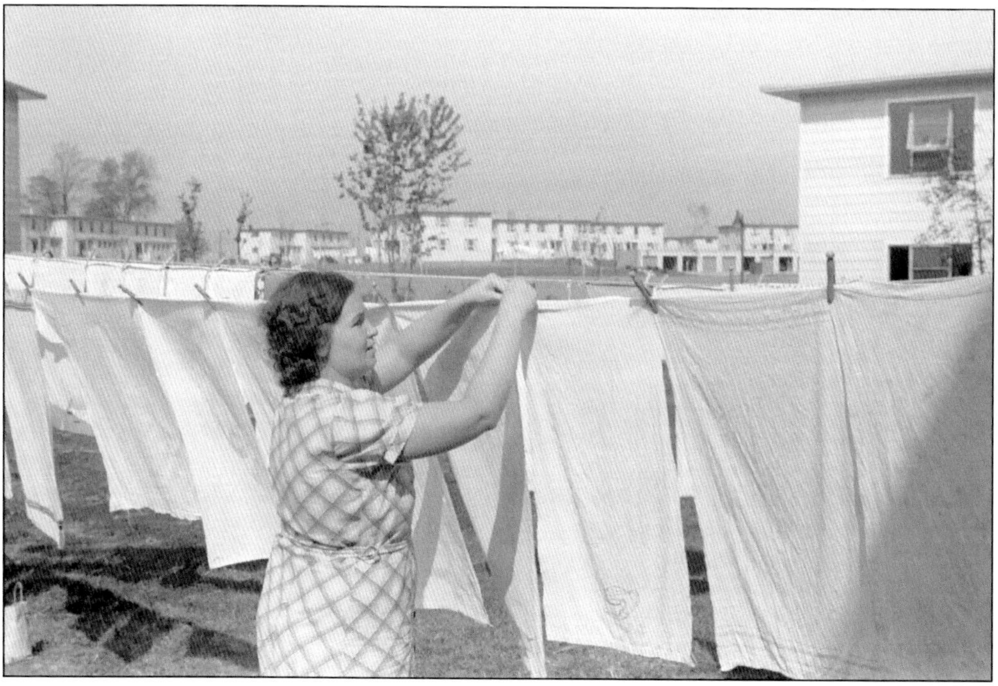

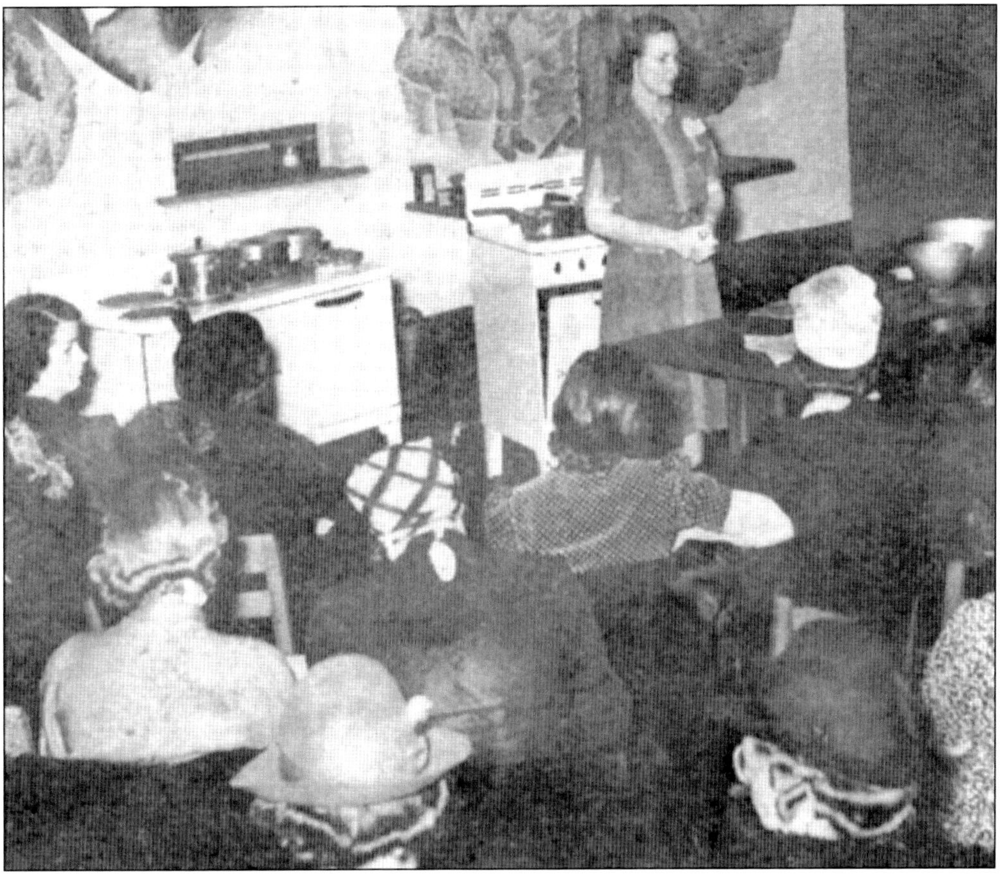

Homemaking classes were popular partly because one of the topics covered was how to safely use the new electric stove. New to almost everyone, the electric stoves were actually a deal breaker for some prospective tenants, who backed out of the application procedure when they found out the kitchens were all electric. Accustomed to cooking with gas, the residents felt the new technology was suspect and considered it dangerous. Greenhills was one of the first completely electrified towns in the country. (Above, courtesy of the Greenhills Historical Society; right, courtesy of Saundra Fancher Ziliox.)

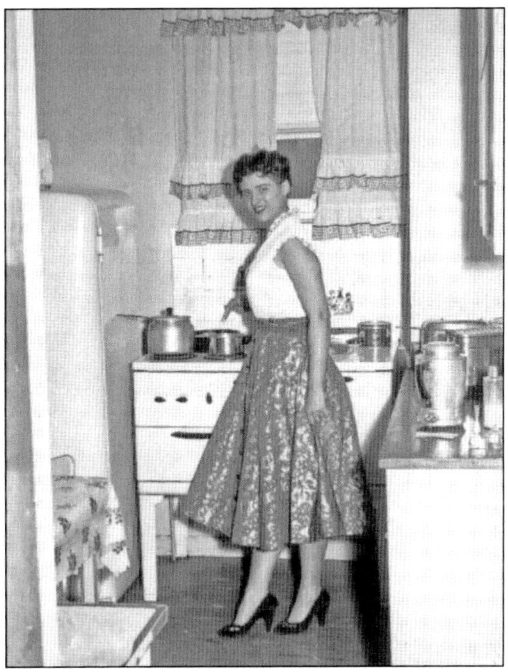

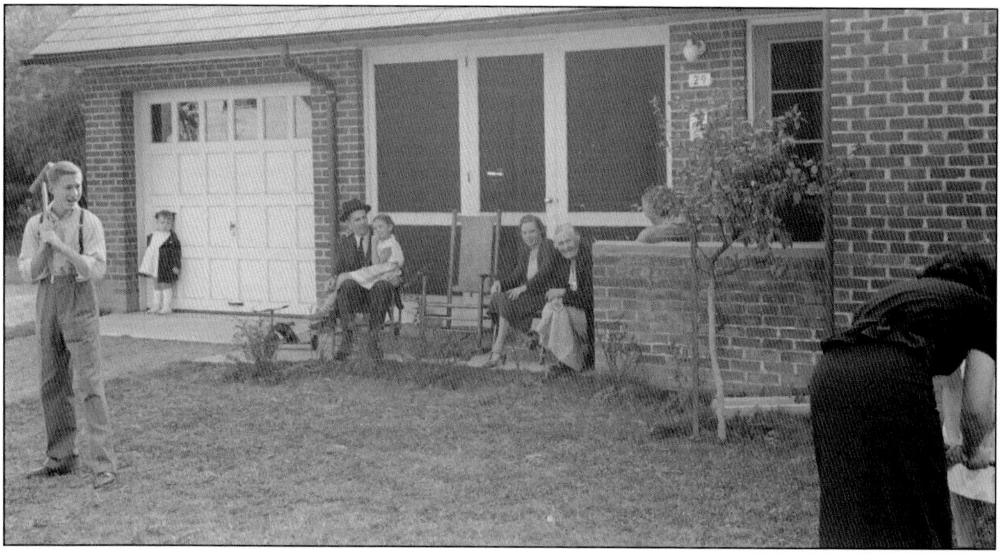

Greenhills and its new tenants were a curiosity to Cincinnati residents and became a destination for Sunday drives. For some residents, it became a matter of routine to look up from the Sunday dinner table and find strangers on their porch looking through the windows. It became such a problem at one point that several streets were actually closed by the police, who made anyone wanting to pass prove that they were residents. That did not last long, as invited guests were also turned away, but the curiosity and interest created by all the publicity about the project did make temporary celebrities of the citizens of Greenhills. (Courtesy of the Library of Congress.)

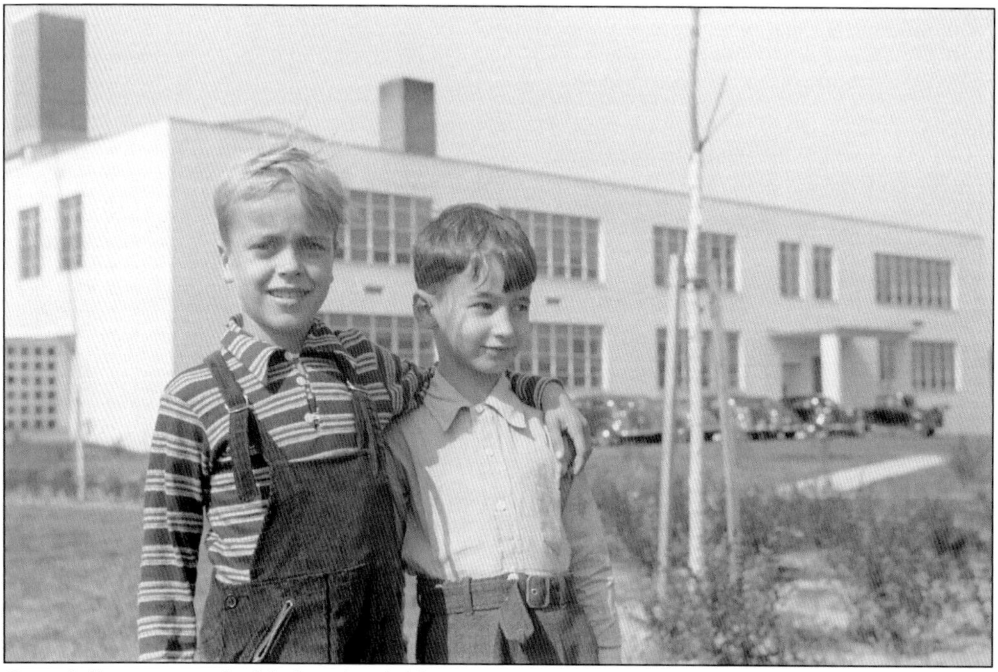

Greenhills was a wonderful place for children. One longtime resident Tom Haverland remembered arriving to his new home from the city, saying he "felt like he had gone to heaven!" There were plenty of fields to explore, paved cul-de-sac streets for bikes, walking paths, playgrounds, and of course the swimming pool. (Courtesy of the Library of Congress.)

Different kinds of heating systems were used in different homes in order to efficiently heat the various spaces, but all homes included radiator units in each room of the dwelling. Large buildings with multiple apartment flats had a central unit maintained by the town, with coal to heat the central boiler. Most townhome units each had individual boilers and their own coal delivered. (Courtesy of the Library of Congress.)

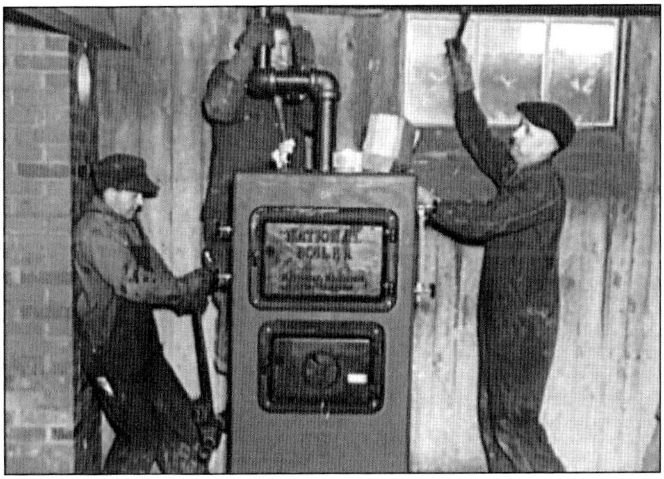

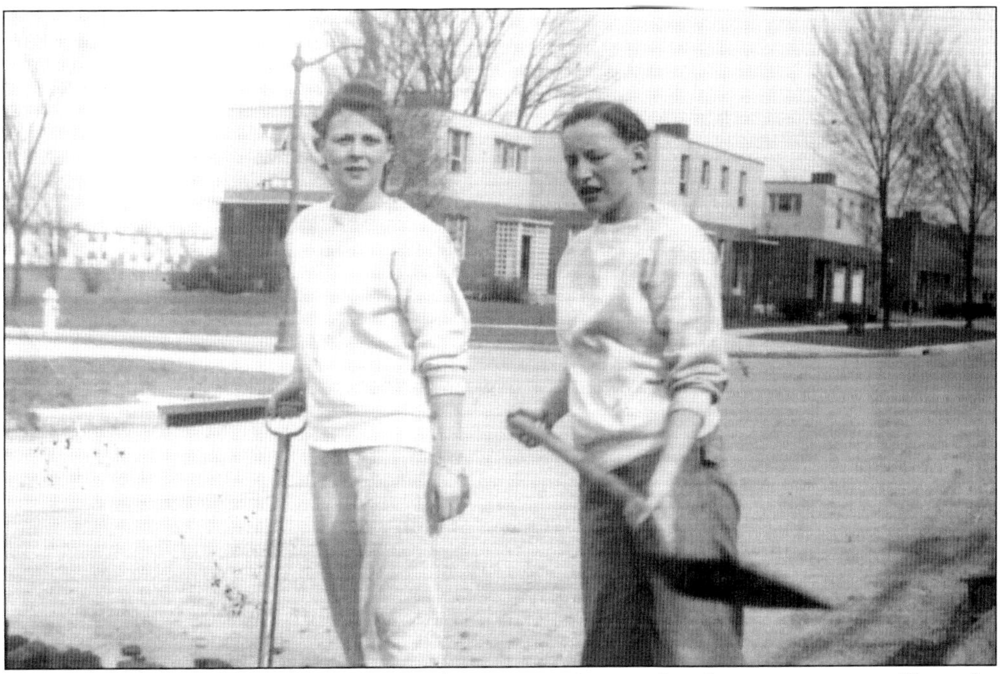

Central heating was a joy to have. Not having to rely on a fireplace as a source of heat for each room made housekeeping easier. Houses without basements had hot water systems, and the coal was delivered right to the service entrance of the house. Houses with basements had steam heating systems, and apartments had central boiler systems. Under the terms of the lease specified in the Greenhills manual, only the heating facilities provided with the houses were to be used unless written consent was obtained from the community manager. Transporting coal to the furnace area became a regular chore for some homeowners. (Courtesy of the Greenhills Alumni Association.)

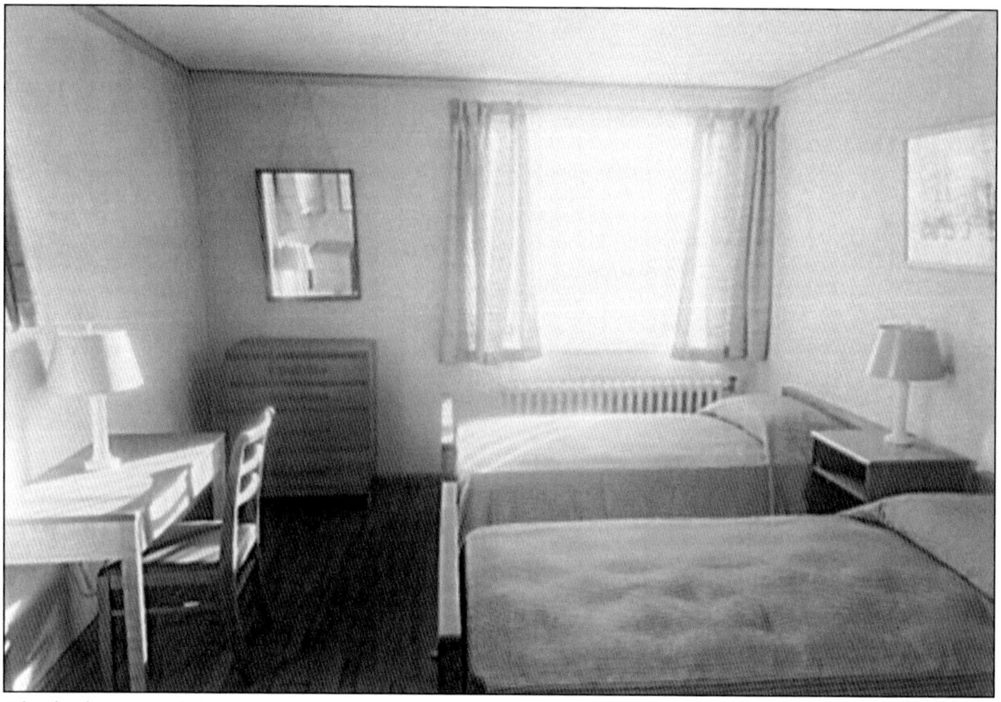

The bedrooms of the newly designed houses in Greenhills had closets, a rare feature in homes at the time. Also, most units had linen closets right off the bathroom, a great bonus feature and space saver. (Above, courtesy of the Library of Congress; below, courtesy of the Village of Greenhills.)

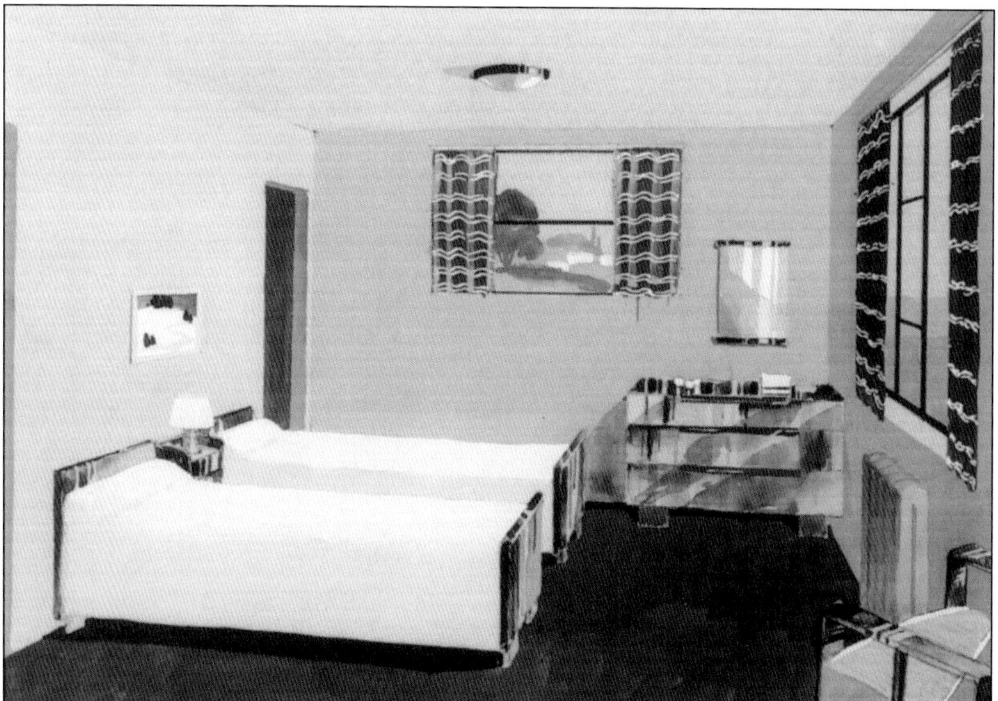

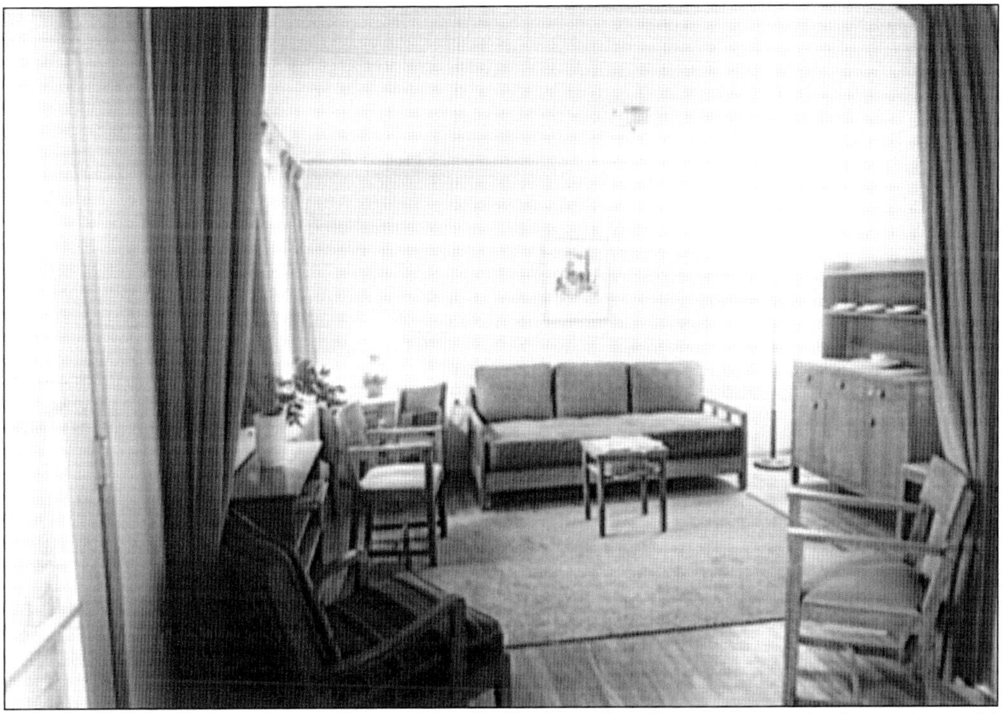

Furniture was specifically made to scale for the homes. All of the pieces matched in style to add ease in decorating. The furniture was built well and offered at an inexpensive rate. The windows were measured at a certain distance from the floor to offer more space to allow the placement of furniture. The walls were solid, and nails were not allowed to be used to hang pictures on the wall. Instead, there were picture rails at the ceiling level. (Above, courtesy of the Library of Congress; below, courtesy of the Village of Greenhills.)

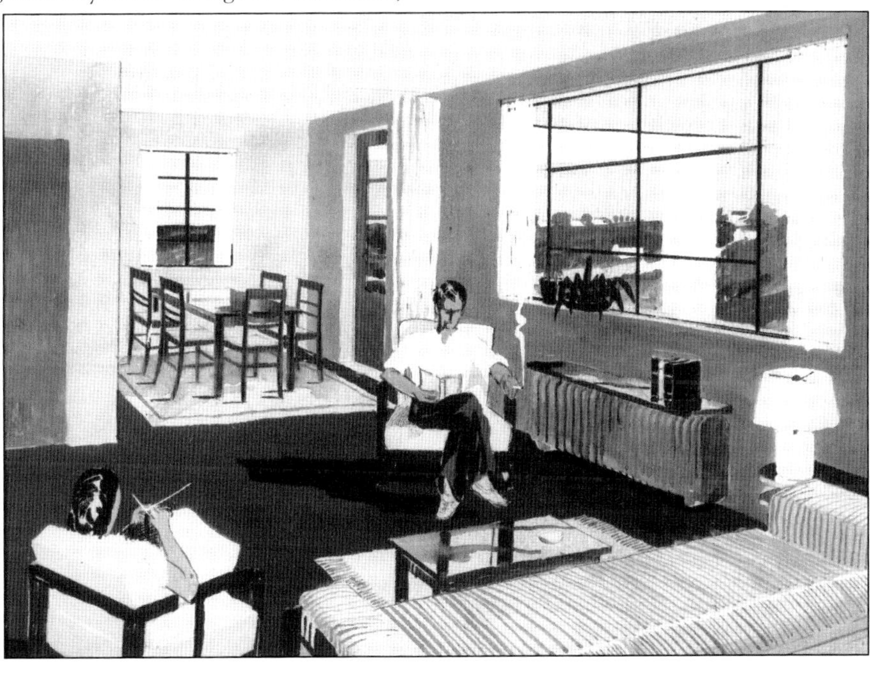

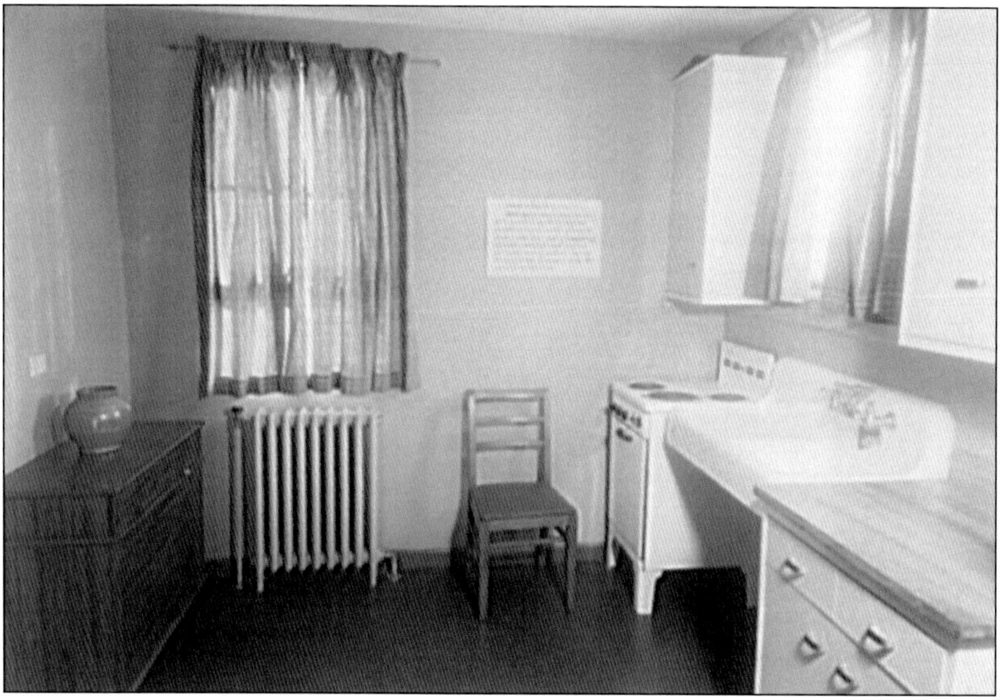

Kitchens were designed with space for a small table and chairs. The kitchens had a window that looked upon the green space outdoors, where the children would be playing. The appliances were of the latest design and offered to each unit. The sinks were deep enough to be useful, and the butcher-block counters were maintained by the service department. Each counter had the style marked on the underside, so that when they were removed for sanding, cleaning, and resealing, the service department could reinstall the refinished counter. (Above, courtesy of the Library of Congress; below, courtesy of the Village of Greenhills.)

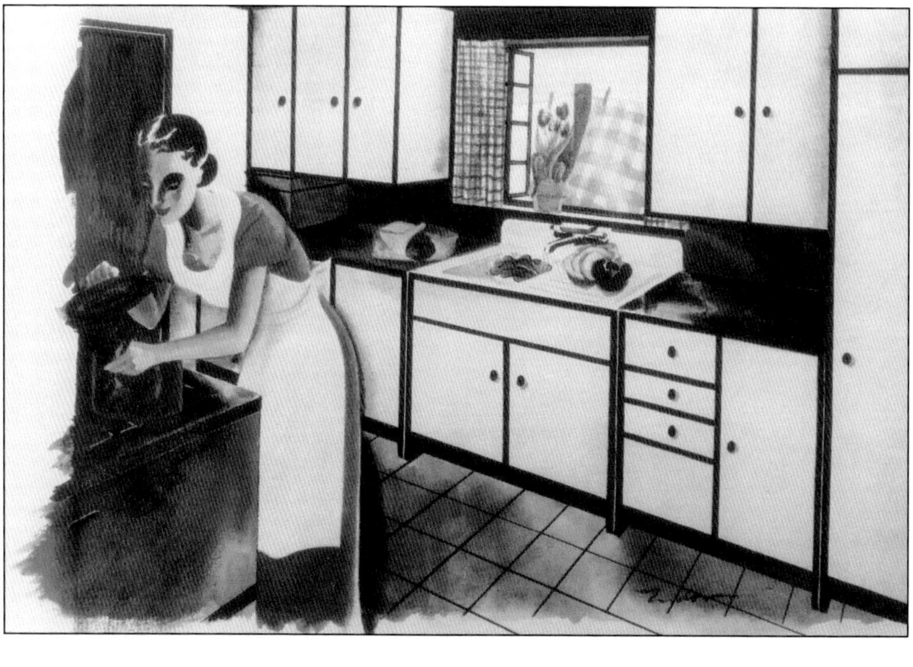

The ONCE OVER

by H. I. PHILLIPS

SPRING CHAOS

(Greenbelt, Mo.—There is further confusion in the model U. S. homes here. Because the front yards were designed as back yards tenants didn't know where to hang the wash. The lawns being in the back yards, it has now been discovered that the hose faucets for watering them are located in the front yard. —News item.)

Out where the hose is
  That's where the lawn's not;
Not where the hose is
  You'll find the grass plot.

Out in the back yard
  There is the front. Oh,
Not in the front yard
  Where you'd expect so!

TO CLARIFY

The front's where the back is,
  The back is the front. See?
The "Keep Off the Grass sign
  Is not where it should be.

To go on the front lawn
  You go to the back yard;
The back's not a back yard—
  It's front. Boy, is life hard!

LET'S GET THIS STRAIGHT

The place for the hose now
  Is out on the front lawn;
But that makes it tough, for
  The front to the back's gone!

Back where the lawn is
  The faucet is not, so
You go to the front for
  A front-to-the-back flow.

TO REPEAT

The lawn to be wet
  Isn't out by the wetter;
The back lawn's the front,
  By a government letter.

The place for the clothesline
  Is not where it should be;
But back where no folks thought
  It possibly could be.

SUMMING UP

The front lawn's out back
  But the water's out front, sir;
We may get it straight
  But I fear that we won't sir.

This poem tried to explain and clear up the confusion about what others called the "backward houses" in Greenhills. The houses were designed to have the "working" part of the house by the street, for deliveries, unloading, and entering the vehicle, away from the family recreation area. This meant that the kitchen and living room windows faced the back of the house near the green space so parents could watch children at play. (Courtesy of the Greenbelt Historical Society.)

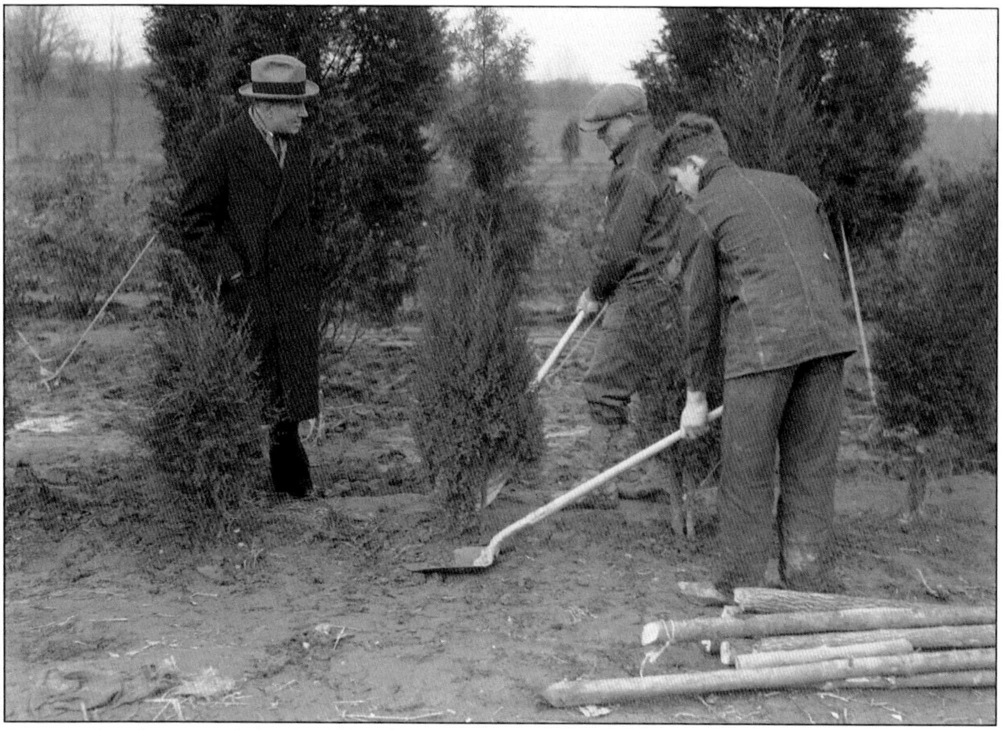

During the clearing of the land for the construction of Greenhills, larger trees were protected on site. Many small saplings were moved to a tree nursery like the one pictured above. Rexford Tugwell encouraged reforestation and the use of native plants and trees. Gardens for personal use were to be planted only close to the house. Large allotment gardens for more substantial gardening were also encouraged. Greenhills had five large community gardens. (Both, courtesy of the Library of Congress.)

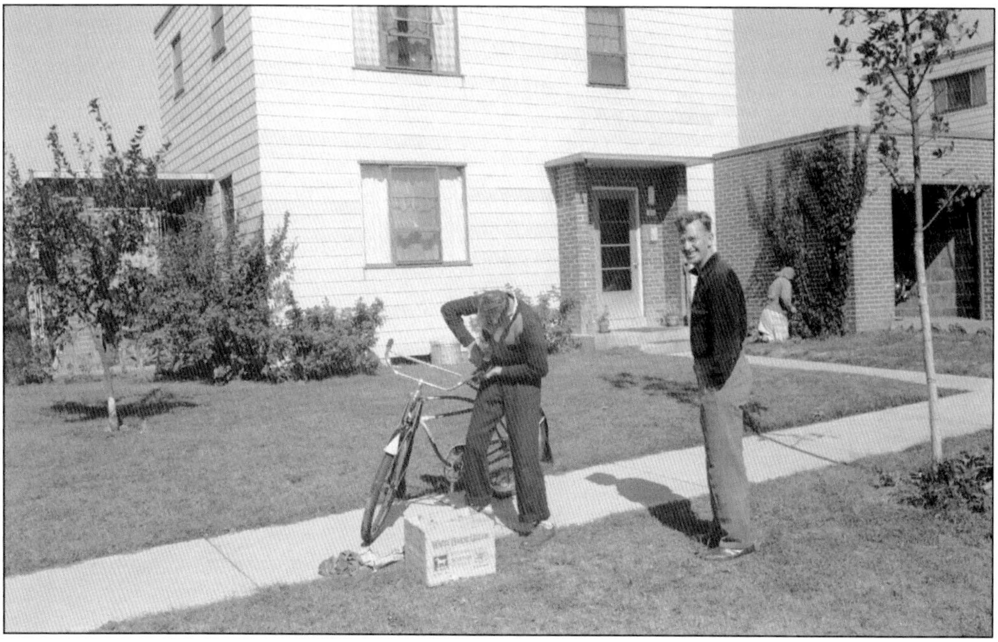

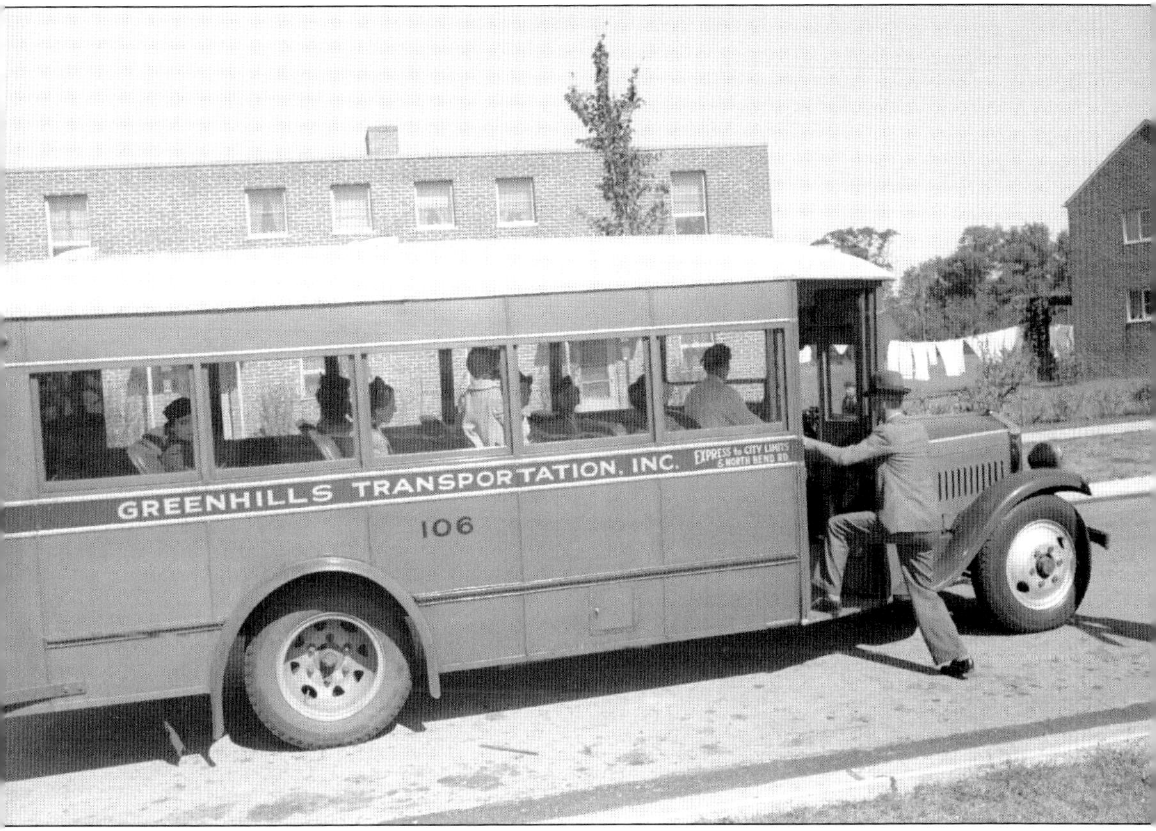

The Greenhills Transportation, Inc. bus service was not only for getting around town in a jiffy, but also for going to work. It even offered to transport people out of Greenhills to events in the evenings. Greenhills was miles from places of employment, so if one did not have a car, then the bus was the mode. Transportation into Cincinnati for early residents of Greenhills was provided by this bus and the driver, Ruth Weber, who was always referred to as "Army." The bus was known to overheat and often had to stop and cool off. Frequently, the passengers had to get out and push the bus up the hill on Winton Road. Early resident Fergus Sullivan remembered one time when, as the bus went through College Hill, a passenger yelled, "Stop here, Army!" and ran in to a hamburger stand, returning with refreshments for all of the occupants of the bus. (Courtesy of the Library of Congress.)

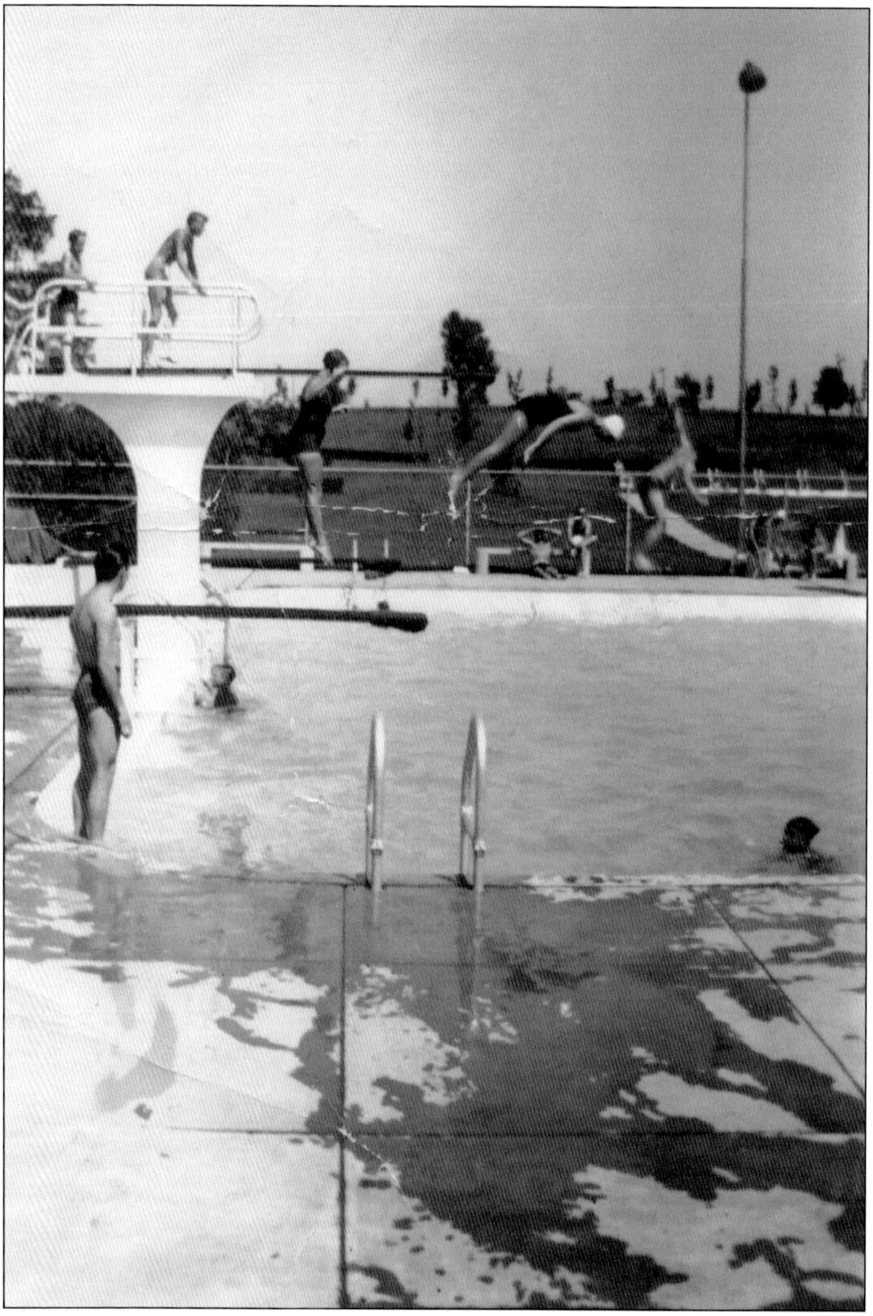

The new swimming pool became the center of summer activity for the families of Greenhills. The pool opened on July 1, 1938, and scores of residents took advantage of the opportunity for a free dip. The pool was for Greenhills residents and their guests, who were admitted only with a card bearing the signature of their hosts, along with 40¢. The cost for residents was 25¢ a day, $3 a month, or $6 for a seasonal pass. The *Greenhills Journal* reported, "The water is changed constantly and filtered and chlorinated in the process. Bathers are required to take shower baths before entering. Use will be from 10:00 a.m. to 10:00 p.m. daily and two qualified Red Cross life guards will be on duty constantly." (Courtesy of the Greenhills Alumni Association.)

Six

Civic Life

If civilization is to survive, we must cultivate the science of human relationships—the ability of all peoples, of all kinds, to live together, in the same world at peace.

—Franklin Delano Roosevelt

The open green spaces of the community offered ample room for outdoor organized activities. There were plenty of playing areas, ball fields, and interior pocket parks in which to play and relax. There were also classes on archery, bird-watching, golf, and agricultural, as well as the garden guild.

The Greenhills Community Building, situated in the center of town, provided a place for all and even served as a church for different religions. In September 1938, before the official incorporation of the village, a community council was formed to be in charge of community activities, which occurred after 5:00 p.m. during the school year.

Any group wanting to meet in the community building had to submit for approval, stating the reason for the meeting. Until Greenhills became an incorporated village, the community council was given the power to establish traffic, fire, police, sanitation, and health regulations It was suggested in a community meeting that a general plan for rules and regulations be created, and the 1940 Greenhills anniversary book stated, "To make the committee truly representative of the community, families arriving before May 30 chose three members; those between May 30 and July 15, three; those after July 15, three; and rural families, two."

The Greenhills Community Building was home to many civic evening programs. It was open by June and was immediately a center for the whole community. It included the public library, which featured 4,000 books, and various artists painted murals and created pieces of art to decorate the interior. As an adult education center, the community building provided classes in many different subjects, including economics, typing, machine and wood shop, and home economics. Classrooms provided plenty of room to seat 50 adults with typewriters for adult education. There were state-of-the-art workshops with sewing and cooking areas for classroom use, plus a living room, dining room, bath, and kitchen for students to learn decorating and cleaning. The music room was the site for the first church services, both Catholic and Protestant. The auditorium was a perfect place for large community meetings and also served as the theater and playhouse and a popular venue for movies.

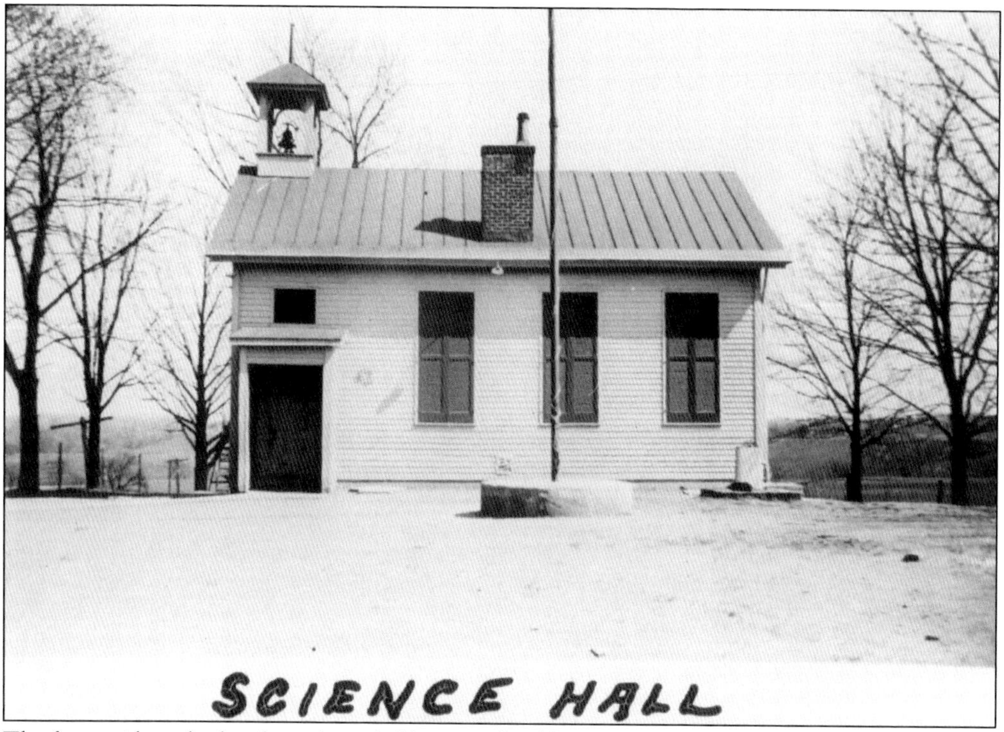

The first residents had to drive their children to school because the local Greenhills school building was not ready, but that soon changed. When the Greenhills Community Building was completed, it also served as a K–12 school. In 1939, the Hamilton County Board of Education created the Greenhills Rural School District, which included all the area owned by the government. The new district was created from five different rural districts: the Science Hall Rural School District, the Newell Rural School District, and portions of the New Burlington, Pleasant Run, and Springdale Rural School Districts. Children in the area of Greenhills had gone to the Science Hall School (above) or the Newell School (below), both one-room schoolhouses, before the community building opened. (Both, courtesy of the Winton Woods City Schools.)

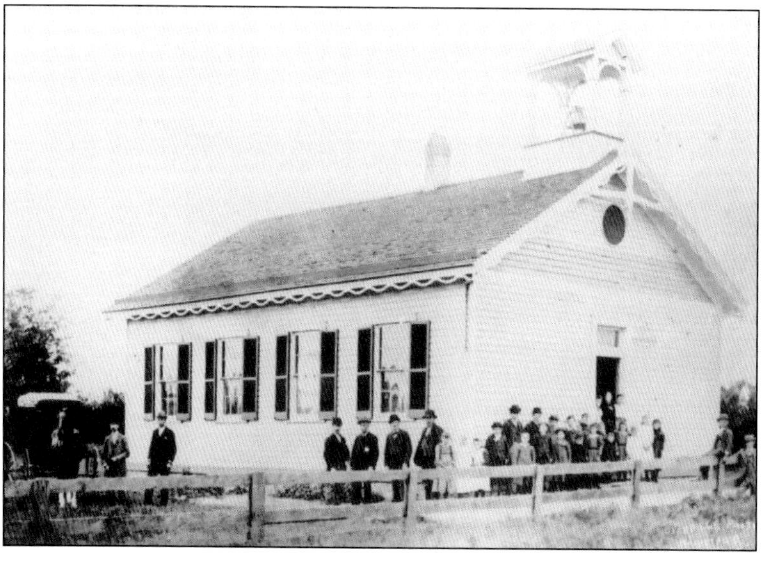

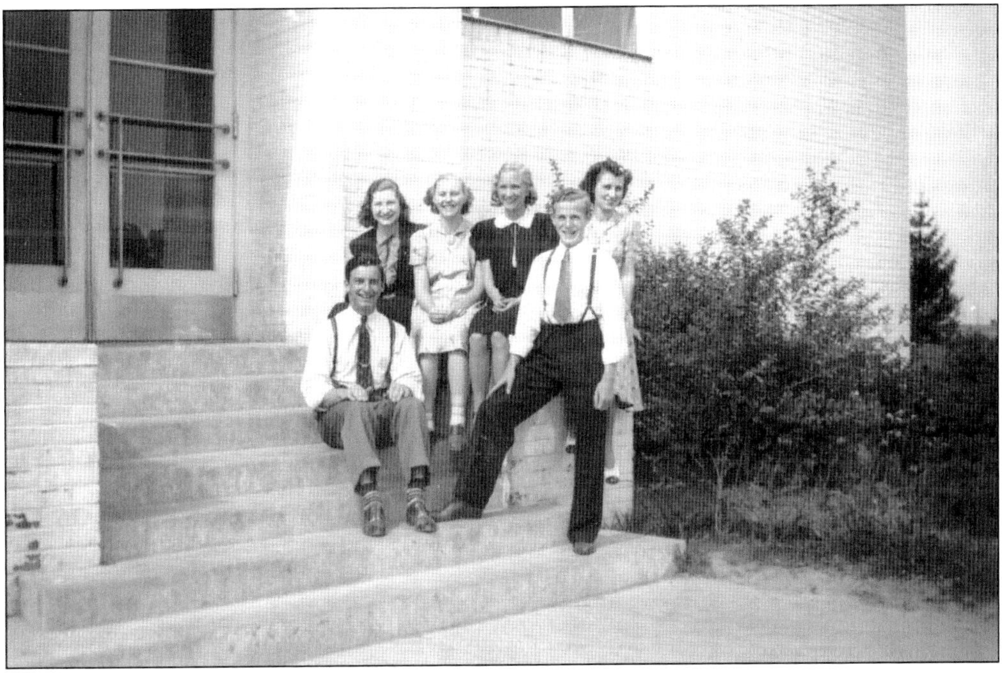

The first Greenhills graduating class, seen here in 1939, includes, from left to right, (first row) Richard Recher and Jimmy Giblin; (second row) Hallie Bowling, Gladys Craig, Elaine Landers, and Ruth Colby. (Courtesy of the Greenhills Alumni Association.)

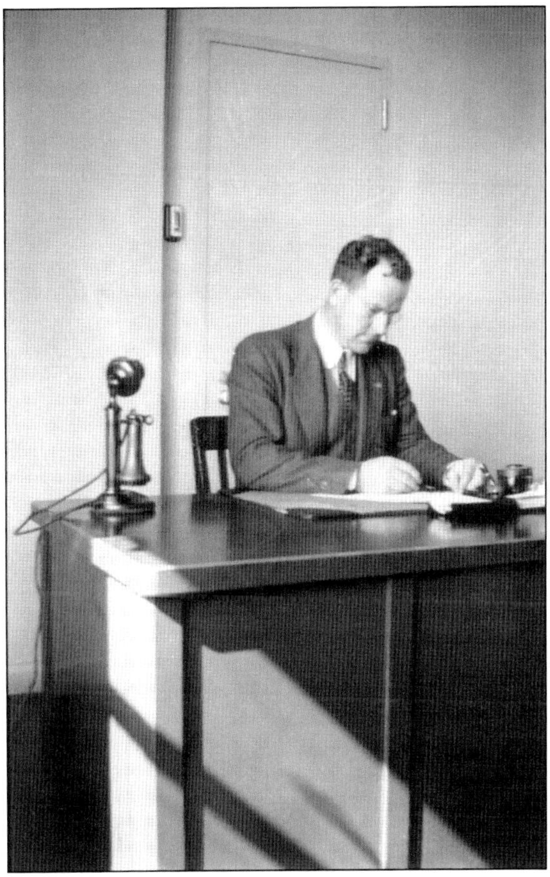

The Greenhills public schools opened in September 1938, and by the end of the year, 458 students were enrolled. R.K. Salisbury (pictured here) was the superintendent, Lincoln Hurst was the principal, and Theodore Rickey was the elementary principal. (Courtesy of the Greenhills Alumni Association.)

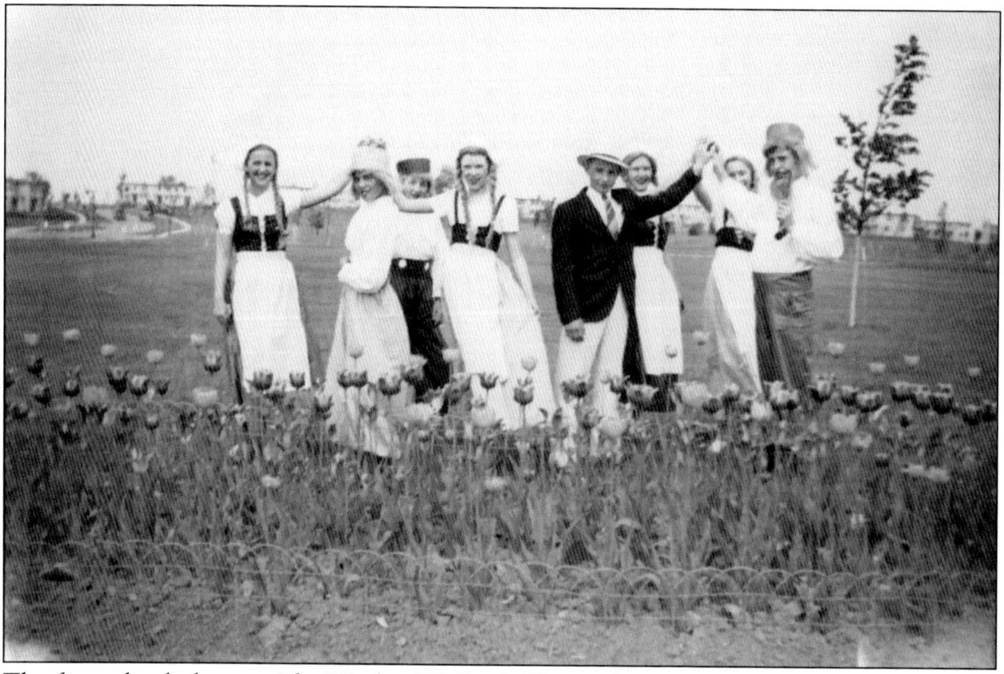

The first school play was *The Winds of Holland.* The student actors, seen here, had the good fortune to find some early spring tulips bordering a yard by the school. (Courtesy of the Greenhills Alumni Association.)

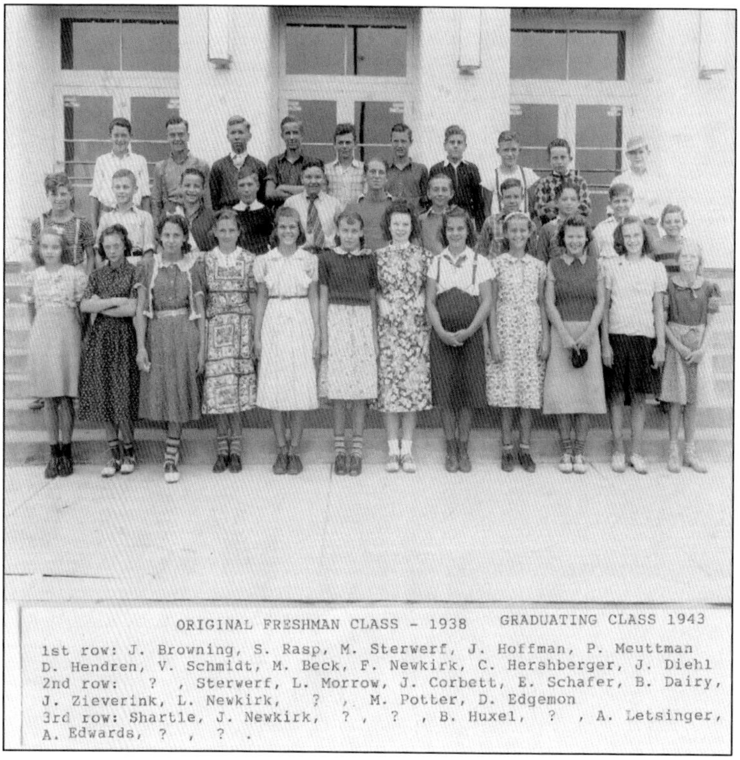

The first high school freshman class, which graduated in 1943, is pictured on the front steps of the community building. (Courtesy of the Greenhills Alumni Association.)

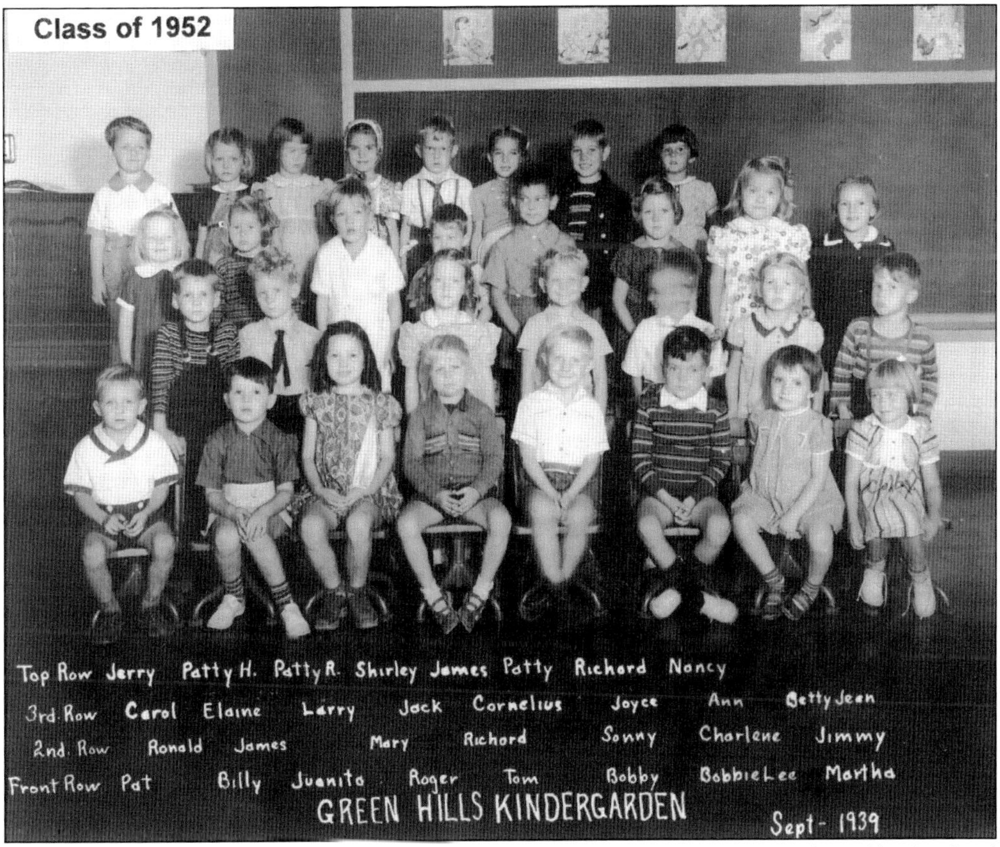

The first kindergarten class of the Greenhills Rural School District, which graduated high school in 1952, is seen above. The Greenhills Alumni Association has an archive of all the class yearbooks from the beginning of the school district. The first yearbook was handmade, with photographs printed from negatives. Below is a candid shot of an early elementary class in the spacious new Greenhills Community Building. (Both, courtesy of the Greenhills Alumni Association.)

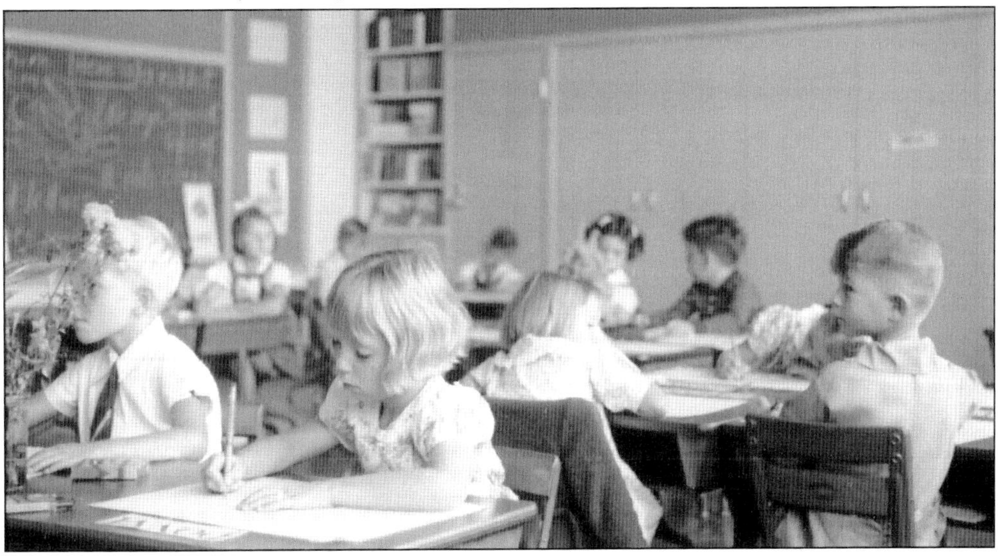

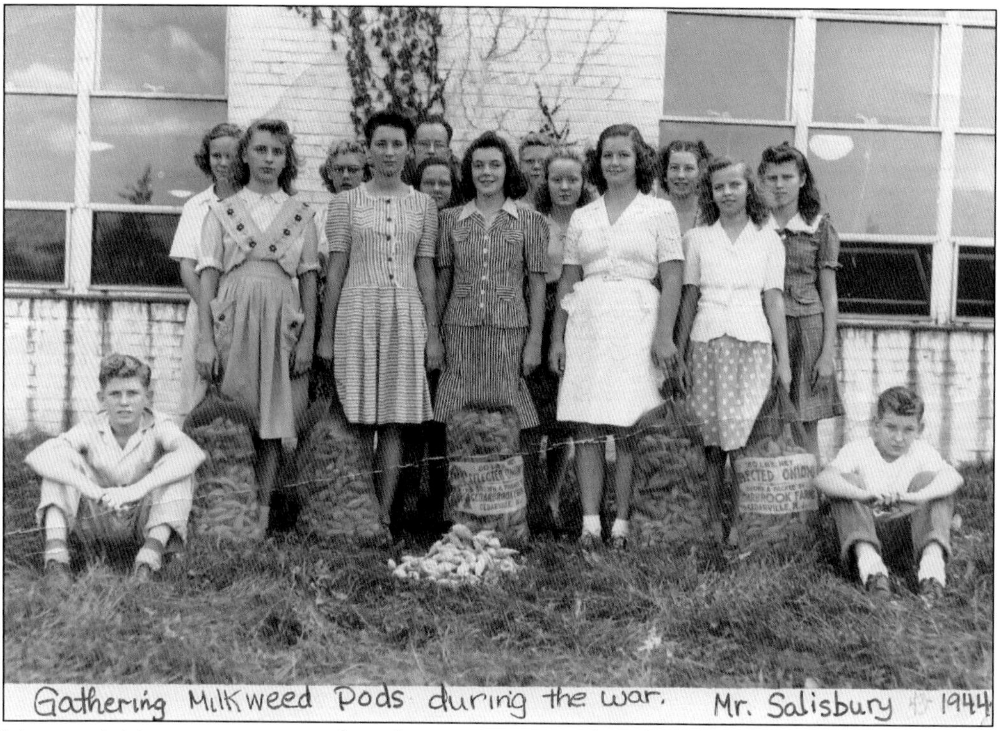

Many activities were encouraged in the community and in the school from its beginning. As World War II was gearing up, allotment gardens became victory gardens. Other wartime pursuits to help the troops were scrap drives, where movie admission could be paid for with pounds of scrap metal and war bonds. Here, R.K. Salisbury's class of students created a project gathering milkweed pods, which were then used for stuffing flotation devices. (Courtesy of the Greenhills Alumni Association.)

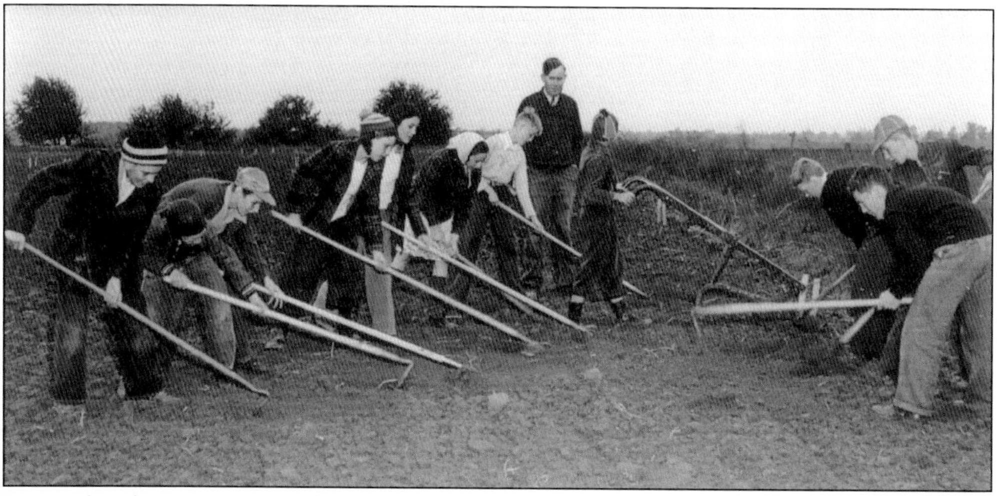

Personal and community gardens were part of the original plans for Greenhills. In 1942, the *Greenhills Journal* reported that teacher Theodore Rickey and the schoolchildren planted 500 pounds of potatoes, 10,000 tomatoes, 500 cabbages, and other vegetables and beans. After it was processed by cafeteria workers, the food was served to schoolchildren all the next year. (Courtesy of the Library of Congress.)

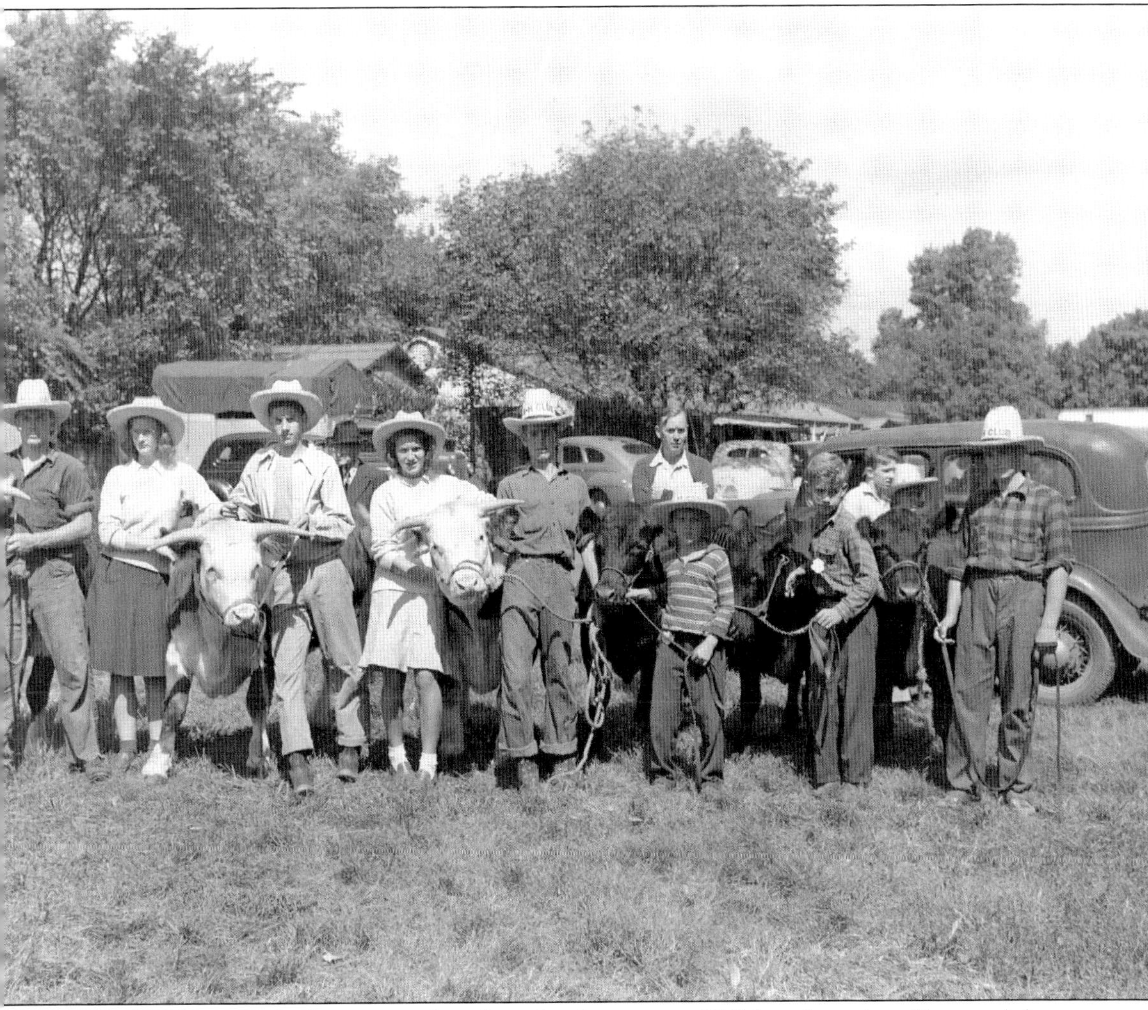

The 4-H club was one of many popular after-school activities. Children from the village and the surrounding farms joined. Some of the members of the steer club are seen here with their projects. Other popular clubs were the horse club, the sewing club, and the cooking club. The Greenhills school was closed for the county fair, where student entries were highlighted. (Courtesy of the Palma family.)

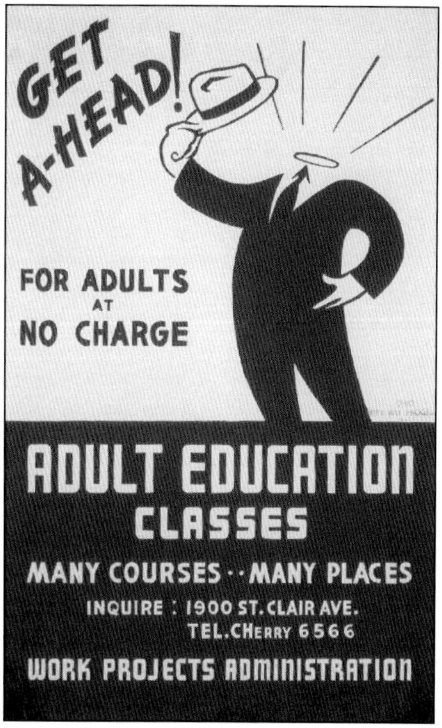

Adult education typing classes were popular at the community building, and an amazing array of classes building job and life skills were offered, including adult art classes (below). All adult classes were offered at night, starting at 5:00 p.m. (Left, courtesy of the Library of Congress; below, courtesy of the Lippmeier family.)

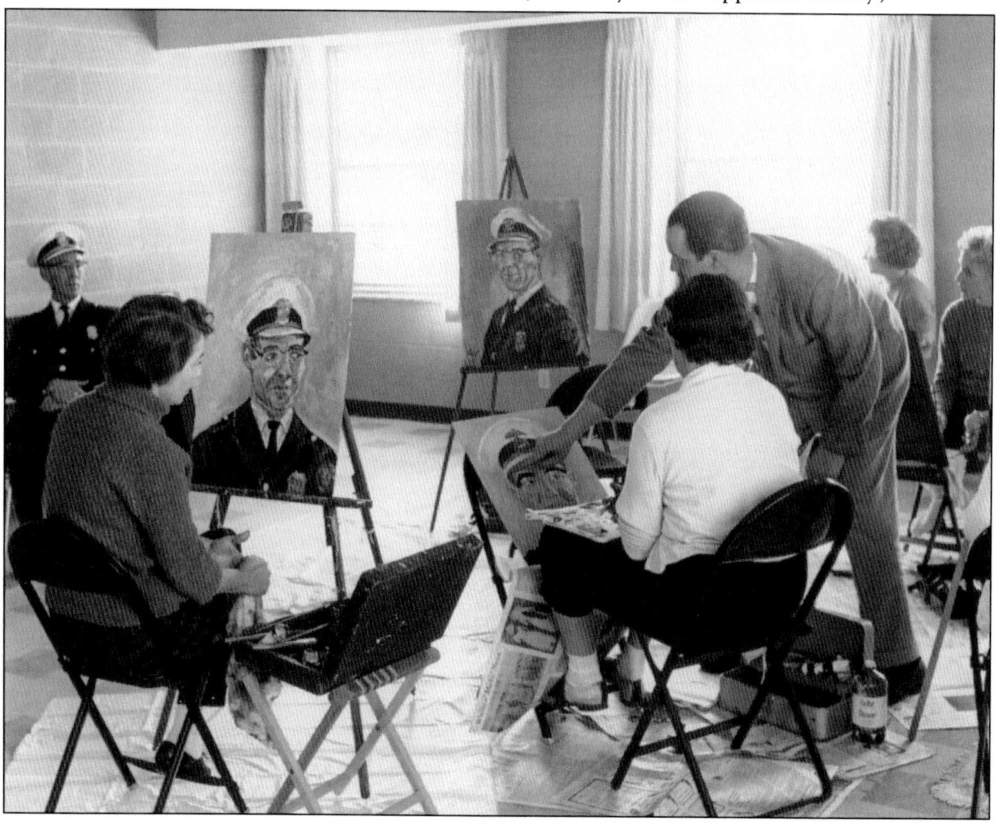

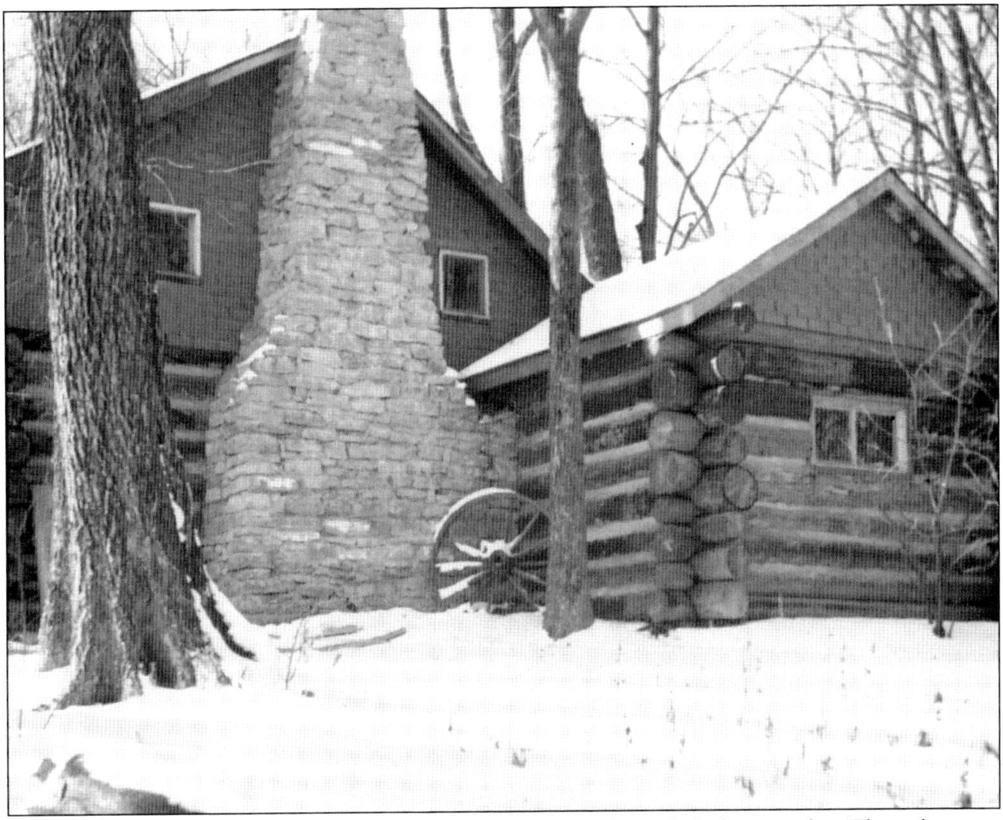

A group of volunteers built the Boy Scouts cabin out of discarded phone poles. The cabin was used for many years thereafter. (Courtesy of the Lippmeier family.)

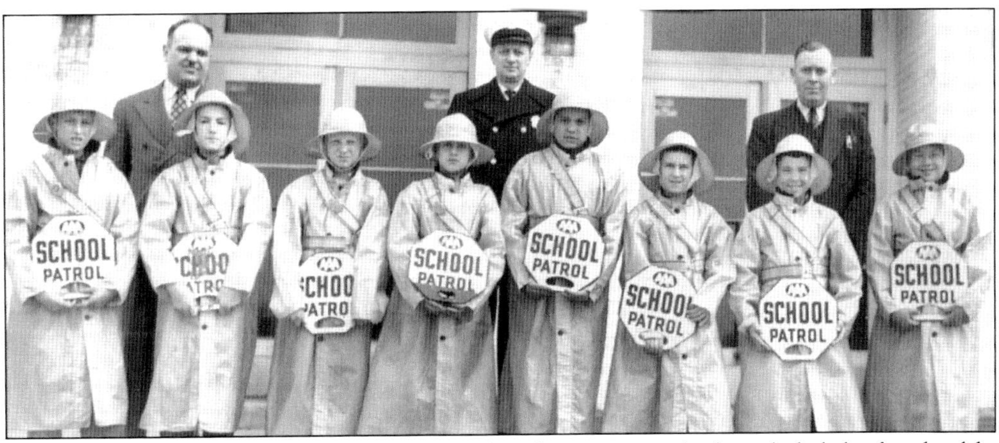

In the early years of Greenhills, the public safety department, which included the fire, health, and safety squads and the police department, took pride in training the volunteers who helped as school crossing guards. (Courtesy of the Lippmeier family.)

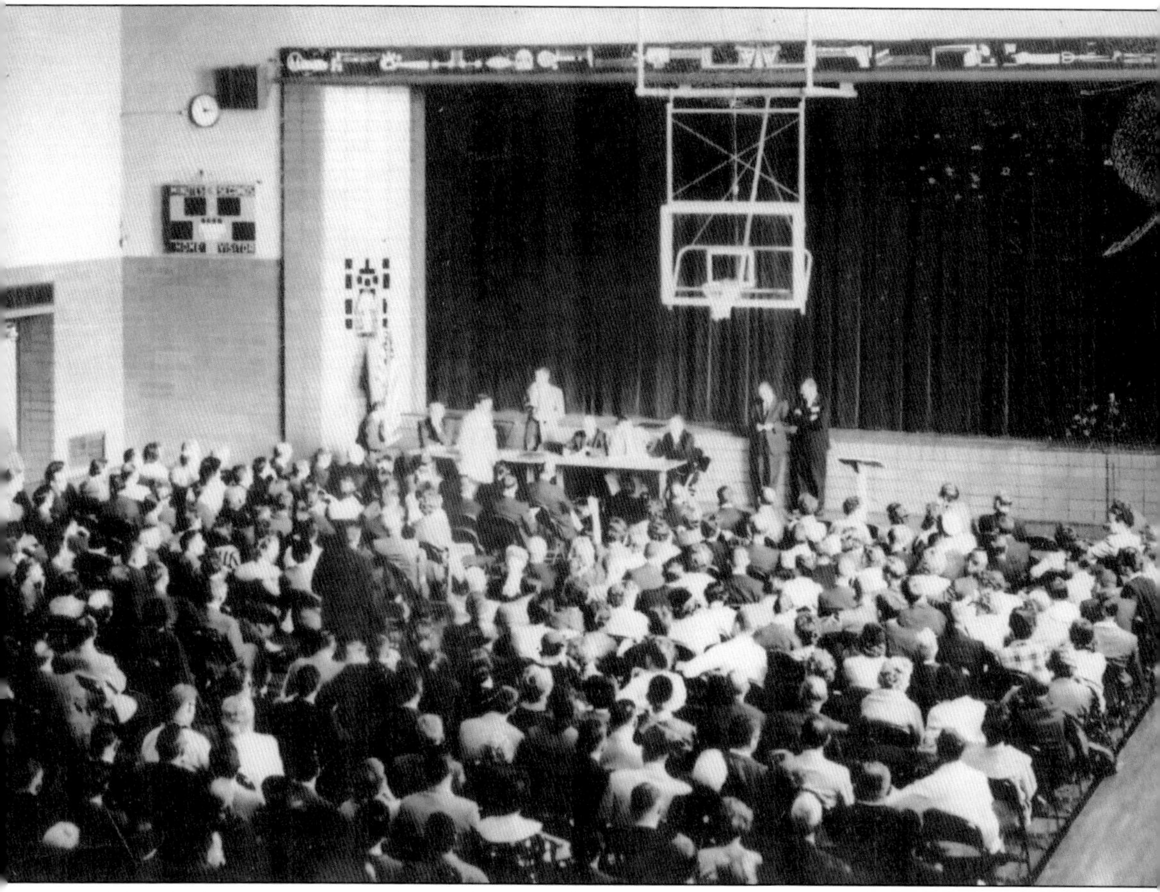

Many early civic events were held at the Greenhills Community Building, filling its large auditorium to capacity. Boy Scout Troop 400 used the gymnasium for large events, and it served as a venue for services for all religious denominations until church buildings were constructed. (Courtesy of the Greenhills Alumni Association.)

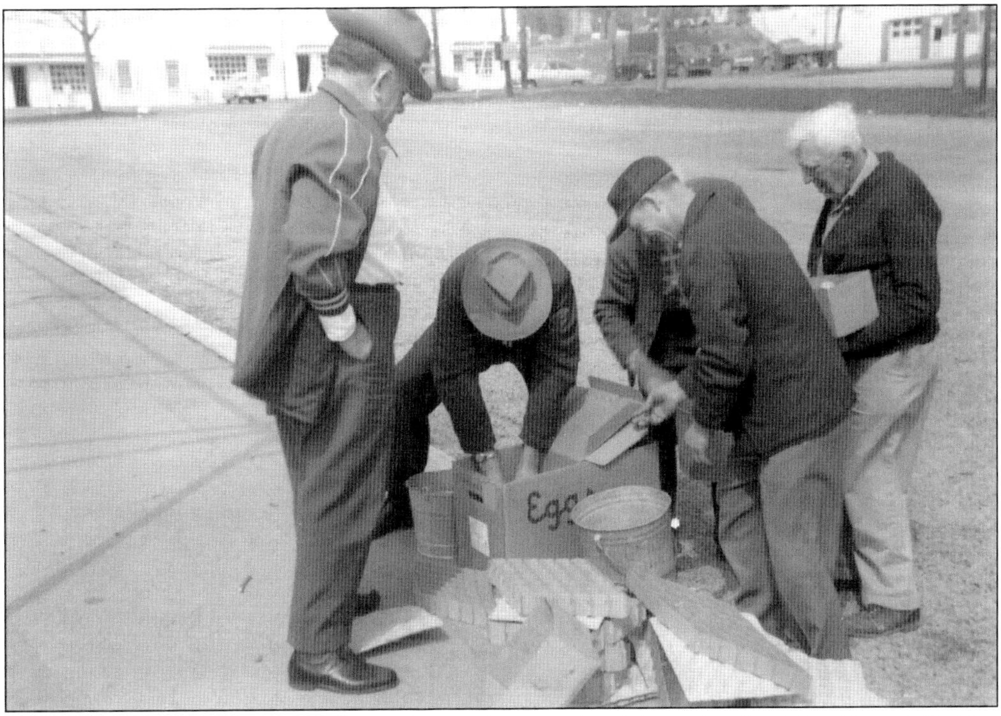

The Easter egg hunt is an annual tradition that is still celebrated today. The Greenhills Fire Department has always volunteered to run the well-attended event. (Both, courtesy of the Greenhills Historical Society.)

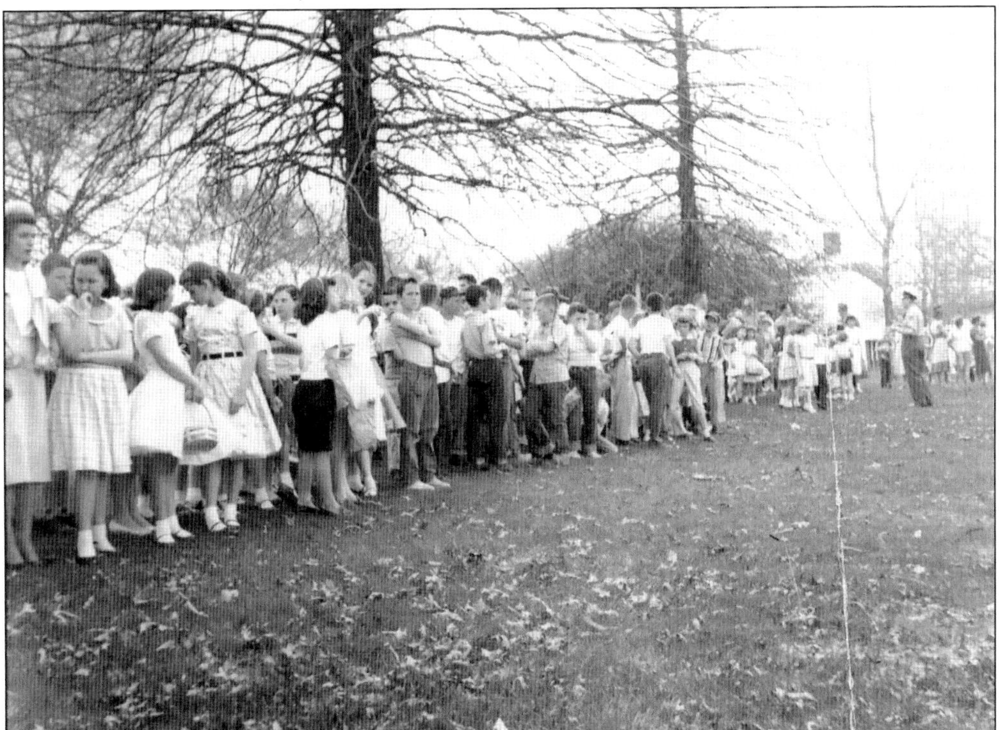

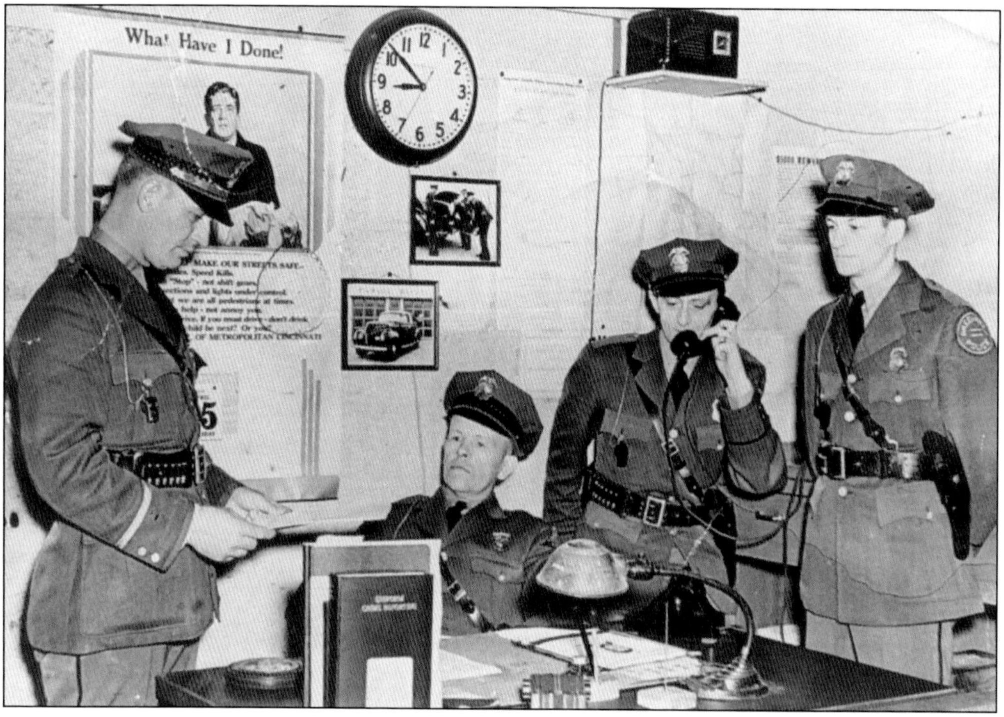

The early days of the Greenhills Police Department are seen in these photographs. The police department was located in the south end of the shopping center and shared space area with the volunteer fire department. Directly below, in the lower level of the shopping center, were the jail cells. (Both, courtesy of the Lippmeier family.)

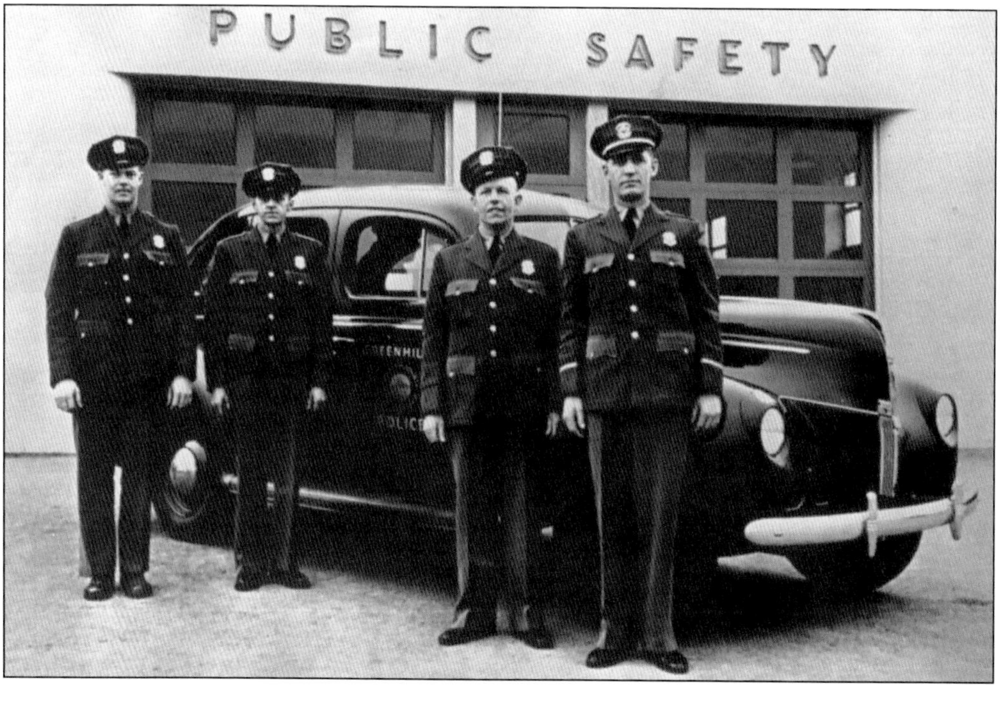

In this collage, early Greenhills public safety and fire department volunteers demonstrate their talents in protecting the community. (Courtesy of the Palma family.)

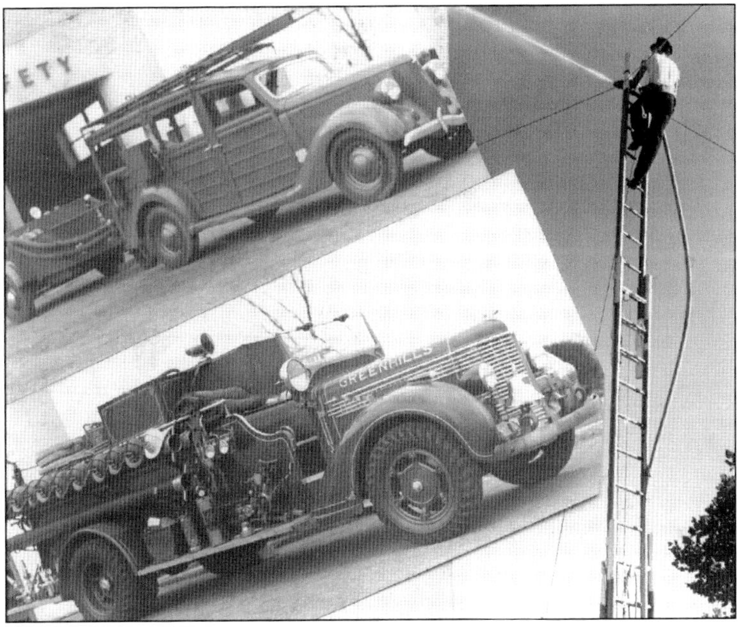

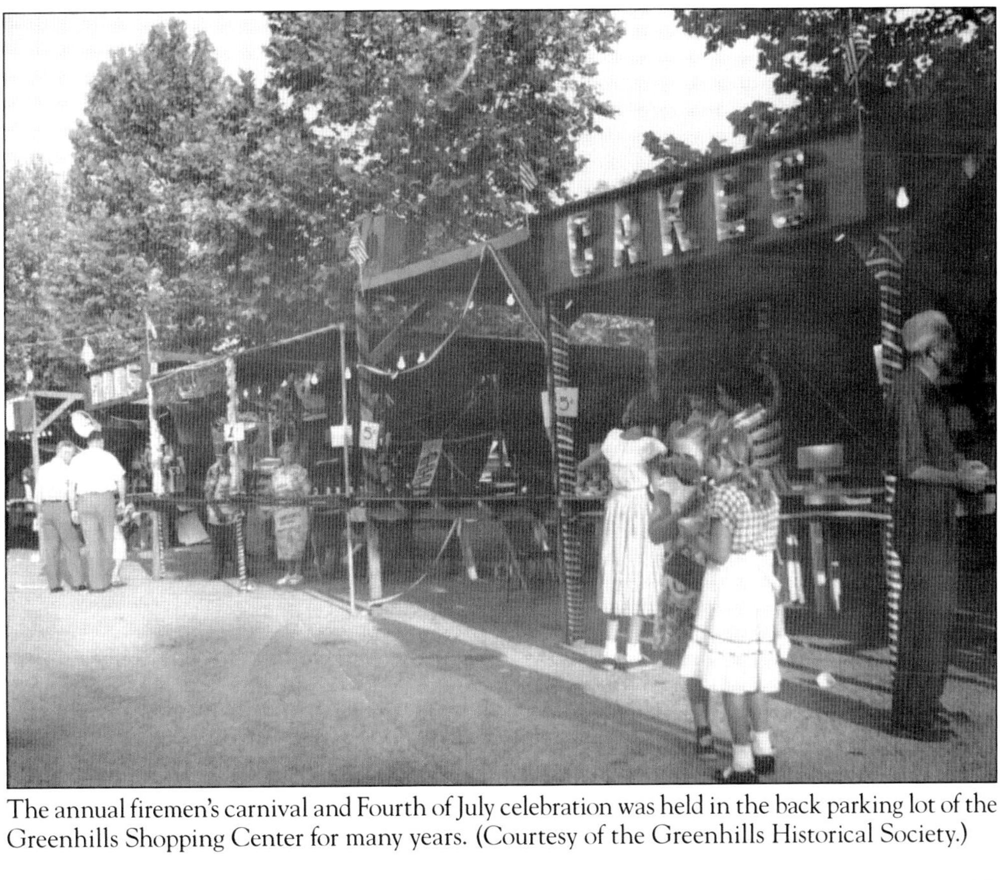

The annual firemen's carnival and Fourth of July celebration was held in the back parking lot of the Greenhills Shopping Center for many years. (Courtesy of the Greenhills Historical Society.)

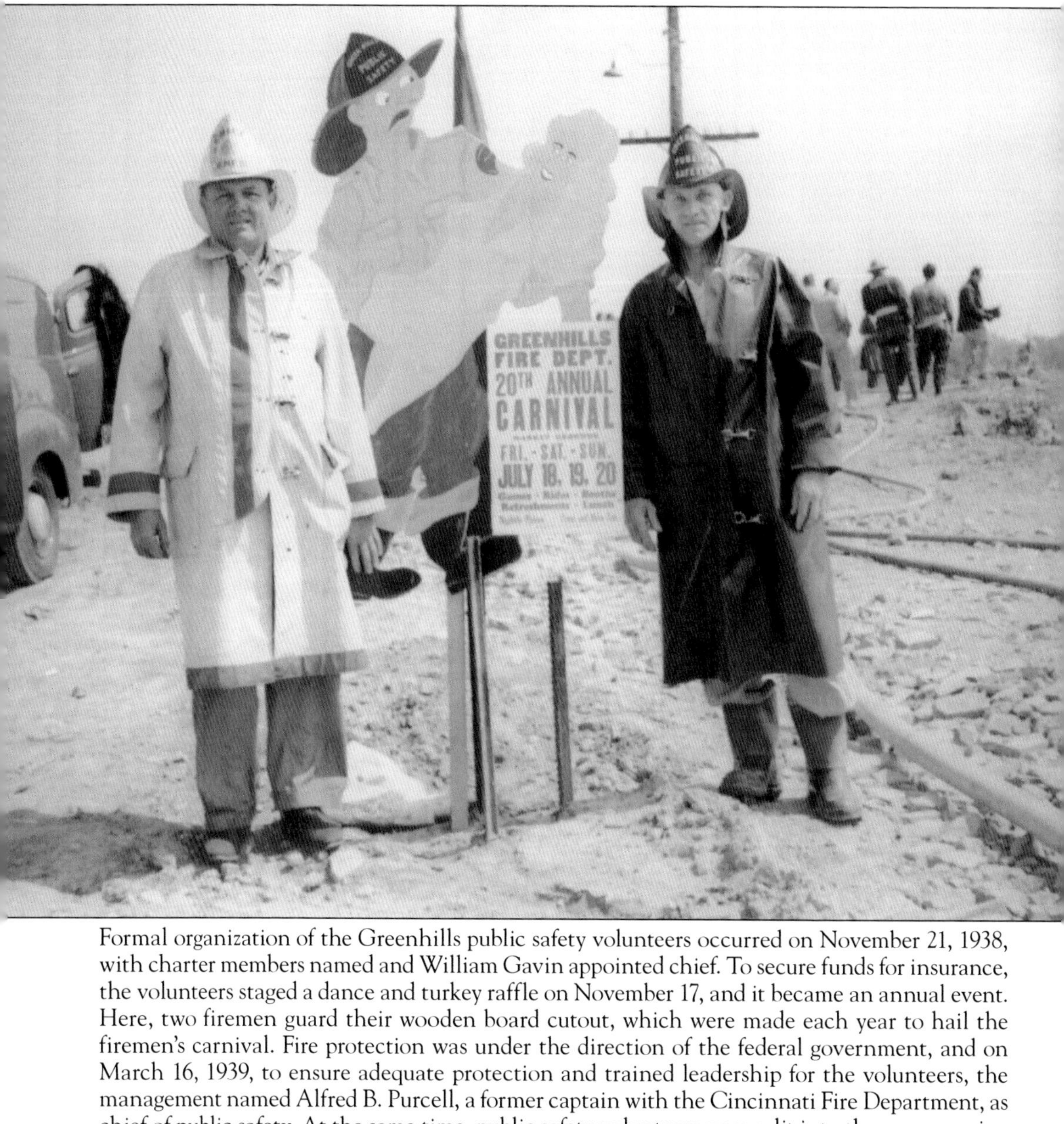

Formal organization of the Greenhills public safety volunteers occurred on November 21, 1938, with charter members named and William Gavin appointed chief. To secure funds for insurance, the volunteers staged a dance and turkey raffle on November 17, and it became an annual event. Here, two firemen guard their wooden board cutout, which were made each year to hail the firemen's carnival. Fire protection was under the direction of the federal government, and on March 16, 1939, to ensure adequate protection and trained leadership for the volunteers, the management named Alfred B. Purcell, a former captain with the Cincinnati Fire Department, as chief of public safety. At the same time, public safety volunteers were split into three companies: firefighters, traffic, and reserves. (Courtesy of the Greenhills Historical Society.)

Seven

THE COOPERATIVES

Cooperatives are not only a business . . . they are a movement for the betterment of mankind, irrespective of his race, color or creed, and regardless of where he may live. Cooperatives are US . . . not THEY.

—Greenhills Eighth Anniversary Booklet

During the Great Depression, the New Deal stimulated great change in the overall view of how the government worked with cooperatives. The government encouraged the "self-help" cooperative movement, stressing the mutual aid and barter system. Cooperatives produced a variety of goods for trade and self-use, and organized exchanges between laborers, farmers, services, goods, and community members. One of the New Deal's first acts was to set up a Division of Self-Help Cooperatives, under the Federal Emergency Relief Act, which provided technical assistance and grants to self-help cooperatives and barter associations.

Greenhills was the first of the three greenbelt towns—and the first town in the country—to use cooperatives as a way to engage everyone in the commercial vitality of its existence. At the first general meeting at the end of April 1938, residents decided that the store facilities should be leased to a cooperative. Consequently, Greenhills Consumer Services, Inc. was organized by the residents of Greenhills and by members of cooperative organizations from Cincinnati in May 1938. Financing was obtained through loans from the Consumer Distribution Corporation of New York, an organization founded and financed by Edward A. Filene of Boston to assist the cooperative movement in the United States. Herbert E. Evans was named the executive trustee, in charge of designing and equipping the stores, employing personnel, supervising purchases, stocking merchandise, and acting in the capacity of general manager.

The first-anniversary edition of the *Greenhills News Bulletin* reported, "One of the community accomplishments that the residents of Greenhills can view with pride is the progress that has been made by the Greenhills Consumer Services, Incorporated, the corporation through which the residents of the village operate their own commercial enterprises."

Any person over the age of 18 was eligible to join the cooperative. The membership fee for residents was $10 per year. Receipts were saved, and any profits of the cooperative were shared in proportion to their purchases. Each member had one vote and helped make all management decisions in regular meetings.

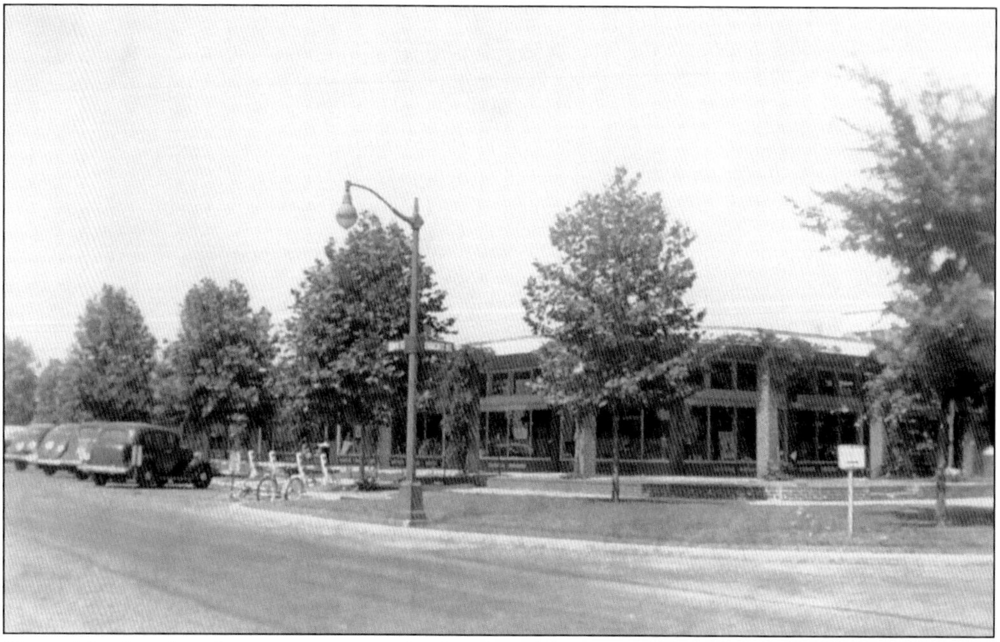

One of the first few shopping centers of its kind in the country, the Greenhills Shopping Center is a significant contributing building in the Greenhills historic district, as listed in the National Register of Historic Places. Greenhills was the first of the three greenbelt towns to have consumer cooperation services established and open the stores for business. On December 15, 1938, the *Greenbelt Cooperator*, from Greenbelt, Maryland, reported, "Greenhills, Ohio, younger sister to Greenbelt, has already surpassed Greenbelt in some respects. It is the first of the government housing projects to develop cooperatives." (Above, courtesy of the Greenhills Historical Society; below, courtesy of the Palma family.)

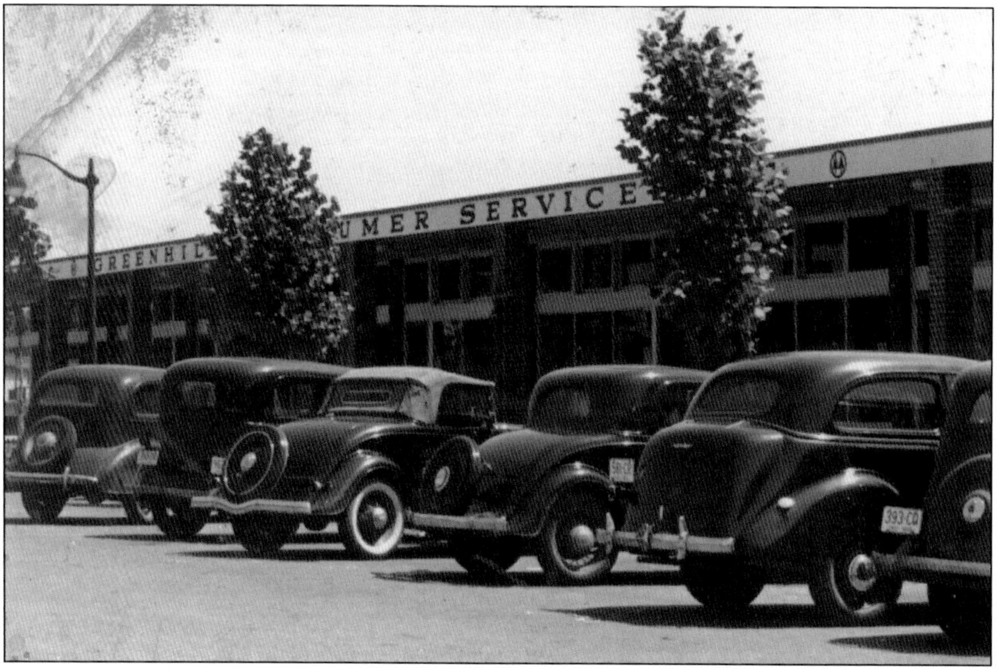

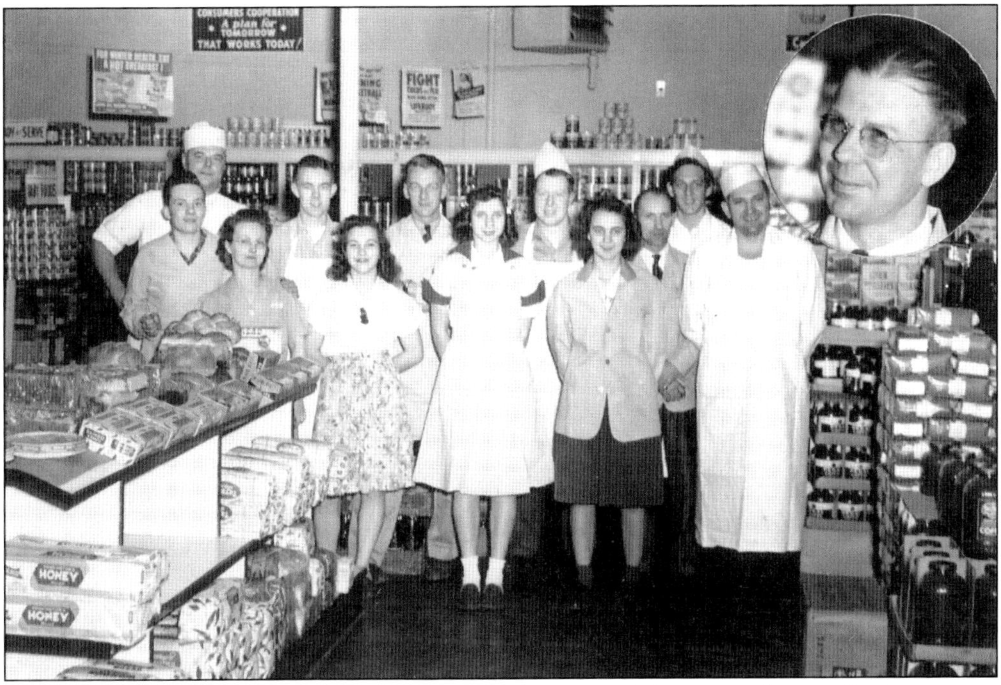

The cooperative food store opened its doors on July 11, 1938, and the meat and vegetable departments opened on October 1. The service station opened on August 13, and the dry cleaners and barbershop opened on October 31. The general merchandise store, with drug and prescription services and a soda fountain and lunch counter, opened on December 3. A beauty shop opened the next May. The cooperative drugstore and lunch counter became a great neighborhood hangout; it was a good place to catch up on Greenhills gossip and news. (Both, courtesy of the Palma family.)

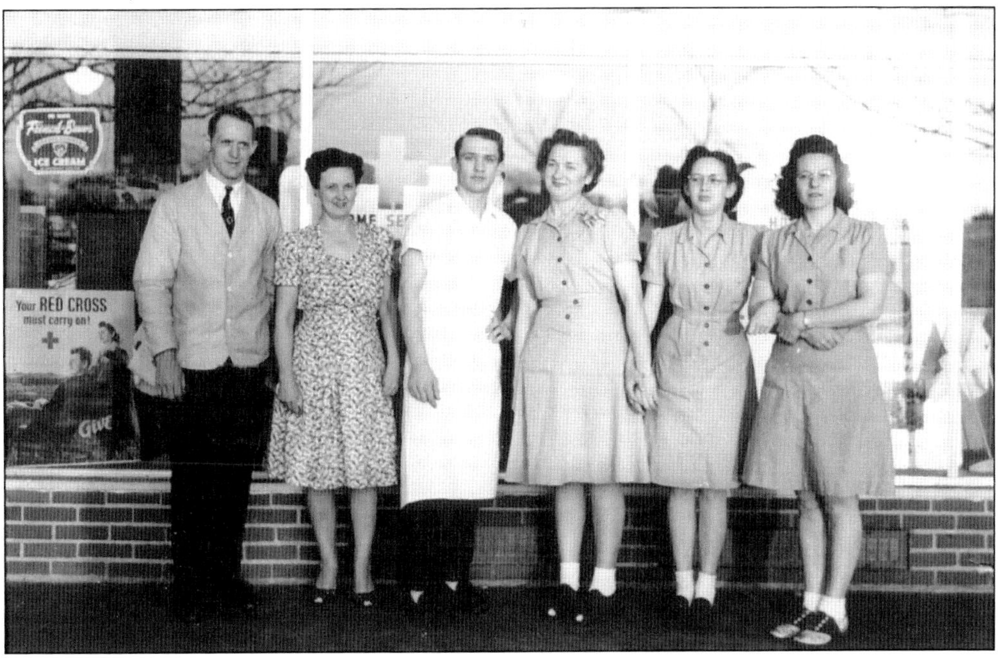

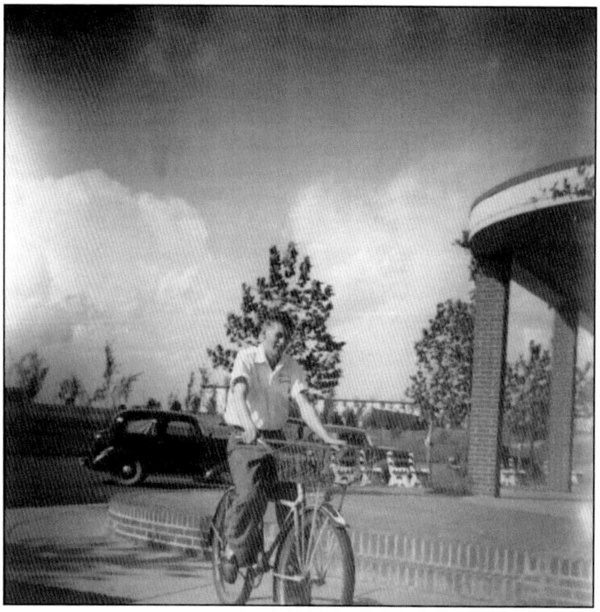

The shopping center was unique because of the colonnade, which covered patrons from one end of the shopping center to the other. It also had access steps through its structure in places from the front to the lower level. When real estate agents sold potential clients on the community assets, they boasted about the convenient center of the town with a community building, an outdoor swimming pool, tennis courts, town administration buildings, and the myriad of stores for all needed conveniences. This made life very attractive to all generations of families. (Left, courtesy of the Greenhills Historical Society; below, courtesy of the Palma family.)

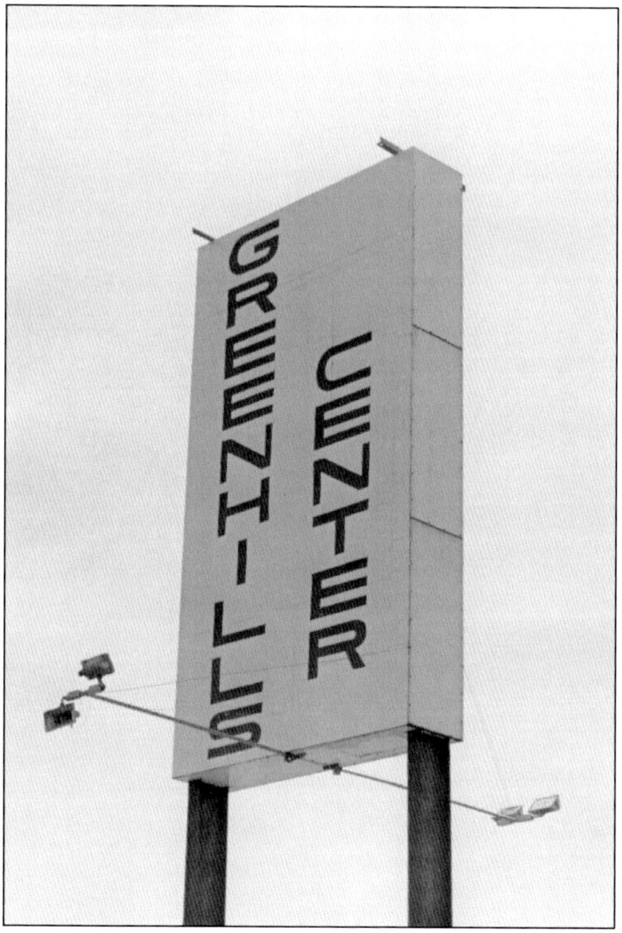

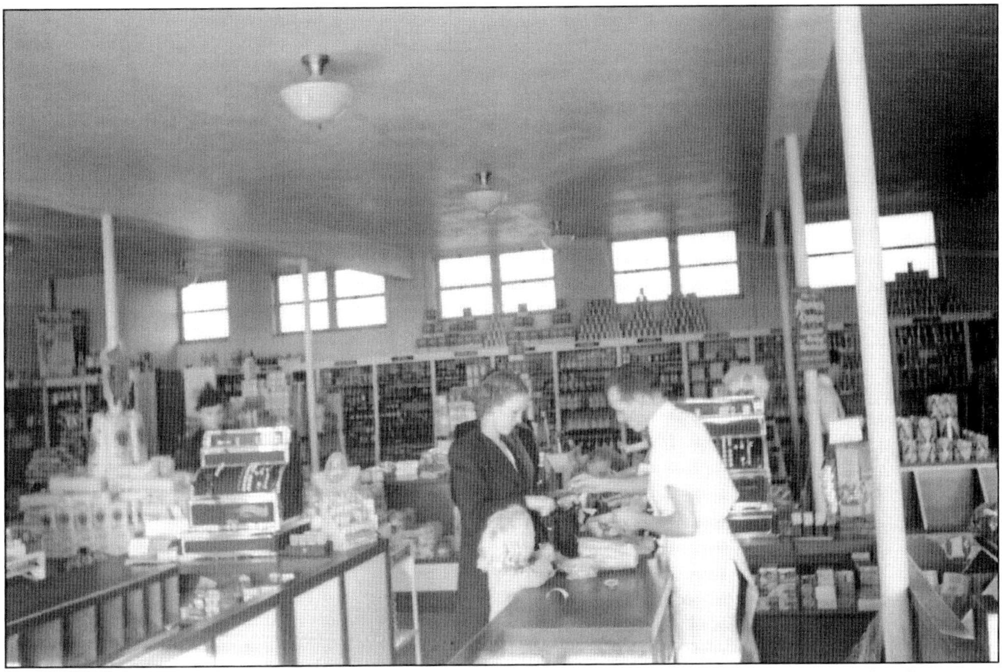

The cooperative (above) soon carried everything needed for daily life and was a hub of activity. By 1962, there were more than 50 stores and services provided for the residents in the shopping center. One of the most popular was what began as Knapps Food Locker (below), where residents could rent freezer storage lockers for their groceries. It also held a large party room for neighborhood events. At the time, this venue was the only place beer could be served. "Party at the freezer" was the phrase used for many memorable events in the early years of village life. (Both, courtesy of the Library of Congress.)

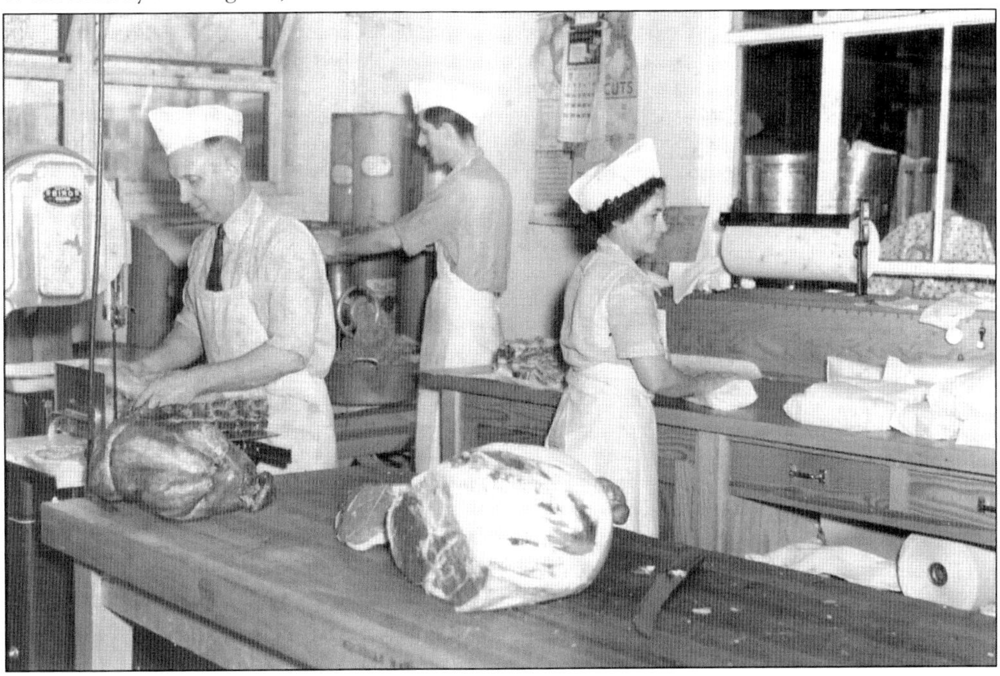

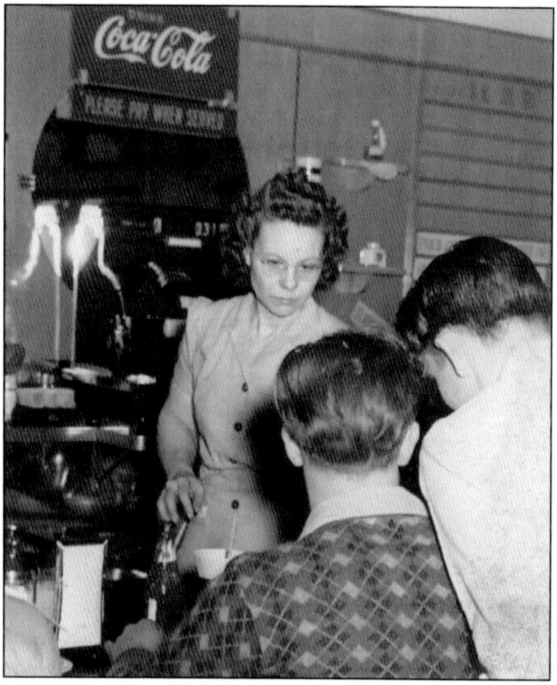

A congressional investigation was conducted by a house subcommittee to see if there was a cooperative monopoly promoted by the Federal Housing Authority to exclude private enterprise, but the greenbelt communities were found to be innocent of any wrongdoing. In 1947, the beauty shop, barbershop, filling station, and dry cleaners were privately owned and operated under leases provided by the cooperative. (Left, courtesy of the Library of Congress; below, courtesy of the Palma family.)

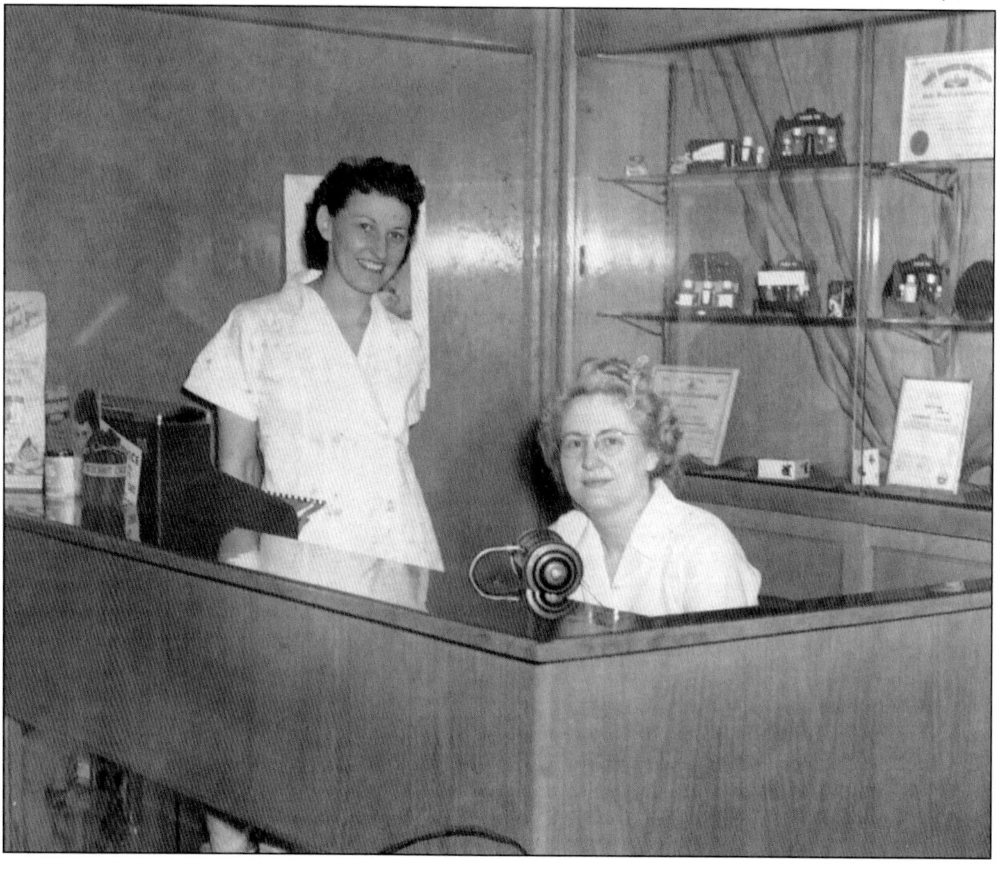

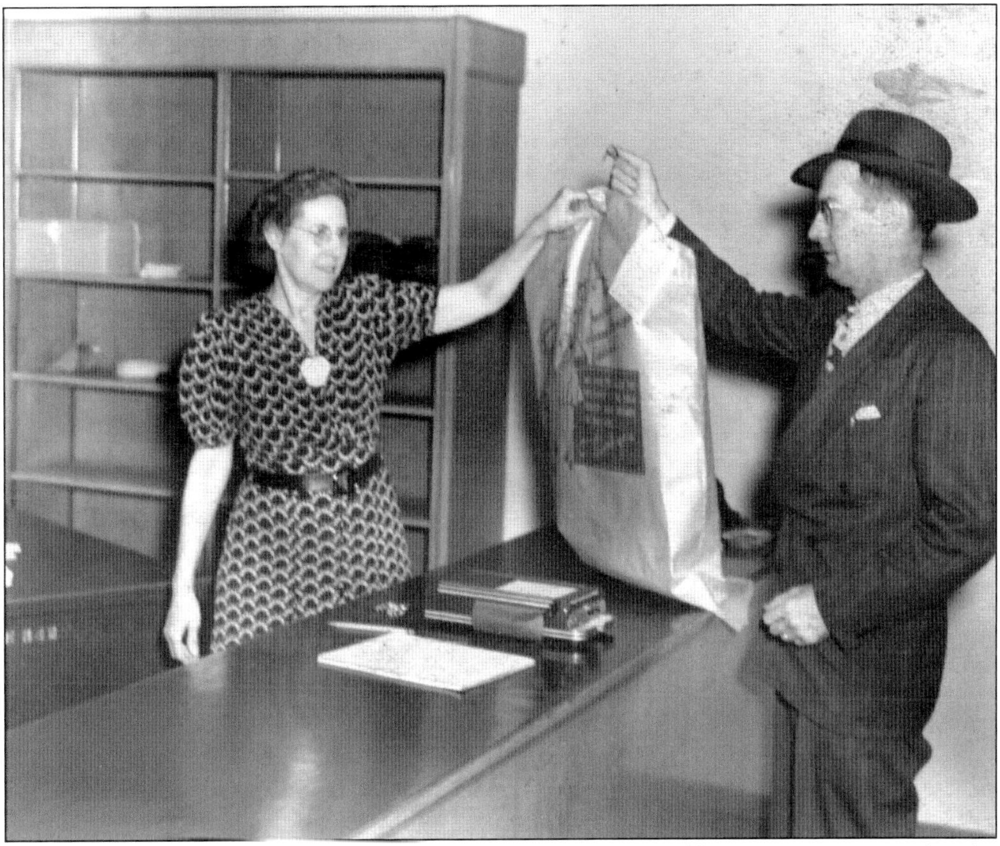

The shopping center was a big part of everyday life for residents. Above, a man retrieves his dry cleaning, and below, local women shop and catch up on the news. (Both, courtesy of the Library of Congress.)

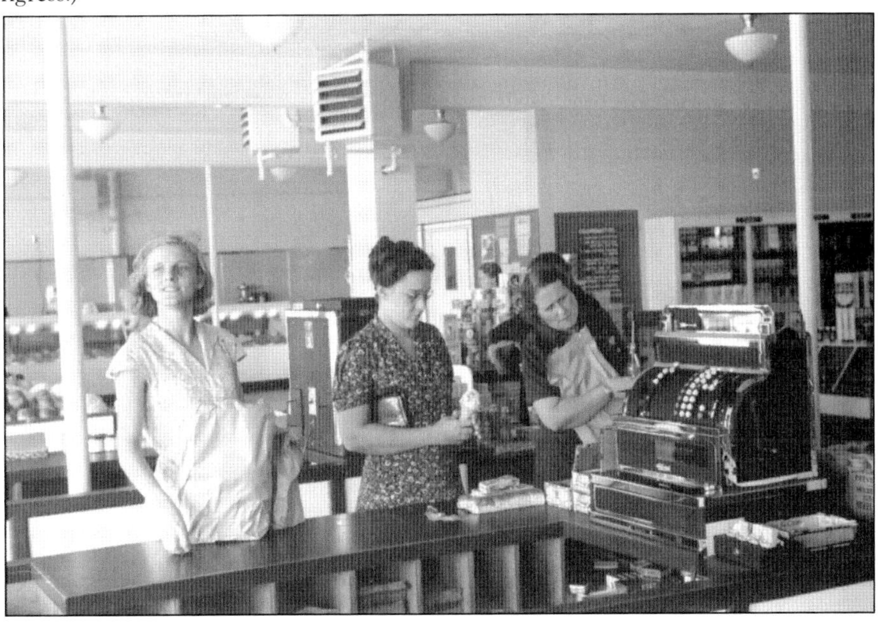

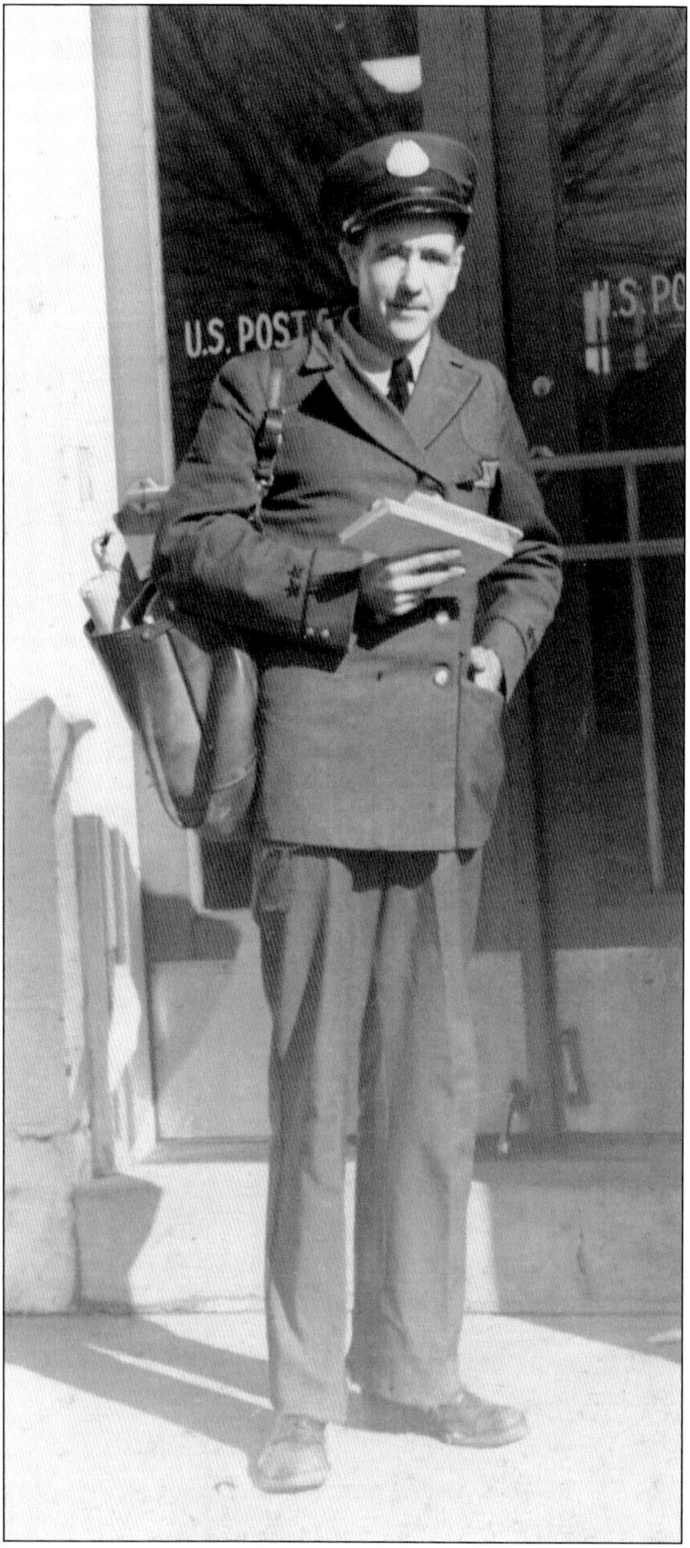

Along with the cooperative and private businesses, the shopping center also included a post office located adjacent to the administrative offices. The village still has a contract post office today, which occupies the same building. (Courtesy of the Palma family.)

Eight

PUBLIC ART AND CULTURE

The organization of the Project has proceeded on the principle that it is not the solitary genius, but a sound general movement which maintains art as a vital, functioning part of any cultural scheme.

—Holger Cahill

As President Roosevelt's second New Deal program was announced, continuing the ever-increasing effort to bring the nation's people out of poverty, the government launched its best-known relief agency, the Works Progress Administration (WPA). The WPA's most controversial program, Federal Project Number One, or Federal One, featured a Professional Projects Division that offered work to artists, musicians, dramatists, and writers. Within the WPA, Federal One became the umbrella organization for all the arts. Artists created thousands of murals and sculptural works to beautify the walls and halls of public buildings. Musicians established symphony orchestras in 30 cities as well as hundreds of smaller musical groups. The Federal Theater Project financed playwrights, actors, and directors, as well as historians who documented American history by interviewing former slaves.

Harry Hopkins, President Roosevelt's administrative assistant, appointed Holger Cahill as the national director of the Federal Art Project (FAP) of the WPA. Cahill, an authority on American folk art, had been a curator at the Newark Museum in New Jersey and then at the Museum of Modern Art in New York City. With the goal of developing an artist's work relief program, Cahill started plans immediately for the WPA/FAP. His wishes were to reach out to every artist, regardless of their talent level.

Eligible FAP recipients had to demonstrate their financial need for relief and had to provide proof of an artistic career. This program grew into what is today one of the most voluminous cultural outreach programs in American history. In 1939, Cahill remarked, "The American public as participant in the experience of art has developed a wide tolerance and a deep interest . . . we now have a sweeping renaissance of democratic interest in American art which runs through every economic level of our society, from the richest to the poorest."

The Greenhills Community Building includes treasures of New Deal art, including three 1938 WPA murals, a bas-relief and frieze, all specially commissioned for the building. John C. Walker, the director of the Resettlement Division of the WPA, wrote that the "murals are intended not as collectors' items for a museum, but as active agents in the daily life of the community."

These pieces brought community members face-to-face with art in their everyday lives, whether they were playing basketball or reading a book.

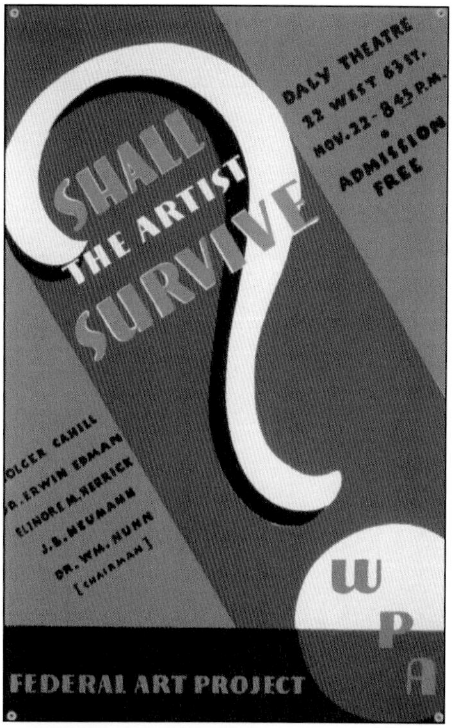

Holger Cahill was born Sveinn Kristjan Bjarnarson in a small valley near the Arctic Circle in Iceland, on January 13, 1887. In 1935, having long since changed his name, he was appointed director of the Works Progress Administration (WPA) and Federal Art Project (FAP) until its end in June 1943. In 1938, Cahill organized a countrywide exhibition, *American Art Today*, for the New York World's Fair. This poster touted the need for the arts. (Courtesy of the Library of Congress.)

Historically, involvement in the arts has been something only the elite in society could afford. The Depression affected all income levels, including higher-income citizens, which meant funding for the arts plunged, leaving many artists with no work and no money. Director Harry Hopkins, President Roosevelt's longtime aide, defended the program, telling his critics, "They've got to eat just like other people." (Courtesy of the Library of Congress.)

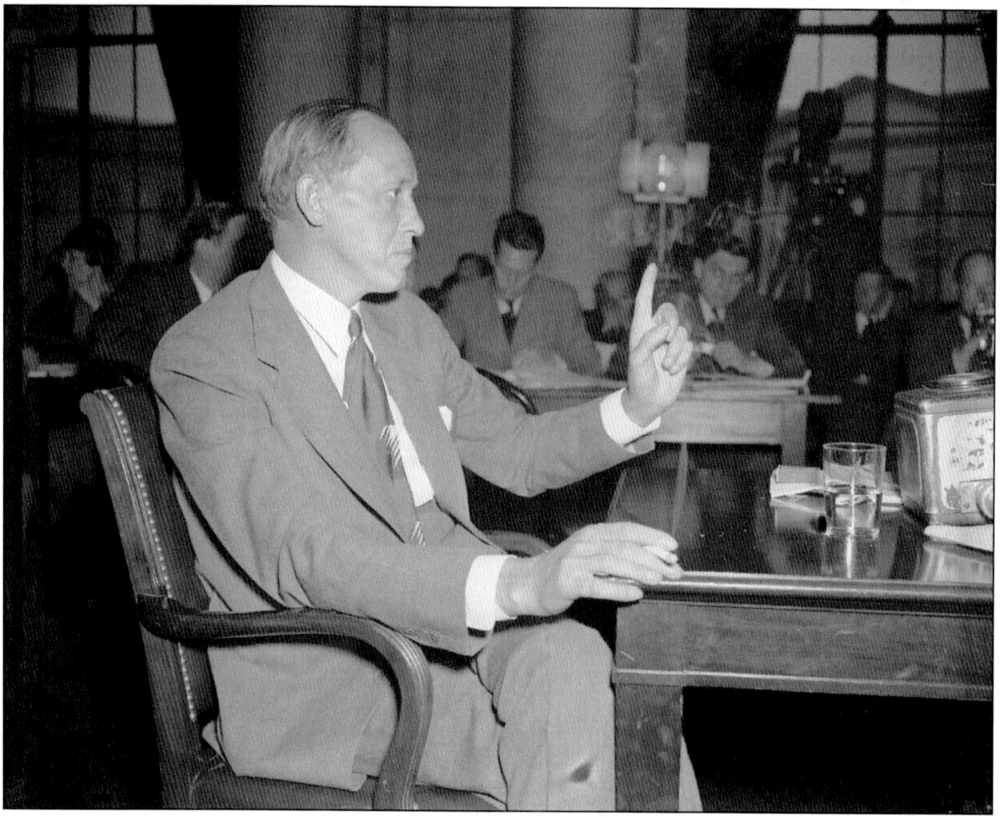

The program put artists of many types back to work, from creators of posters and playbills to actors and musicians. The WPA provided many musicians, including the ones in the Cincinnati Federal Symphonic Orchestra, a wage, and even in some cases, the musical arrangements themselves. (Courtesy of the Library of Congress.)

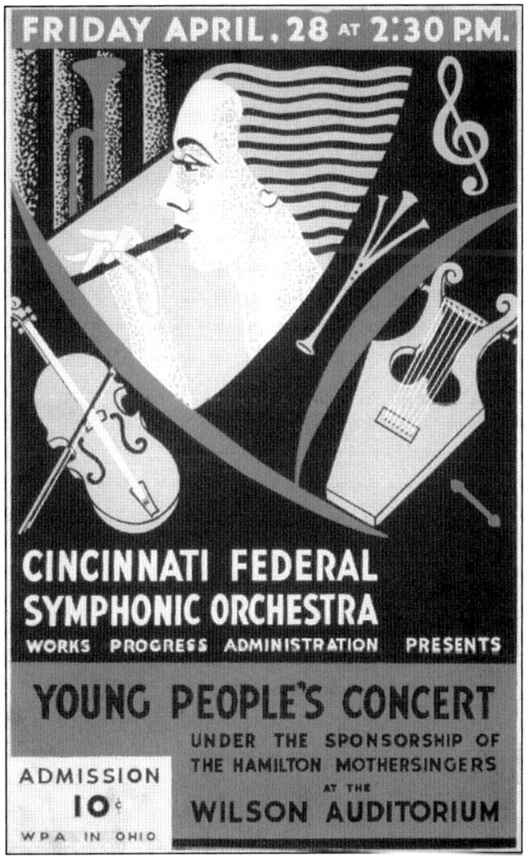

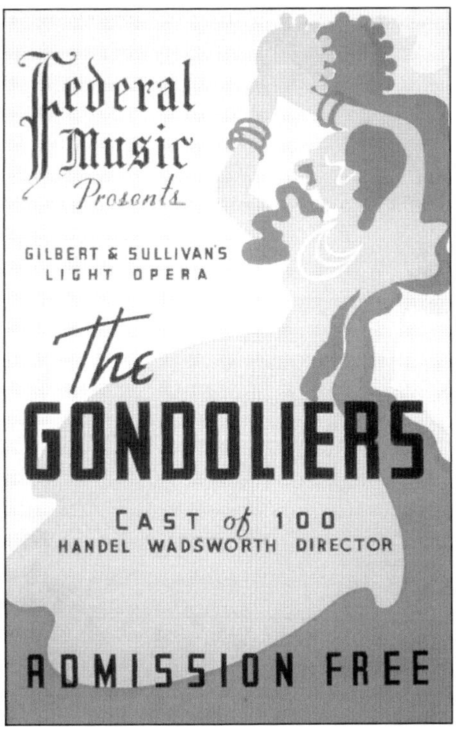

The first public concert in Greenhills was coordinated by the federal music division, which toured musicians through the area, always stopping in Greenhills. (Courtesy of the Library of Congress.)

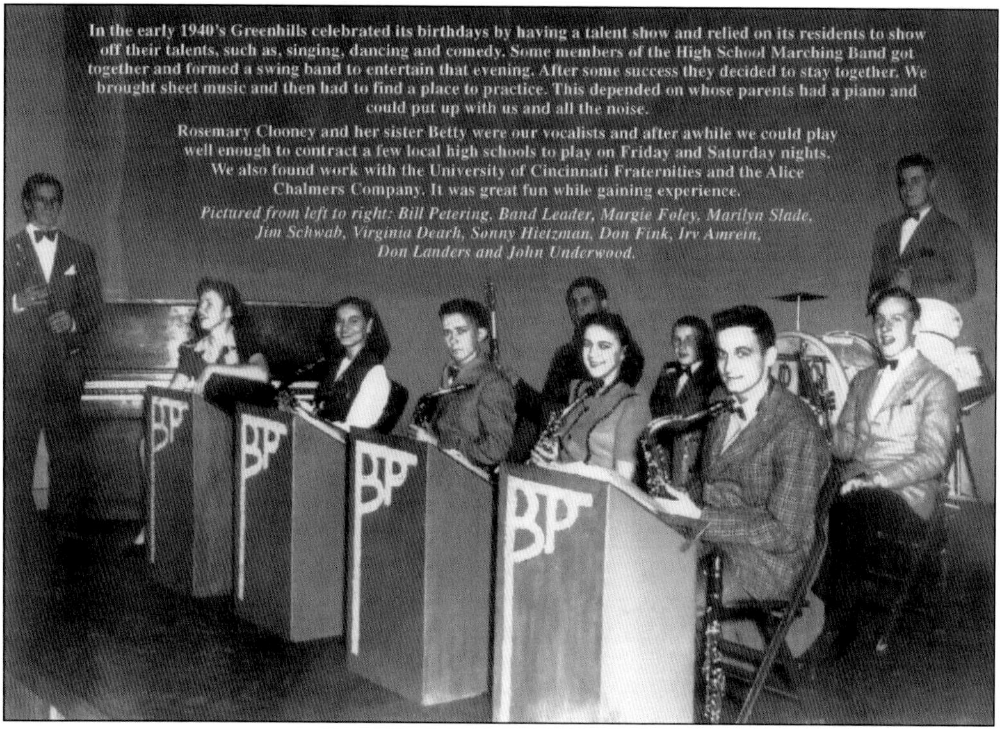

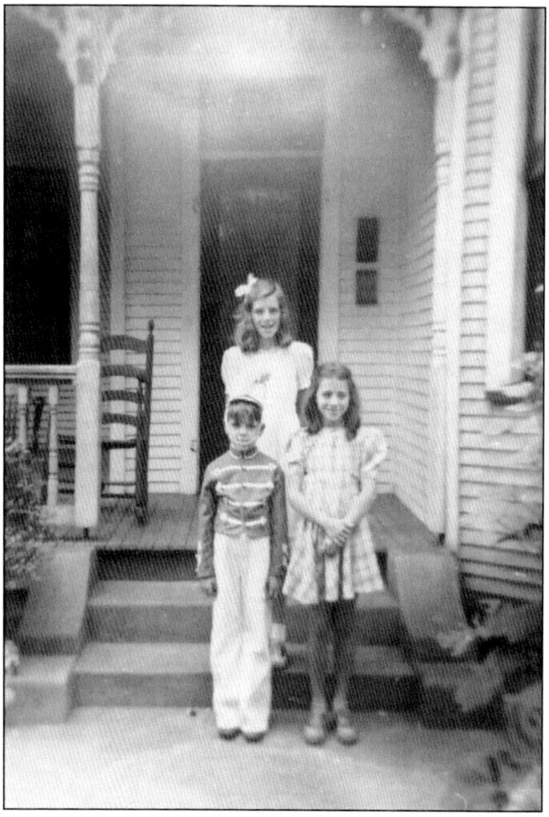

Perhaps spurred on by the idea that one could make a living in the arts, while at Greenhills High School in the early 1940s, a boy by the name of Bill Petering formed a band to perform the popular music of the time. The Bill Petering Band (pictured above) offered a venue for Betty and Rosemary Clooney, just teenagers at the time, to hone their vocal skills. Betty and Rosemary often lived with their Aunt Jeanne and Uncle Roy Dudenhoefer in Greenhills, which offered convenience to perform in the Cincinnati region. Pictured here, before coming to Cincinnati, the Clooney children lived in Ironton, Ohio. Pictured left is Rosemary, age 12, and Betty, age 9. The little lad in the soldier's outfit is brother Nick Clooney at the age of 6. Nick Clooney became a famous American journalist, anchorman, and television host while Rosemary Clooney achieved stardom as a singer and Hollywood actress. (Above, courtesy of the Petering family; left, courtesy of the Nick Clooney family.)

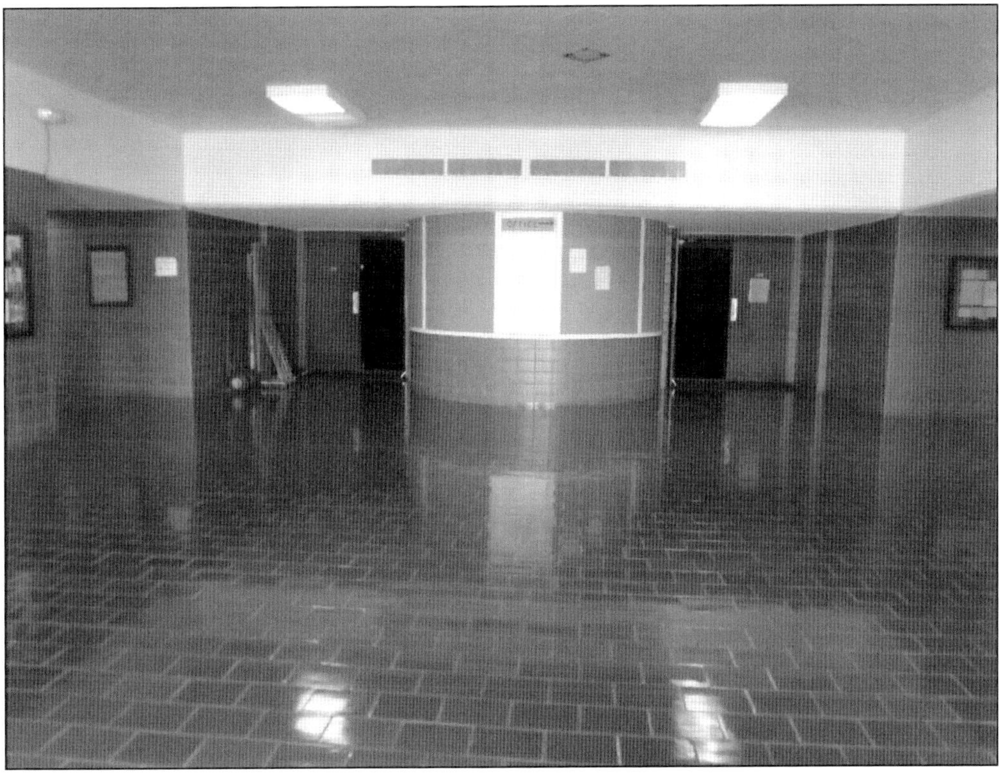

The Greenhills Community Building was equipped with a full-fledged theater, which included a stage with footlights and backdrops, a movie projection booth, a box office, and gymnasium. (Courtesy of Dan Derner.)

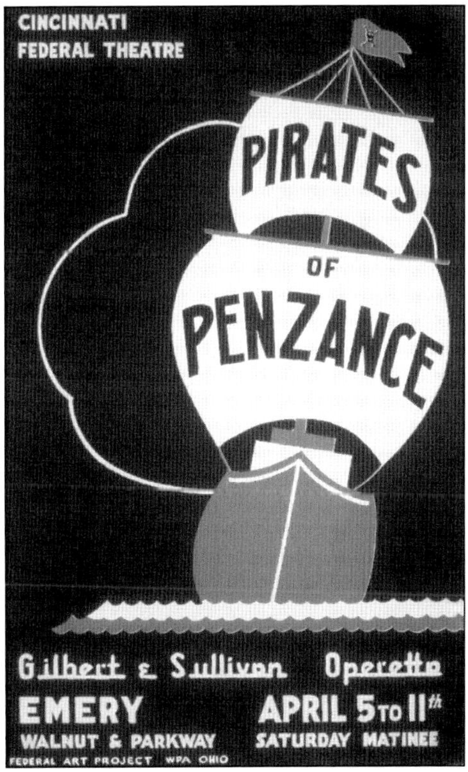

The local communities enjoyed seeing regional theater that was easily accessible, but the federal work program also offered playwrights a way to circulate play script booklets to local theater groups in small outlying communities. They also employed actors and actresses with tour work in companies, offering regional theater at larger venues. (Courtesy of the Library of Congress.)

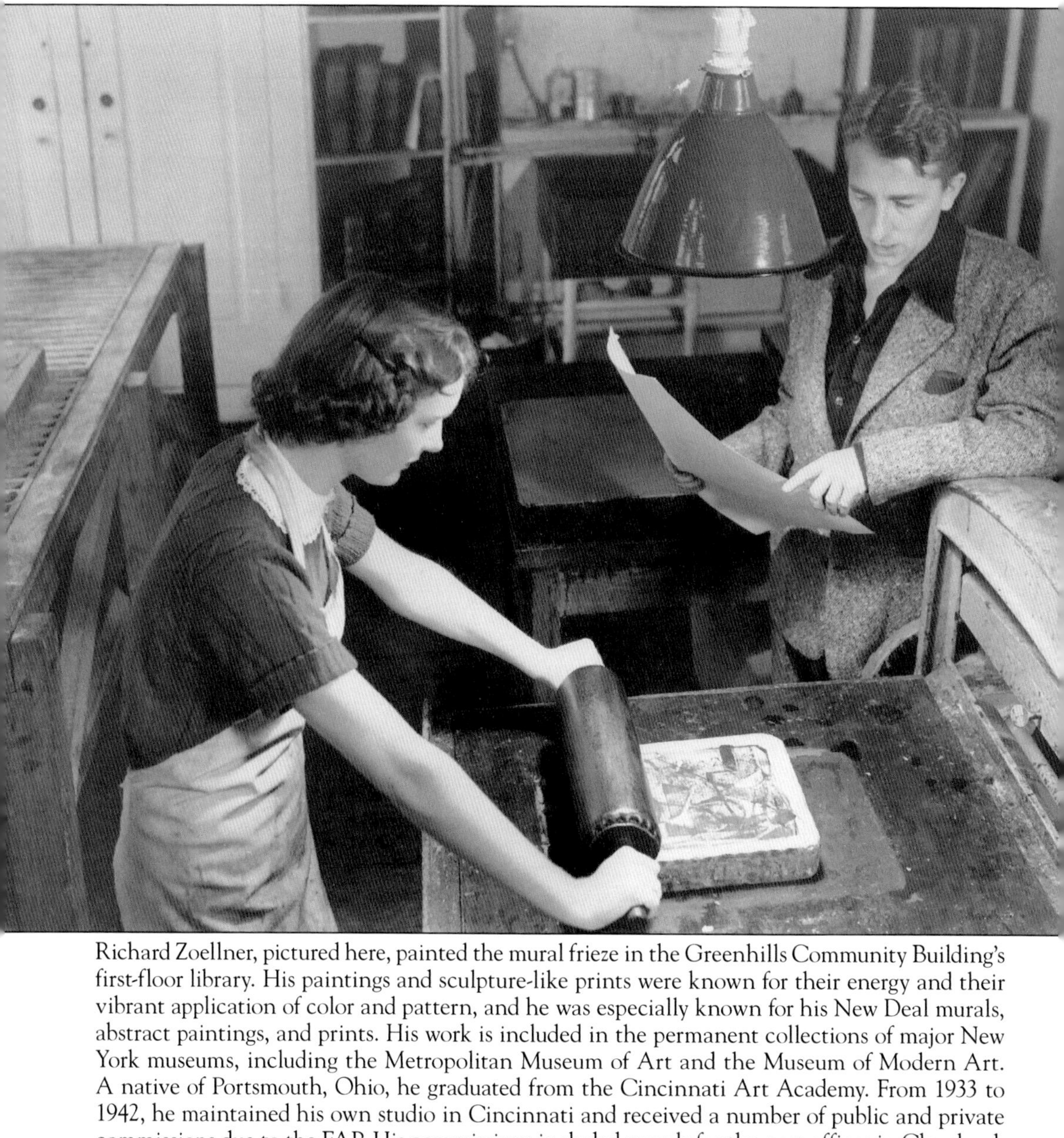

Richard Zoellner, pictured here, painted the mural frieze in the Greenhills Community Building's first-floor library. His paintings and sculpture-like prints were known for their energy and their vibrant application of color and pattern, and he was especially known for his New Deal murals, abstract paintings, and prints. His work is included in the permanent collections of major New York museums, including the Metropolitan Museum of Art and the Museum of Modern Art. A native of Portsmouth, Ohio, he graduated from the Cincinnati Art Academy. From 1933 to 1942, he maintained his own studio in Cincinnati and received a number of public and private commissions due to the FAP. His commissions included murals for the post offices in Cleveland, Georgetown, Hamilton, Medina, and Portsmouth, Ohio, and Mannington, West Virginia. Other commissions included paintings for US Marine hospitals and murals for the Cincinnati Zoo. He was a professor at the University of Alabama's Department of Art from the 1940s until 1979. (Courtesy of the University of Alabama.)

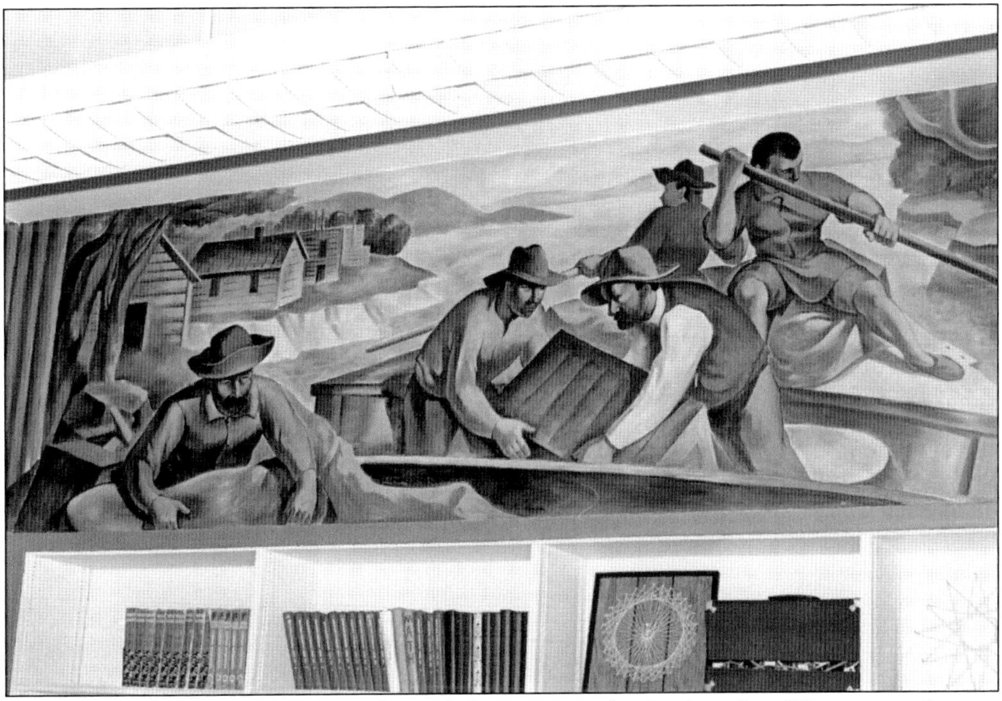

Richard Zoellner's frieze above the library shelves is painted in bright colors. The paint technique almost mimics the look of colored chalks. Called *Ohio River Influence*, it depicts the Ohio River's influence on the building of Cincinnati and its environment. One scene depicts the great Ohio River flood of 1937, which he personally experienced while painting the mural. The 360-degree mural wraps around the top of the library's bookcase and continues briefly down a center area and two sidewalls, ending with his signature. (Both, courtesy of the Lippmeier family.)

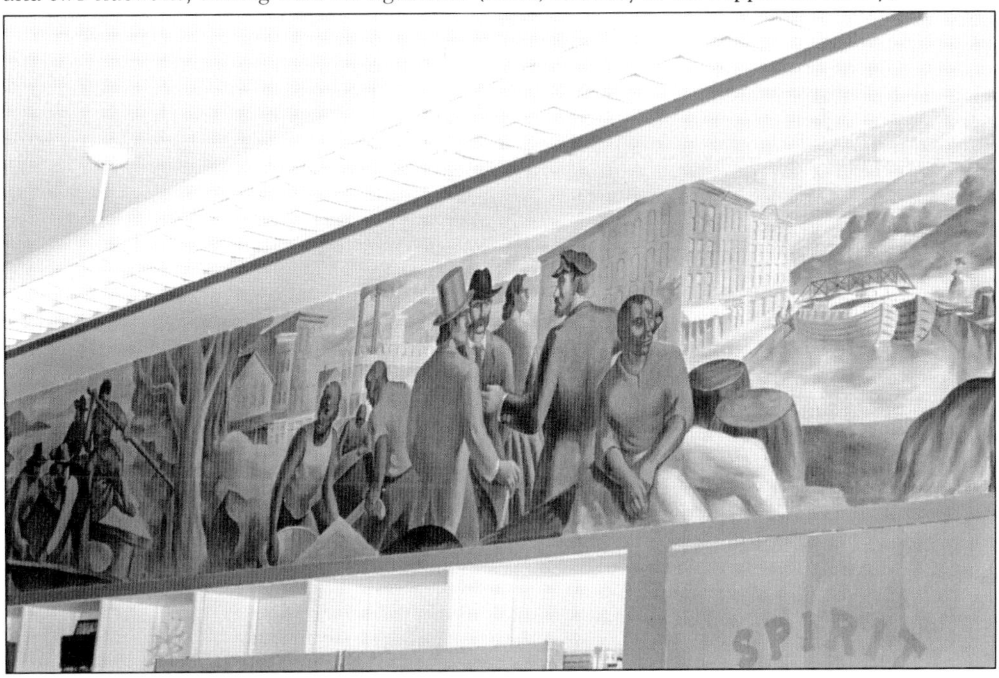

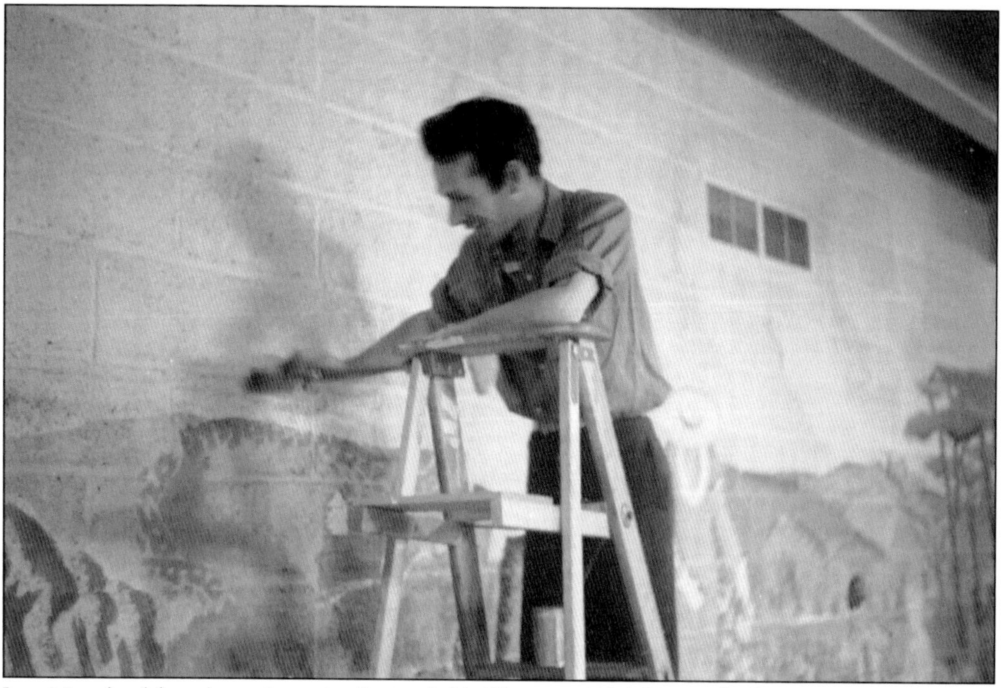

Leo Murphy (above) was born in Springfield, Ohio, in 1906. He studied at the Cincinnati Art Academy and was a member of the Cincinnati Association of Professional Artists. He exhibited throughout the 1930s and 1940s at the Cincinnati Art Museum, the Golden Gate Exposition in San Francisco, and the 1939 World's Fair in New York. Leo Murphy painted a mural in the lower level of the Greenhills Community Building in an area that was used as a cafeteria and a large community gathering place. The mural measured eight feet high and spanned 180 feet around the perimeter of the room. Murphy used a unique method of painting directly on the cement block, a technique that was only used for this mural and never used again. The mural was of fine quality, and its method created a misty, three-dimensional effect, as if one could walk right into the mural's scene. (Both, courtesy of the Library of Congress.)

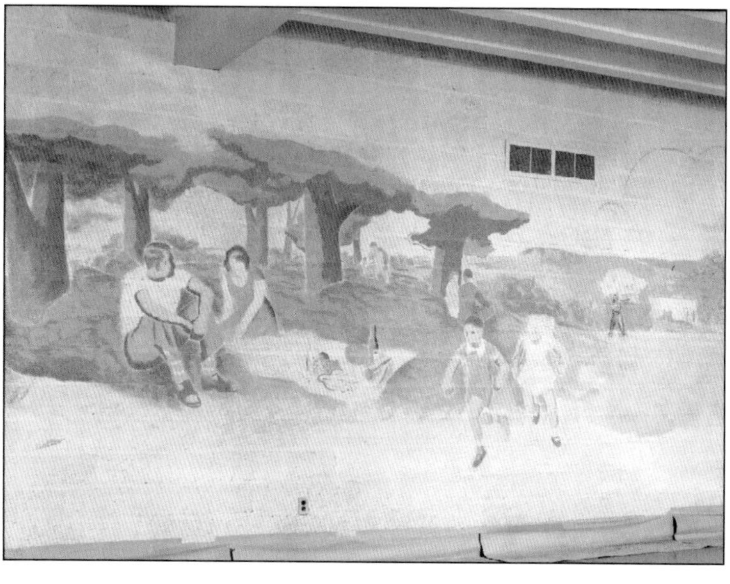

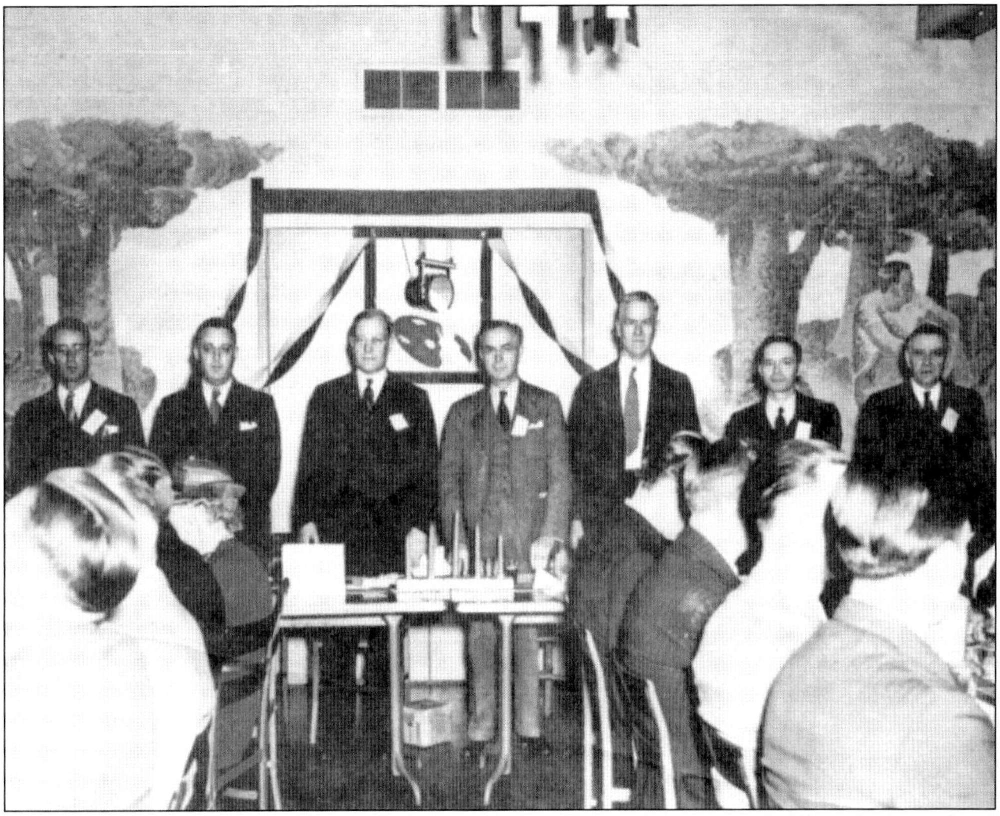

Meetings, the canteen, dances, dinners, and even spillover classes were held in the lower-level room with the beautiful Murphy mural, which depicted lighthearted reflections of everyday life in the community. Unfortunately, in the 1970s, the mural was painted over and lost forever. An assessment of the mural showed that the compounds of paint that covered the mural had bound to the underlying layer, making it un-restorable. The room is now used for school district storage. (Both, courtesy of the Greenhills Historical Society.)

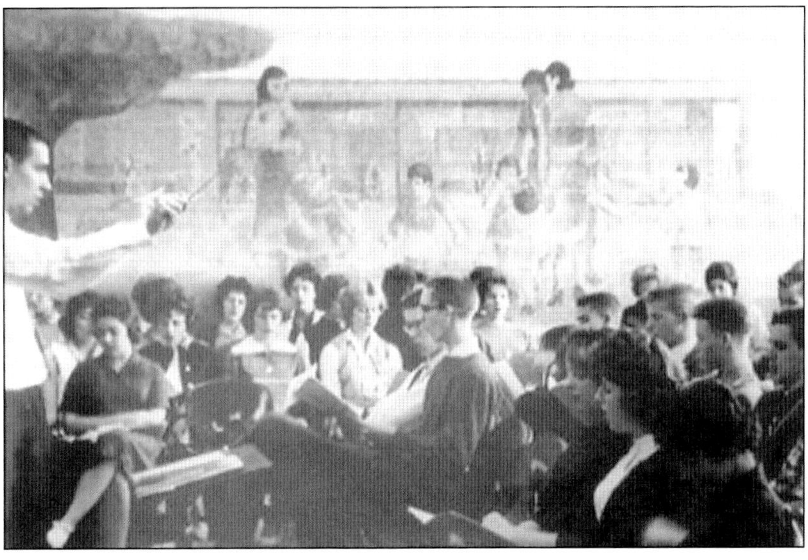

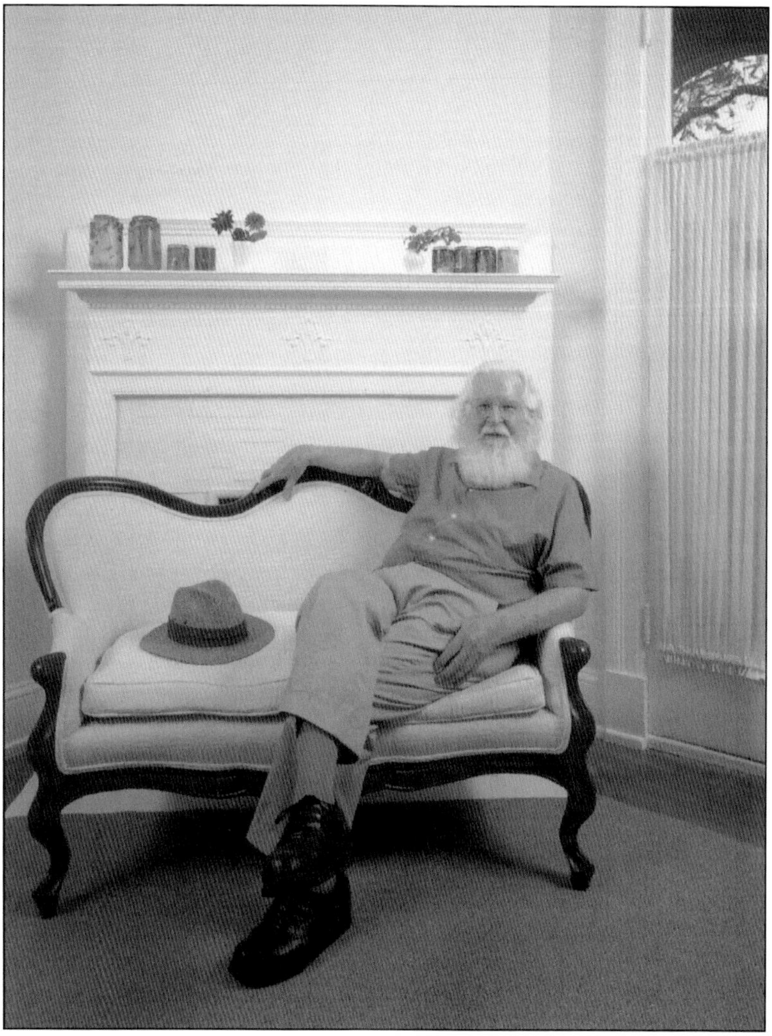

Paul Chidlaw was born in Cleves, Ohio, in 1900. He lived and worked in Cincinnati and also traveled and studied in France. He was a contemporary of Picasso and Matisse and was active in the French Modern Art movement. His singular genius as an artist and teacher made him a legend as Cincinnati's leading modernist. He was an instructor at the Art Academy of Cincinnati. His artwork was whimsical and used pastels with vivid color. (Courtesy of Cal Kowal.)

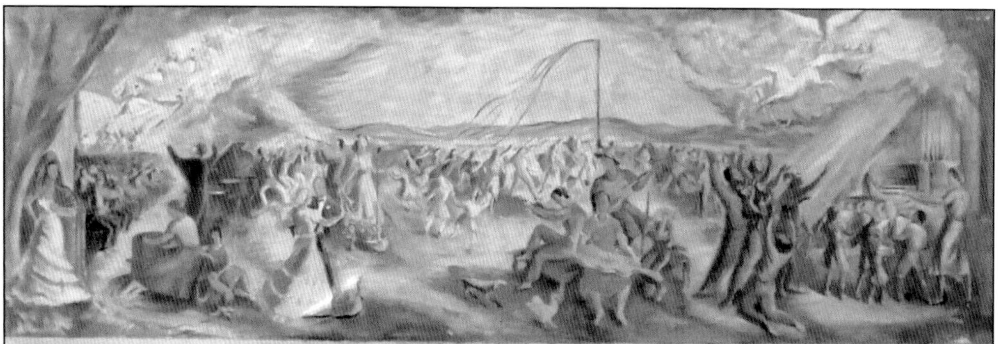

In the period leading up to the construction of the community building, artists were requested to submit cartoon or maquette proposals of the murals that would decorate the building. This is the only maquette left in Greenhills, which was submitted by Paul Chidlaw. This is the original piece submitted to the WPA administration for review; the finished mural in the second-floor music room is on the opposite page. (Courtesy of Michael Ruzga.)

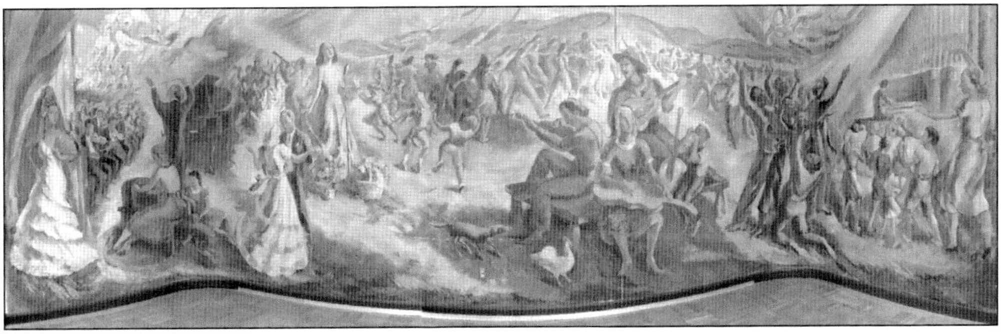

The Joy of Music (above and in detail below), the eventual name of Chidlaw's mural, is painted on a concave wall spanning the full width of the second-floor music room, which currently houses the Greenhills School Alumni offices and museum. The room is now called the Pioneer Room in honor of the school's mascot, but the wall mural is still there. (Above, courtesy of the Dan Derner; below, courtesy of Michael Ruzga.)

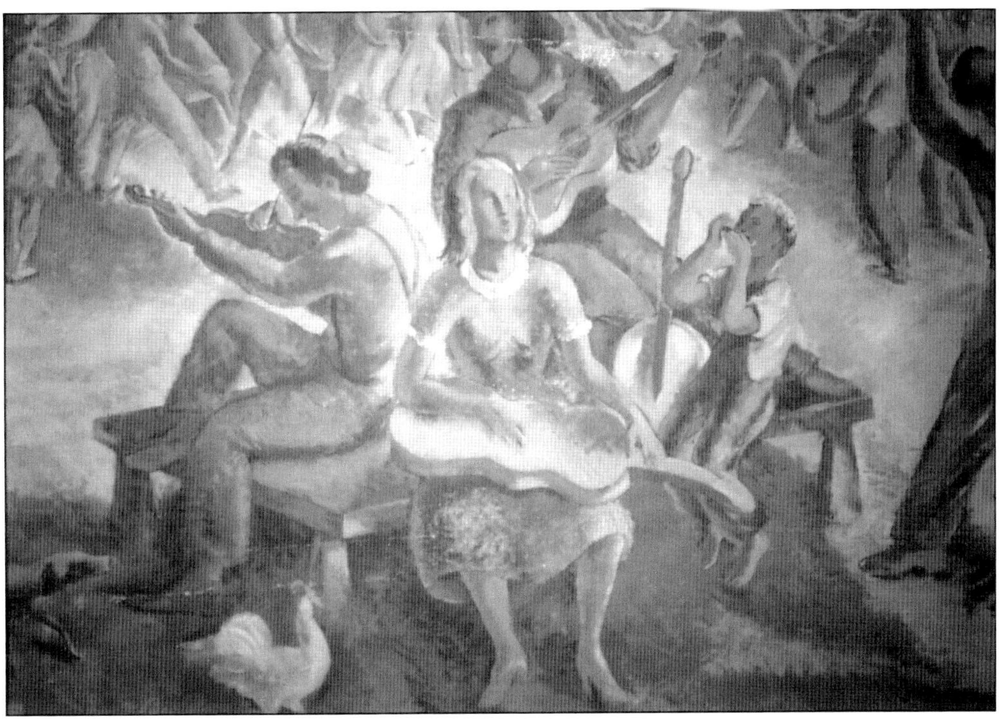

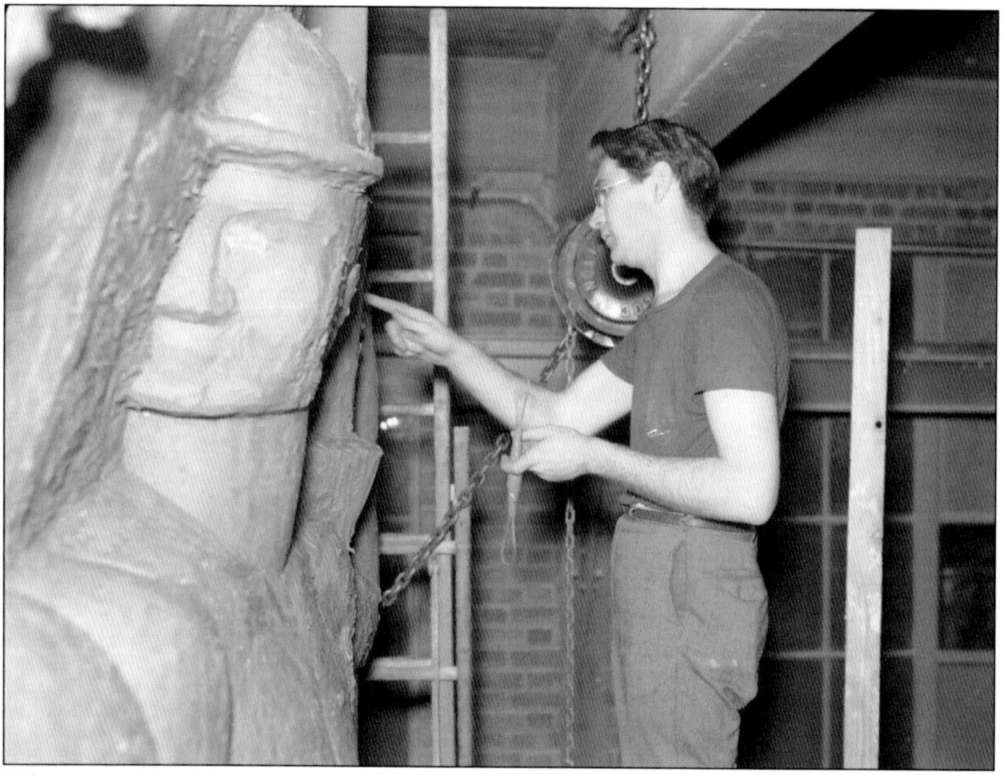

Whitney Atchley (above) attended the Cleveland School of Art in the early 1930s, when he was a member of the Cowan Pottery Group, a flourishing local arts community in northeastern Ohio. The gymnasium/auditorium featured both ceramic bas-relief and frieze spanning the width of the stage, bringing art to basketball players and performers alike. (Above, courtesy of the Library of Congress; below, courtesy of Deborah J. Tilford-Mills.)

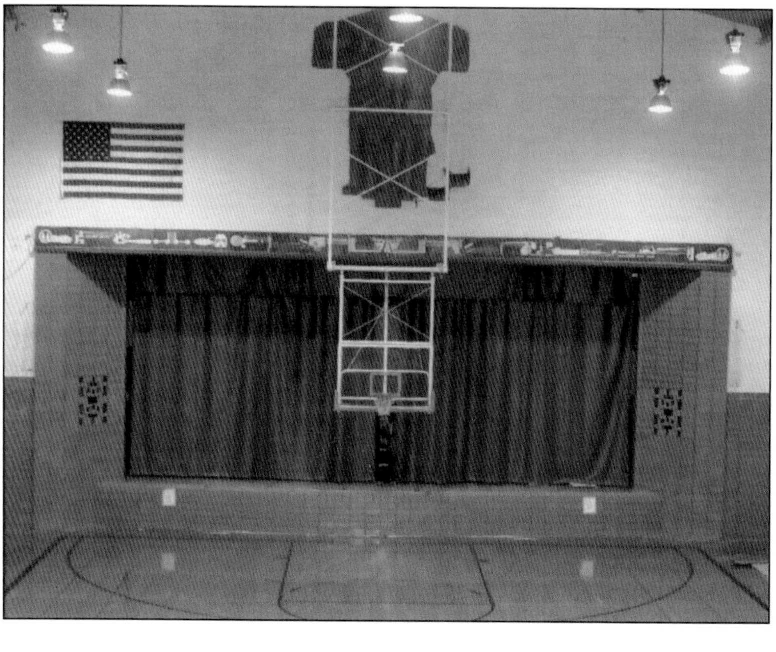

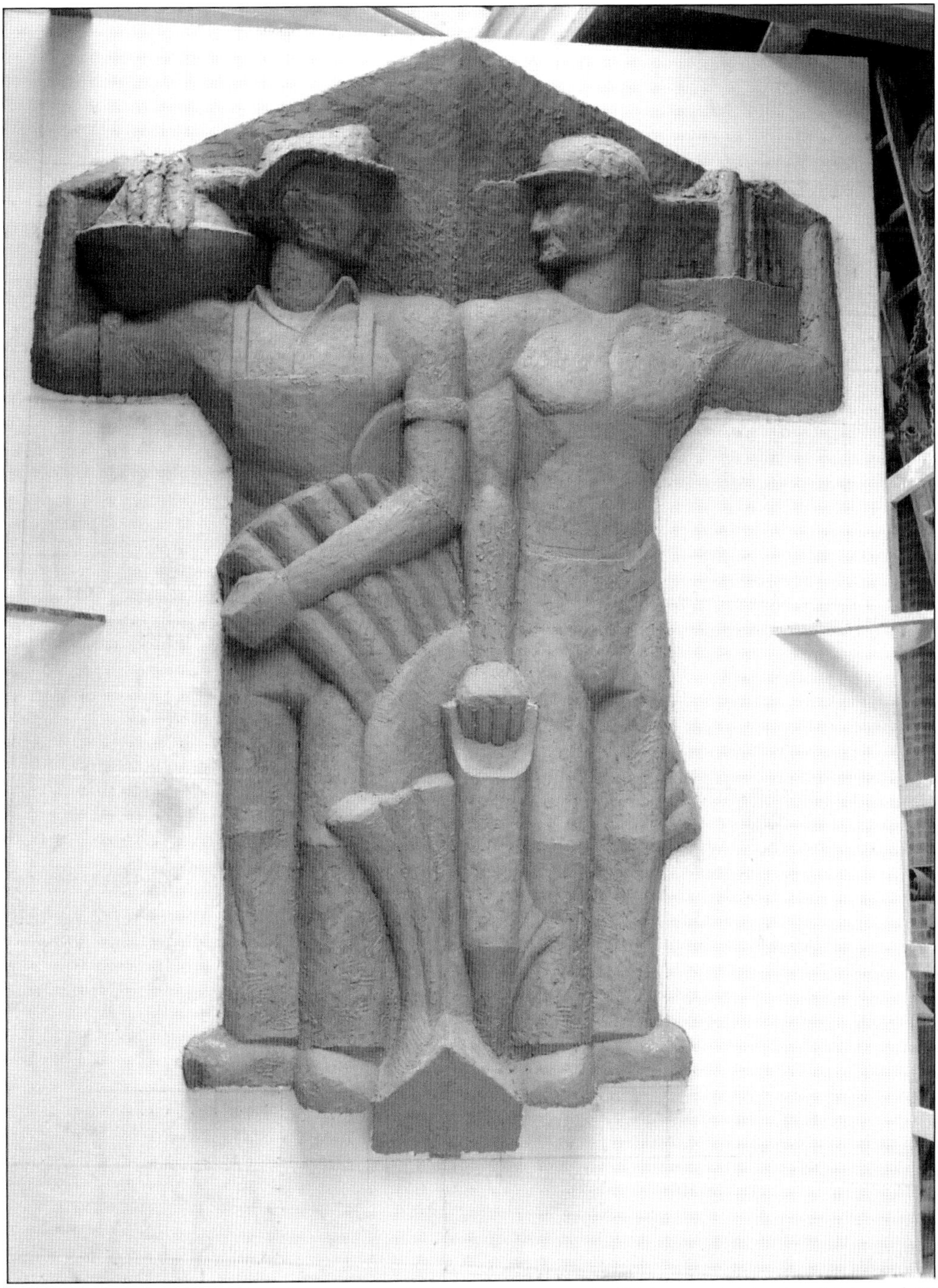

Atchley's bas-relief, entitled *Community Life*, is approximately 13 feet and 4 inches high and 10 feet and 5 inches across. It is mounted over the auditorium stage. It is 17 inches deep. Today, it is obscured by an overhanging steel basketball hoop and backboard. It is terra-cotta, with a reddish-brown glaze and 20 interlocking sections. Following the Department of Agriculture specifications, the ceramic sections are mounted with anchors from the back. The theme is man among industry and nature. (Courtesy of the Library of Congress.)

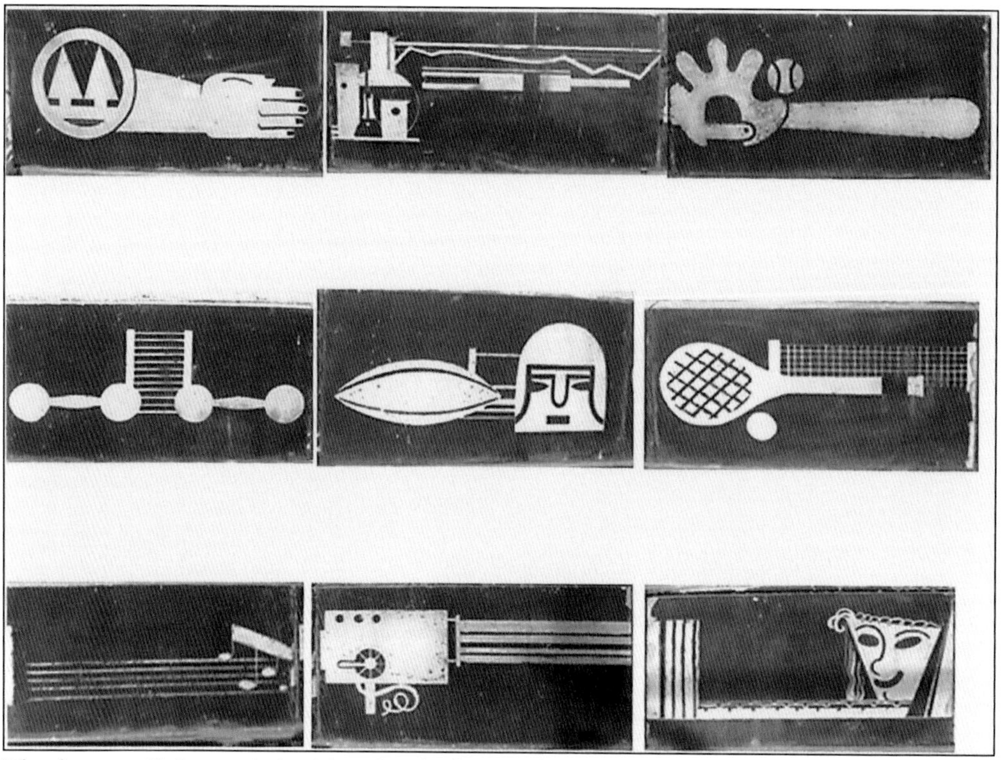

The frieze is 45 feet wide by 16 inches high over the auditorium's stage and is made up of 18 earthenware panels, each 30.75 inches long and approximately the thickness of a heavy plate. It depicts many arts and industries, using stylized symbols common to the WPA movement. White glaze is the base color, and close inspection reveals a small amount of light green used for highlighting areas. (Above, courtesy of Michale Ruzga; below, courtesy of Deborah J. Tilford-Mills.)

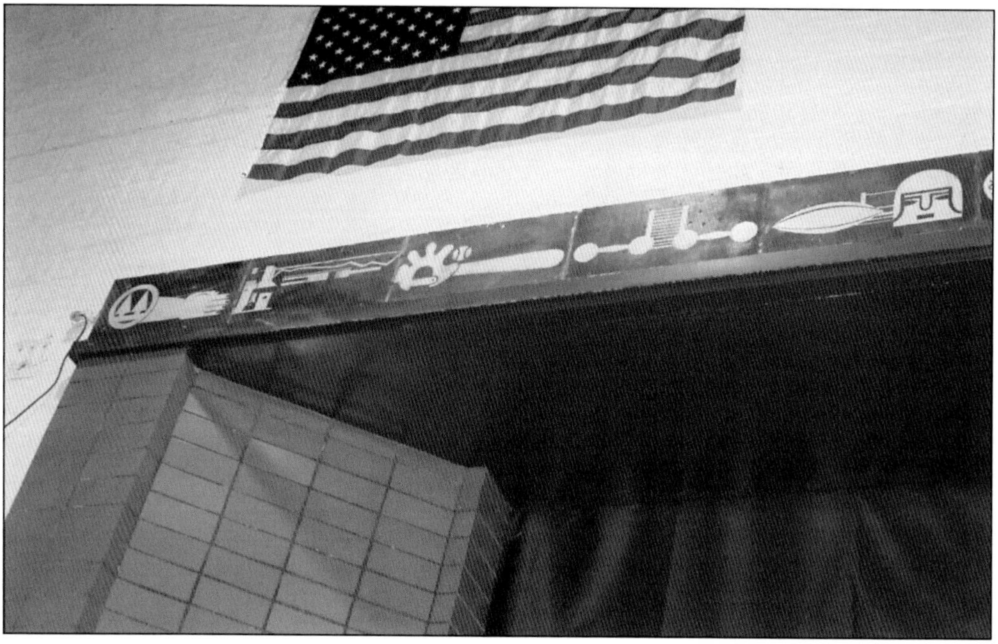

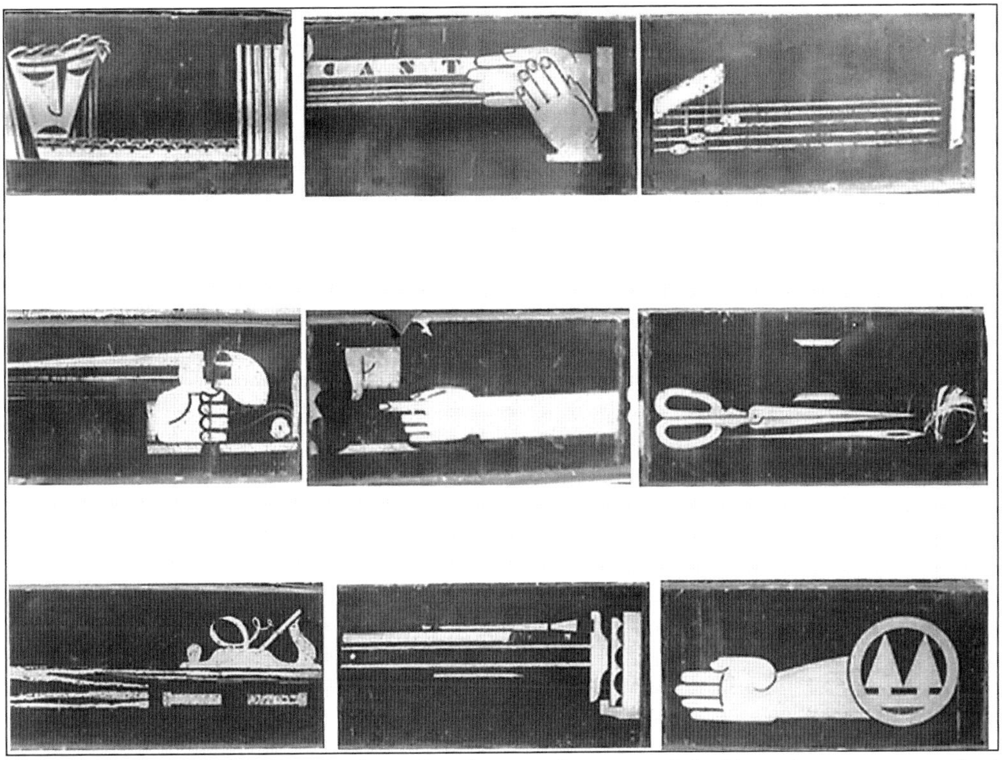

Panels above highlight themes of woodworking, tailoring, and drafting. A very new method used by the artist involved a combination of mica added to the black glaze, which was then applied to the negative spaces on each panel. This created a glowing effect when auditorium lights were lowered, and a spotlight or the ambient light from the movie projector created an almost three-dimensional effect as the mica sparkled and the reflective opaque glaze shimmered. As one stands on the balcony of the third floor overlooking the gymnasium, the view of the bas-relief and frieze (below) is dynamic. (Above, courtesy of Michael Ruzga; below, courtesy of Deborah J. Tilford-Mills.)

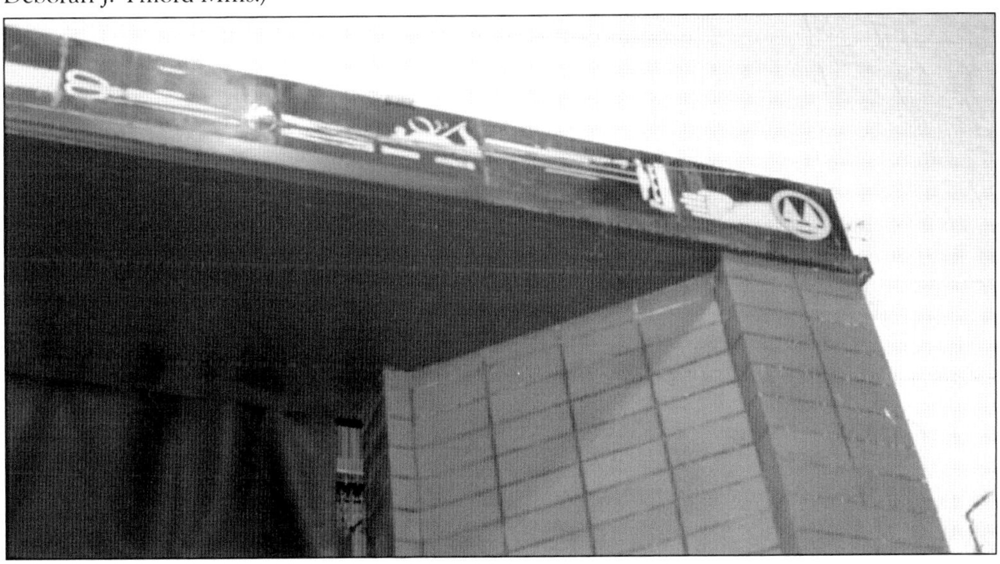

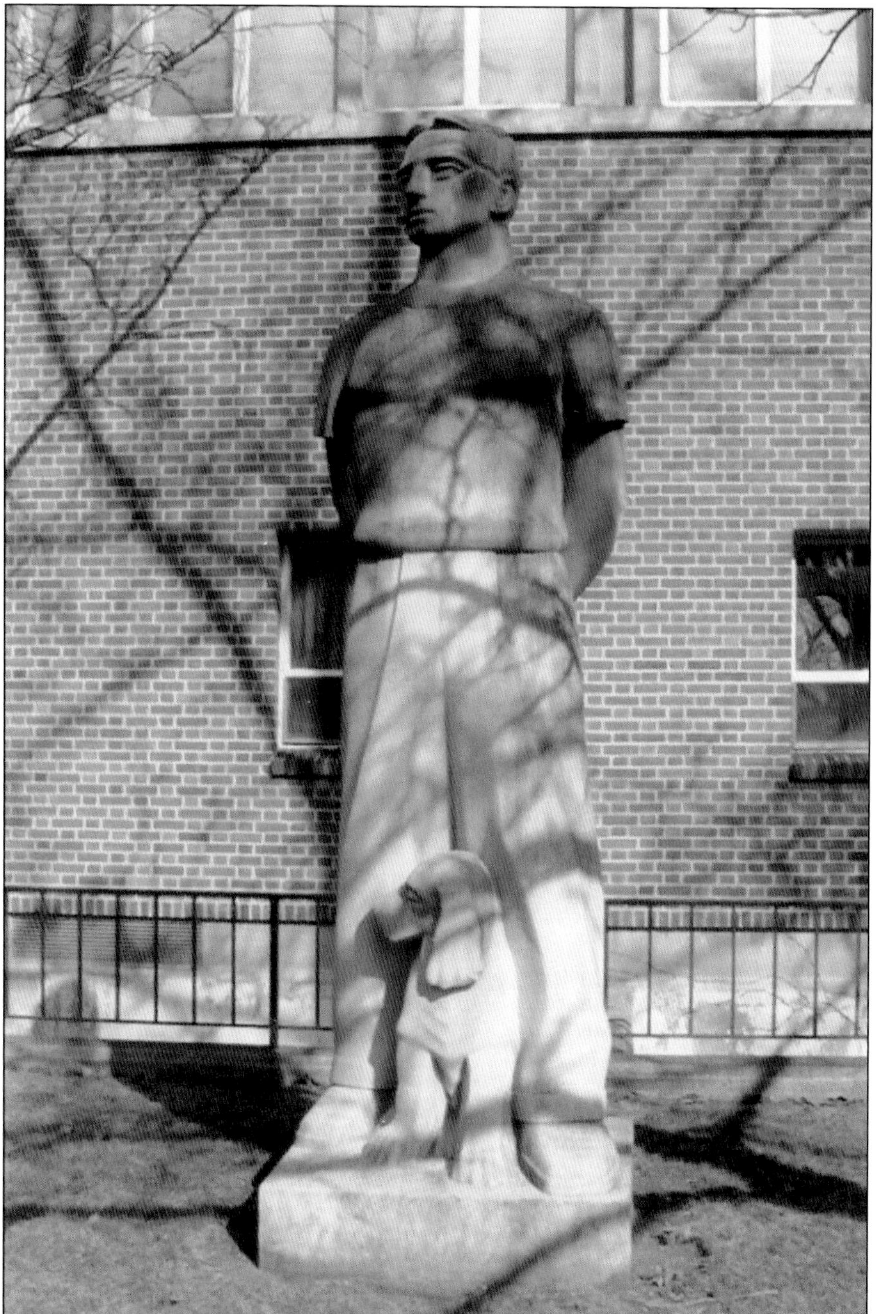

Seth Velsey created a group of sculptures that were to be placed in the main area of the common, at the flagpole in front of the Greenhills Community Building. The November 12, 1939, *Dayton Sunday Journal-Herald* reported, "Seth M. Velsey, Dayton sculptor, is at present at work on limestone sculptures which are to be grouped in a semi-circle around the flagpole in the mall before the administrative building of the Greenhills Community Center, a project which is on its way to completion in Cincinnati." Unfortunately, the artist never finished the entire grouping. (Courtesy of Paul Richardson.)

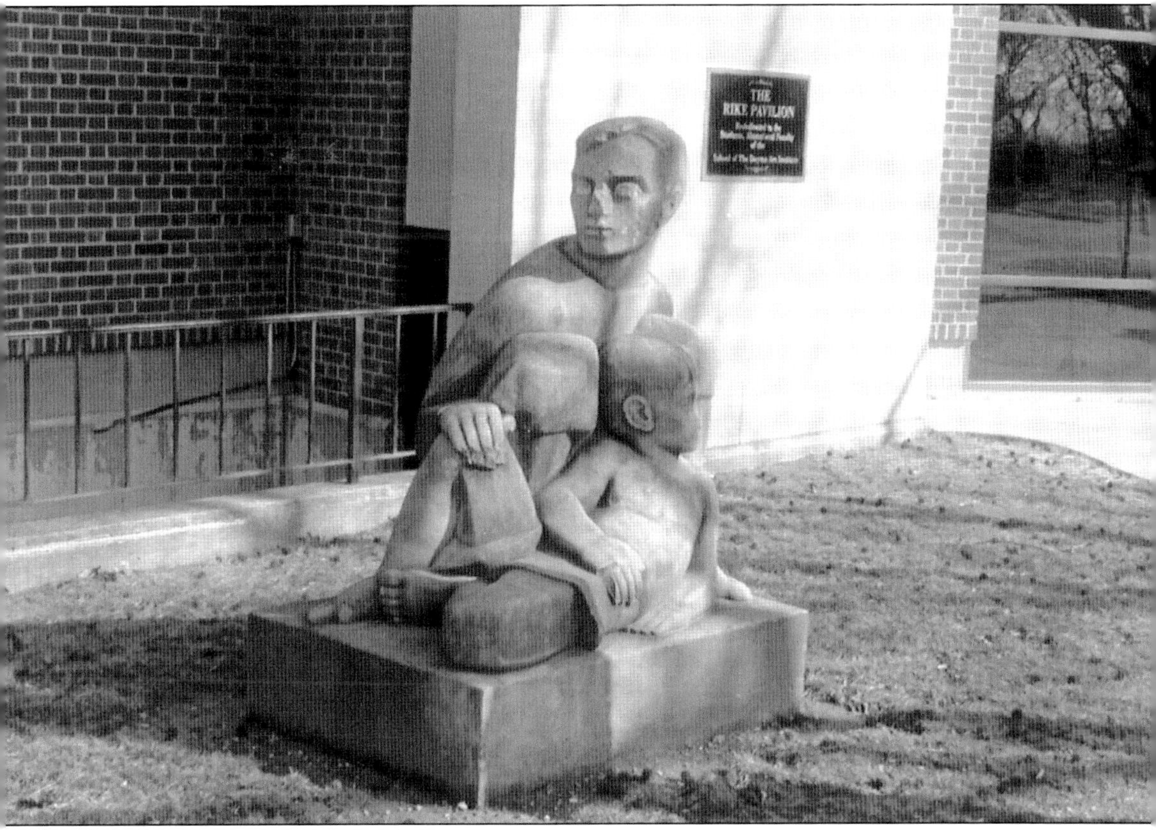

Seth Velsey finished only two sculpture pieces before they were placed in storage in a stone yard when the Farm Security Administration (FSA) was disassembled, and they were never delivered to Greenhills. The sculptures stayed in the storage yard for years. Velsey was an instructor at the Dayton Art Institute, where the sculptures were transported and remain today, situated outside the entrance doors. There has been a constant battle with authorities and legislators ever since in an attempt to convince the institute to have the sculptures brought to Greenhills, where they were intended. (Courtesy of Paul Richardson.)

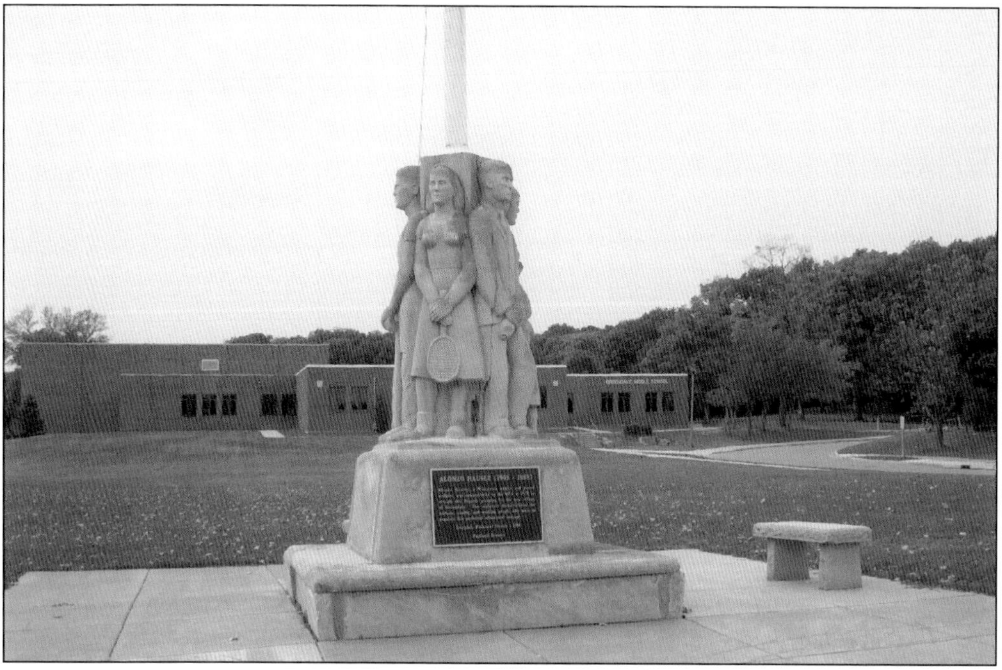

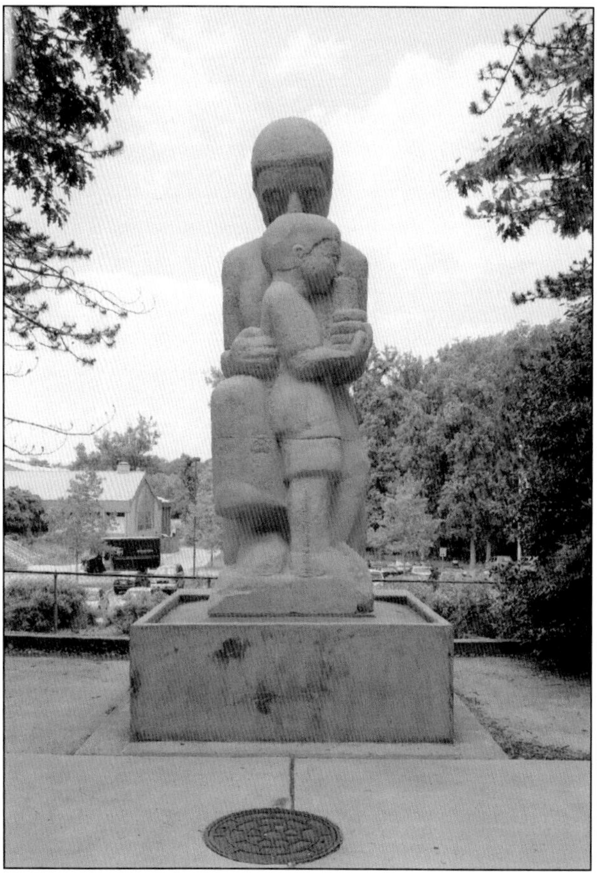

These sculptures, located in the two sister greenbelt towns, show approximately where the sculptures would have been placed in Greenhills. The Greendale, Wisconsin, sculptures (above) are situated around a flagpole, where the Greenhills vignette was to be. The Greenbelt, Maryland, sculpture (left) is in the Roosevelt Center mall area, around the common shopping and entertainment district. (Above, courtesy of Deborah J. Tilford-Mills; left, courtesy of the Library of Congress.)

Nine

Competing Visions

Of the three Greenbelt towns—the others being Greendale, Wisconsin, and Greenbelt, Maryland—Greenhills is the only one to have torn down any of its original homes.

—"Two historic Greenhills townhouses facing demolition," *Building Cincinnati*, September 2009

By the 1990s, older communities like Greenhills had aging, declining populations, rising costs, old infrastructure, and shrinking tax bases. Landlocked, they had nowhere to expand. Fewer children meant closed schools and consolidated districts.

These problems hit smaller suburbs like Greenhills especially hard when the town's original acreage became Forest Park. Greenhills had little commercial development and no industry, limiting its sources of revenue.

As more middle-class families left, more owner-occupied properties became rental units. These apartments increasingly were owned by landlords with no ties to the community. Some buildings deteriorated due to a lack of regular maintenance.

In the Greenhills Shopping Center, longtime businesses moved out and turnover increased. The sleek modern facade of the center was buried under repeated remodeling. In 2008, Johnny's Toys, one of the village's oldest businesses, closed after 32 years, leaving its building vacant.

In 1991, the Greenhills and Forest Park schools merged to form a new school district, renamed Winton Woods. While the combined district meant greater efficiency, it also led to a loss of local identity and pride. Our Lady of the Rosary School also closed its doors in 2006, leaving Greenhills parents with one less option for a neighborhood school.

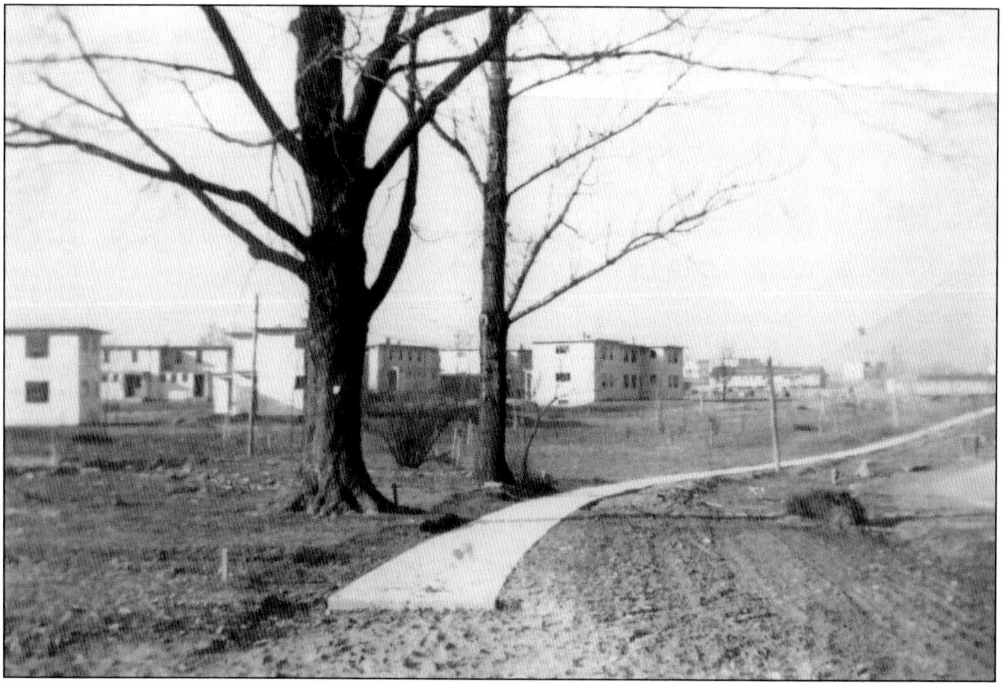

Local government has responded to recent challenges by taking on new powers and working to protect the qualities envisioned in the 1936 rendering of Alcott Lane below: human scale, thoughtful design, and harmony with nature. The village strengthened building codes to prevent blight, and secured grants to renovate the historic pool house and install granite curbing. In the 1970s, the village successfully protected the iconic greenbelt from a court challenge. Of the three New Deal greenbelt towns, only Greenhills has managed to keep its greenbelt largely intact. In 1988, upon Greenhills's 50th anniversary, a consultant was hired to list the original 1938 plat in the National Register of Historic Places as a historic district. The district was included because of its importance to the history of the nation. Greenhills is also designated an American Planning Landmark by the American Planning Association. (Both, courtesy of the Library of Congress.)

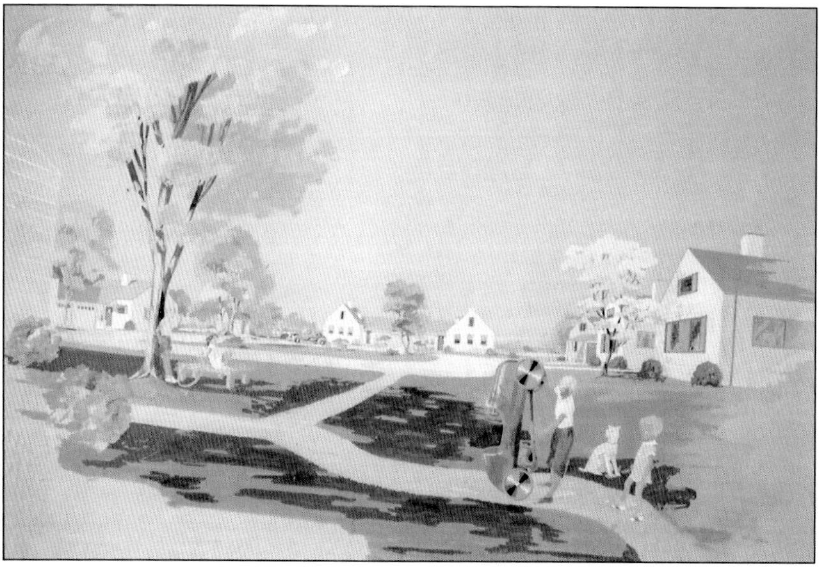

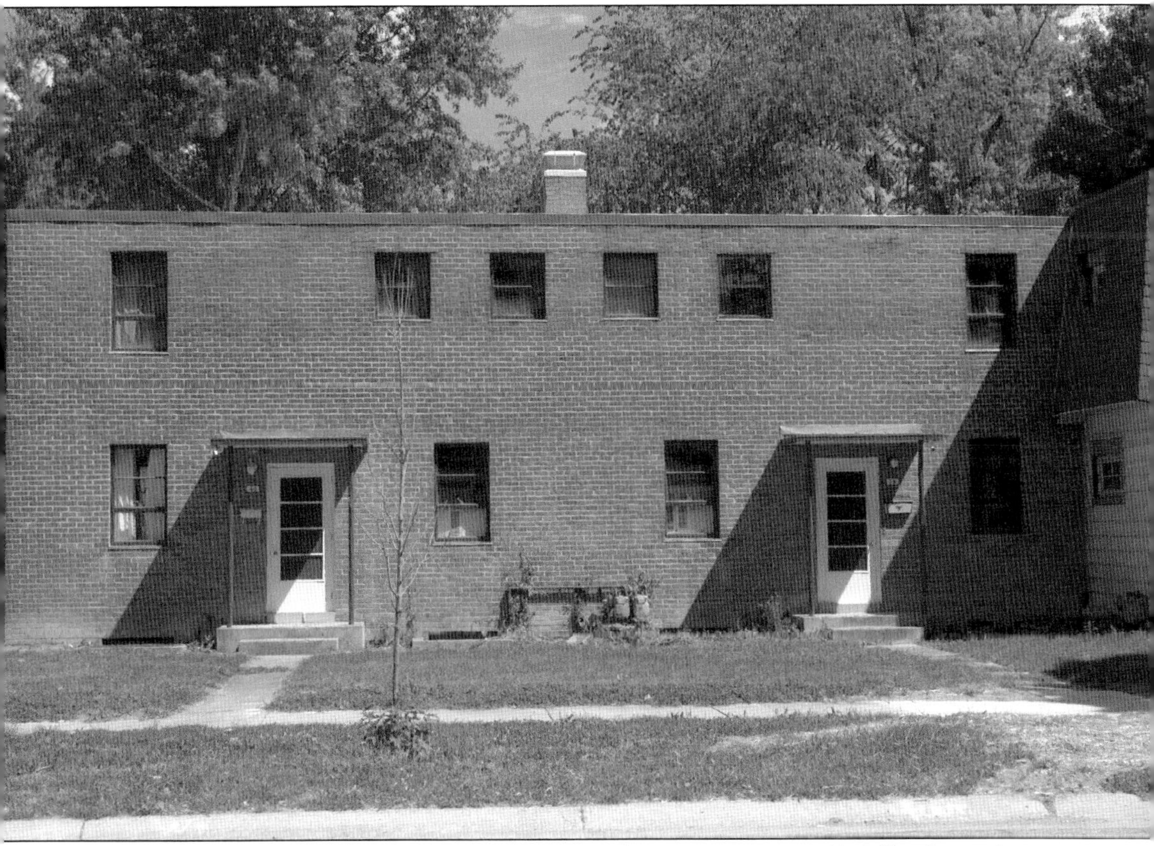

In the early 2000s, Greenhills created an ambitious plan to reinvent itself. Officials sought to grow the tax base by encouraging younger, higher-income families. Selective multifamily buildings in the historic district were removed and replaced with new single-family units. In 2004, voters passed a bond issue to acquire buildings. Beginning in 2000, the village spent more than $3 million acquiring properties, the vast majority of which were rental housing. Some were renovated and sold to private owners or rented at market rates, but many were demolished. From 2000 to 2009, a total of 52 housing units were removed. This vacant, two-family Modernist townhouse on Andover Road, with its original flat roof and steel casements, illustrates the challenges and opportunities of the village's historic buildings. (Courtesy of Margo M. Warminski.)

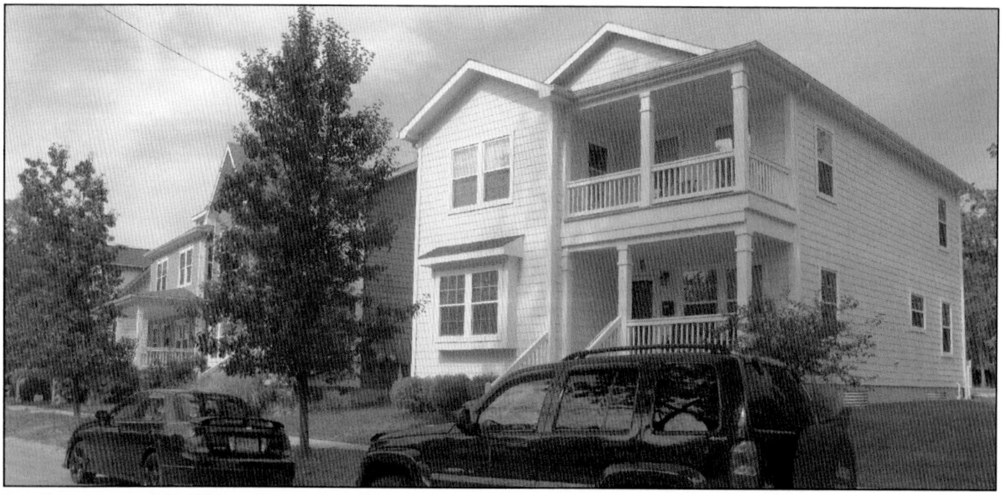

In the area of DeWitt Street and Drummond Road, the village cleared a tract of land for redevelopment. Potterhill Homes, a local homebuilder, was chosen as the developer of DeWitt Landing, a proposed 16-unit development of single-family cottages, bungalows, and American Foursquare-style houses priced from $180,000. DeWitt Landing was structured as a planned development with specific design and setback standards. The new residences differed from traditional village housing in style and siting, as they were larger, taller, closer together, had rear garages, and covered more of the lot, lacking the valuable green space typical of the original Greenhills dwellings. (Courtesy of Margo M. Warminski.)

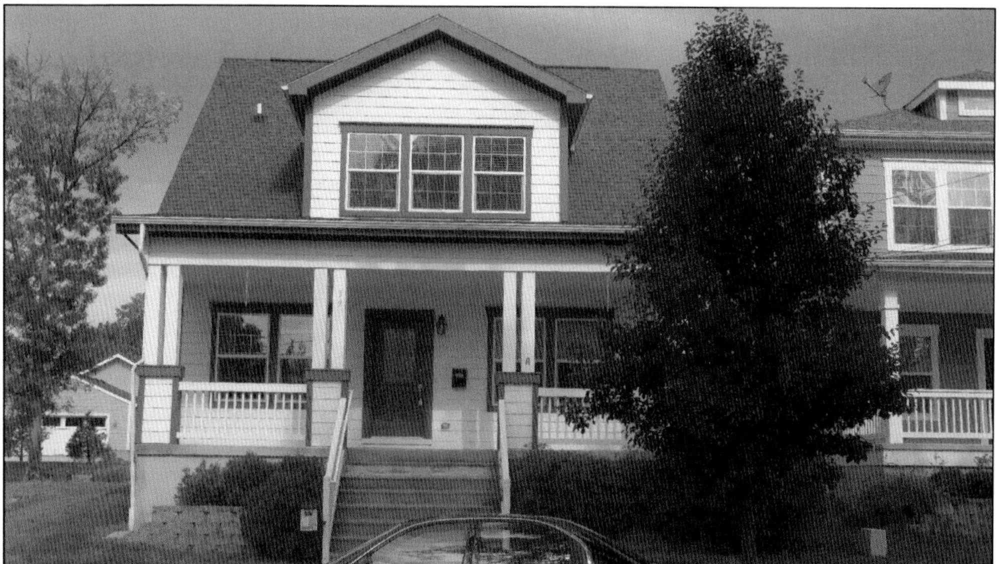

Four new Potterhill homes along Drummond Street were sold to new residents in the mid-2000s. Over time, controversy arose over quality issues and lower-priced homes built with cheaper materials. The development also failed to attract the hoped-for younger families, with many selling to older buyers. Responding to a demand for houses without stairs, five ranch-style homes were built along DeWitt Street in 2007. As of 2012, a total of 10 houses have been built in DeWitt Landing. This bungalow-style residence on Drummond Street has a broad front porch and resembles 1920s houses in Cincinnati neighborhoods like Carthage, Oakley, and College Hill. (Courtesy of Margo M. Warminski.)

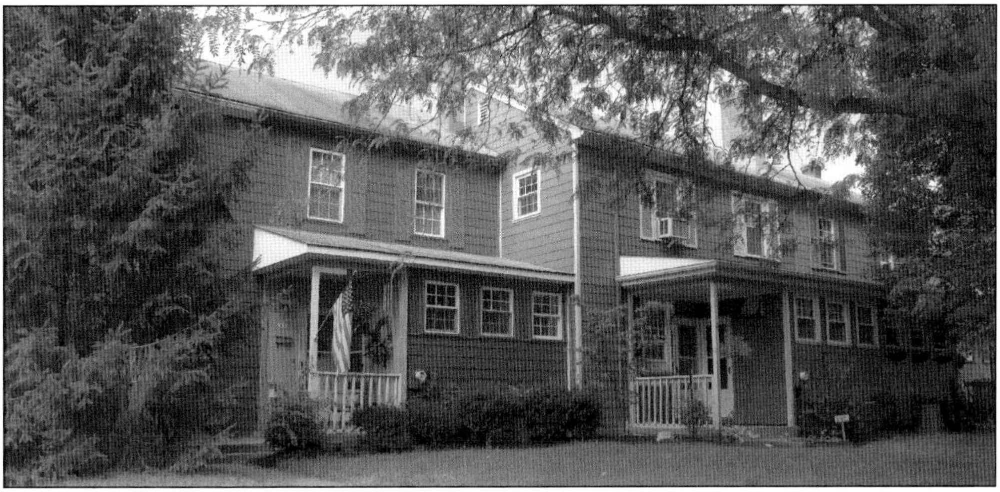

The demolition of the historic village buildings created controversy locally and nationally. Preservationists argued that many of the buildings were sound and could have been renovated. The Greenhills Historical Society (GHS) and the Cincinnati Preservation Association (CPA) worked to encourage the preservation of original buildings and compatible designs for new homes on vacant lots. Their efforts included workshops, symposia, tours, and media coverage. In 2011, architecture and interior design students from the University of Cincinnati studied renovation, reuse, and infill options for the historic district. At the same time, some multifamily buildings in the historic district were renovated for resale by private owners. With their bright paint colors and new windows and shutters, these townhouses on Flanders Lane stand out from their neighbors. (Courtesy of Margo M. Warminski.)

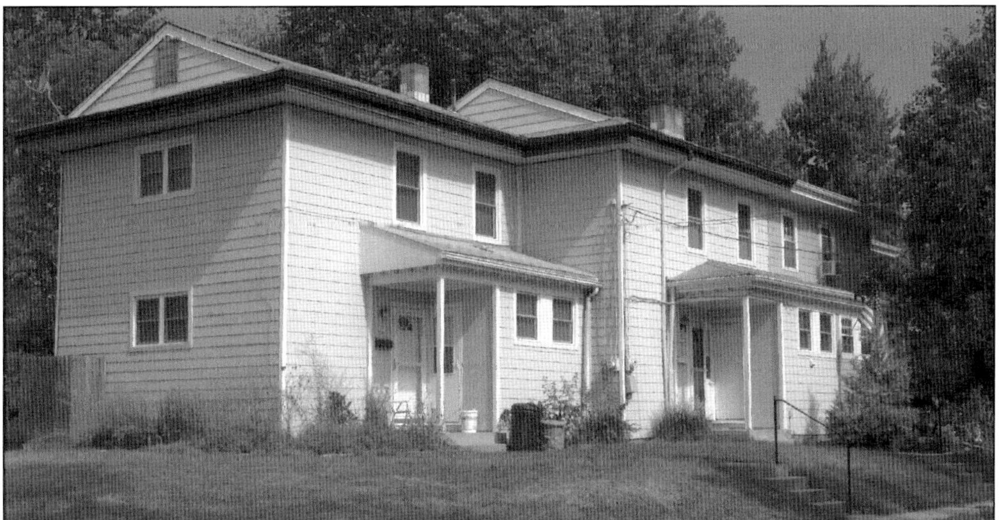

Because of the redevelopment plan's threat to Greenhills's historic buildings, the village was named one of Ohio's most endangered historic places by Preservation Ohio in 2010, 2011, and 2012. A *New York Times* article in February 2009 brought national coverage to the issue. Arguing that Greenhills buildings were worth preserving and that the village was a national treasure worthy of thoughtful development, preservation-minded candidates also ran for village council. The south unit of this four-family townhouse group on Cromwell Street was considered for demolition by the village, but it was renovated for rental use instead. (Courtesy of Margo M. Warminski.)

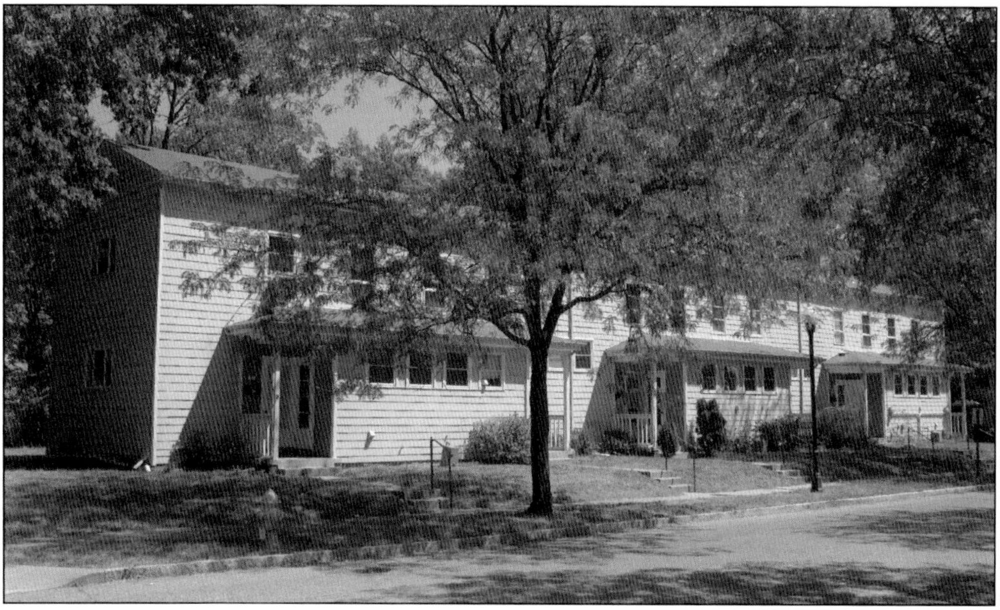

In 2008, a financial collapse and crushing recession brought construction to a halt across the country. As home values dropped and sales slowed, the village found it difficult to sell units or attract new construction. Instead, they became the community's largest landlord. Over the next few years, they renovated several buildings as rentals. As the economy began to recover in 2012, the village put some of its properties on the market, including this vacant six-family townhouse on Flanders Lane. (Courtesy of Margo M. Warminski.)

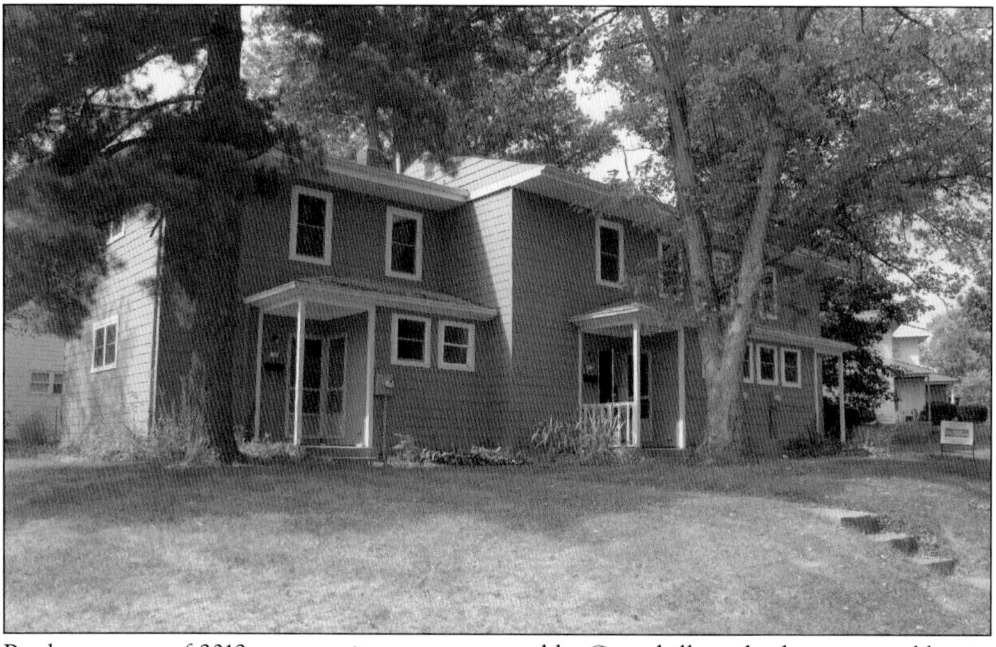

By the summer of 2012, some units were renovated by Greenhills and others were sold as-is. This three-family townhouse on Cromwell Street was partially renovated by the village in 2011 and put up for sale with special financing available to complete the work. (Courtesy of Margo M. Warminski.)

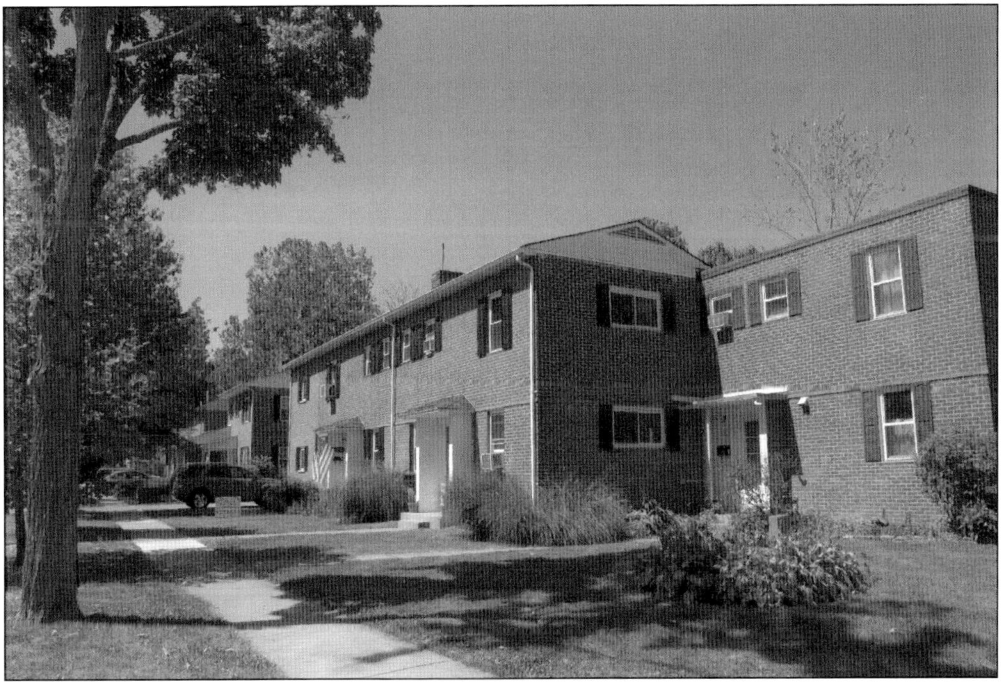

While media attention focused on neglected housing, many Greenhills buildings continued to be well preserved, some by descendants of original village residents. Many of the homes in the village's A and B sections, which have been spared demolition, are well cared for. The hilly topography and proximity to the greenbelt add to the neighborhood's attractiveness. Seen here is the tree-shaded streetscape of Andover Road. (Courtesy of Margo M. Warminski.)

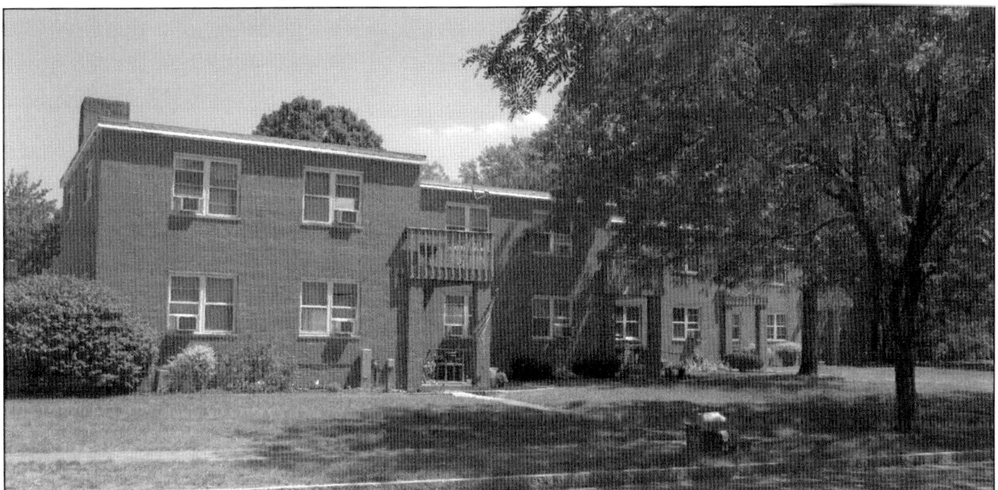

As enthusiasm for early Modern design grew in Cincinnati, Greenhills's forward-looking Modernist- and International-style architecture attracted new interest. This Farragut Road apartment house features units stacked one on another and private balconies. The units are set back for privacy's sake and to create visual interest. Four of these buildings were constructed, with each pair forming an inverted V. Their simple yet sophisticated design is in keeping with the greenbelt towns' architecture of restraint, in which individual buildings are subordinate to the overall design. (Courtesy of Margo M. Warminski.)

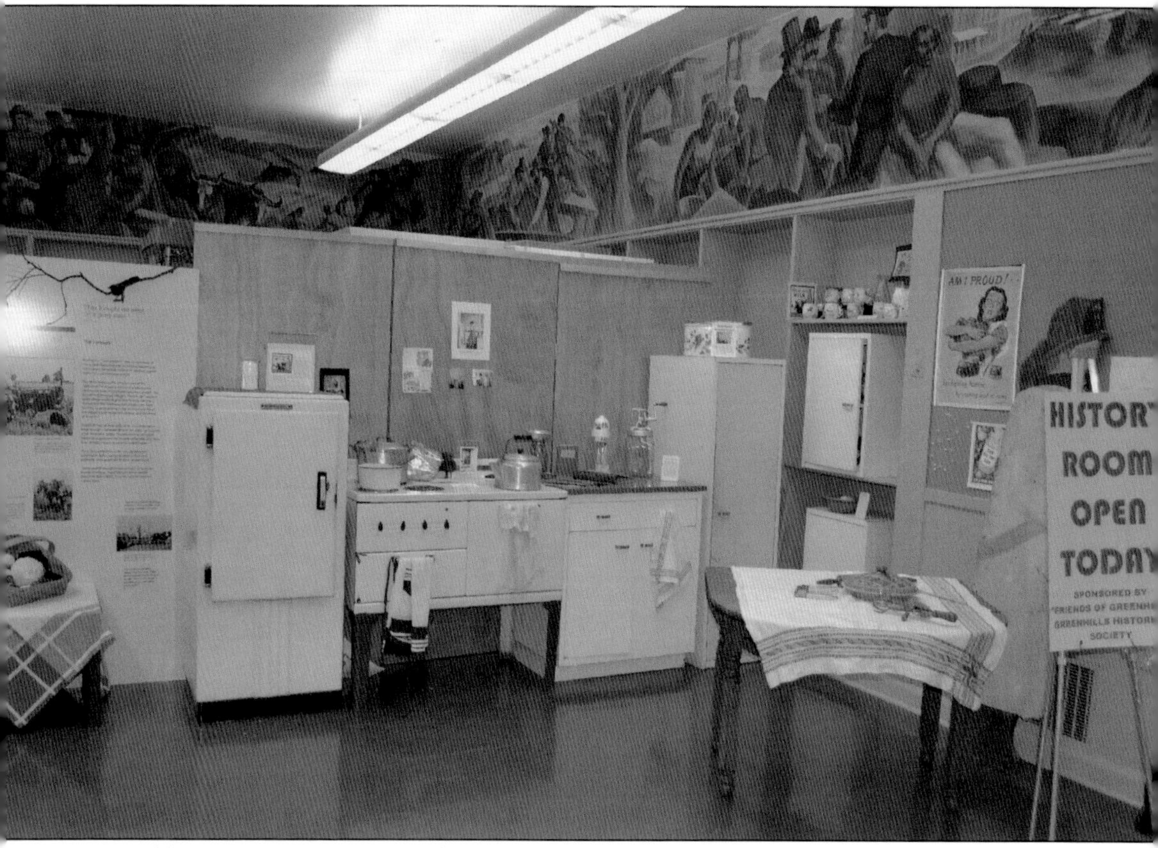

In addition to its preservation advocacy, the Greenhills Historical Society continues to serve as the curator of village history. In 2007, the society used a grant to hire an architectural conservator to assess two original WPA works of art in the Greenhills Community Building gym. GHS relocated its museum in 2009 to the former library on the first floor of the community building. Here, they hold events throughout the year, including open houses and programs on historical topics. The library, seen here, retains an original WPA mural depicting life along the Ohio River. The bookcases remain in place and have been repainted by GHS in their original color. Future projects include replacing hanging fluorescent fixtures with replicas of the original schoolhouse-style lights. (Courtesy of Paul Richardson.)

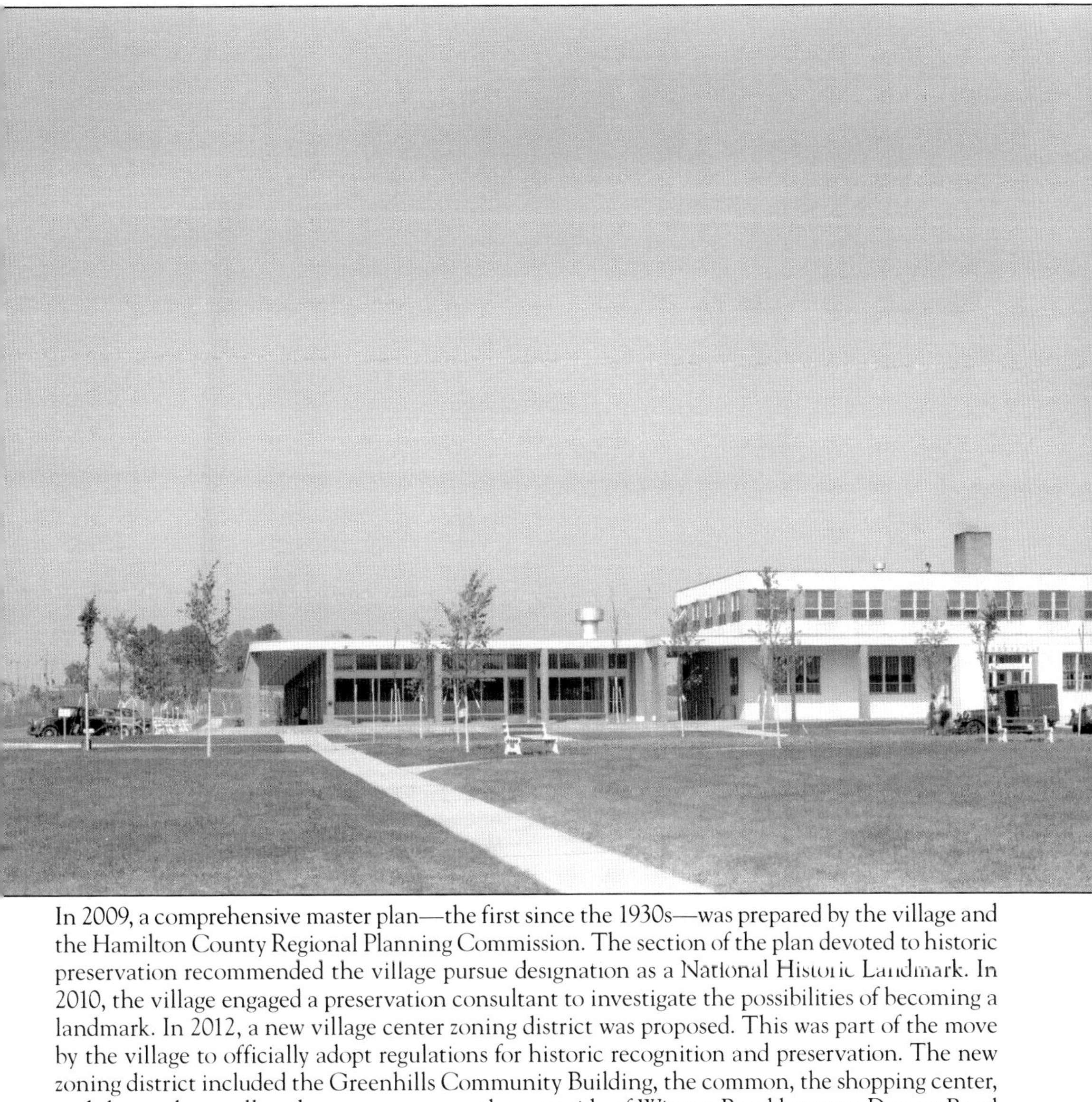

In 2009, a comprehensive master plan—the first since the 1930s—was prepared by the village and the Hamilton County Regional Planning Commission. The section of the plan devoted to historic preservation recommended the village pursue designation as a National Historic Landmark. In 2010, the village engaged a preservation consultant to investigate the possibilities of becoming a landmark. In 2012, a new village center zoning district was proposed. This was part of the move by the village to officially adopt regulations for historic recognition and preservation. The new zoning district included the Greenhills Community Building, the common, the shopping center, and the pool, as well as the green space on the west side of Winton Road between Damon Road and Cromwell Street. This 1939 photograph shows the shopping center in all its Modernist elegance. (Courtesy of the Library of Congress.)

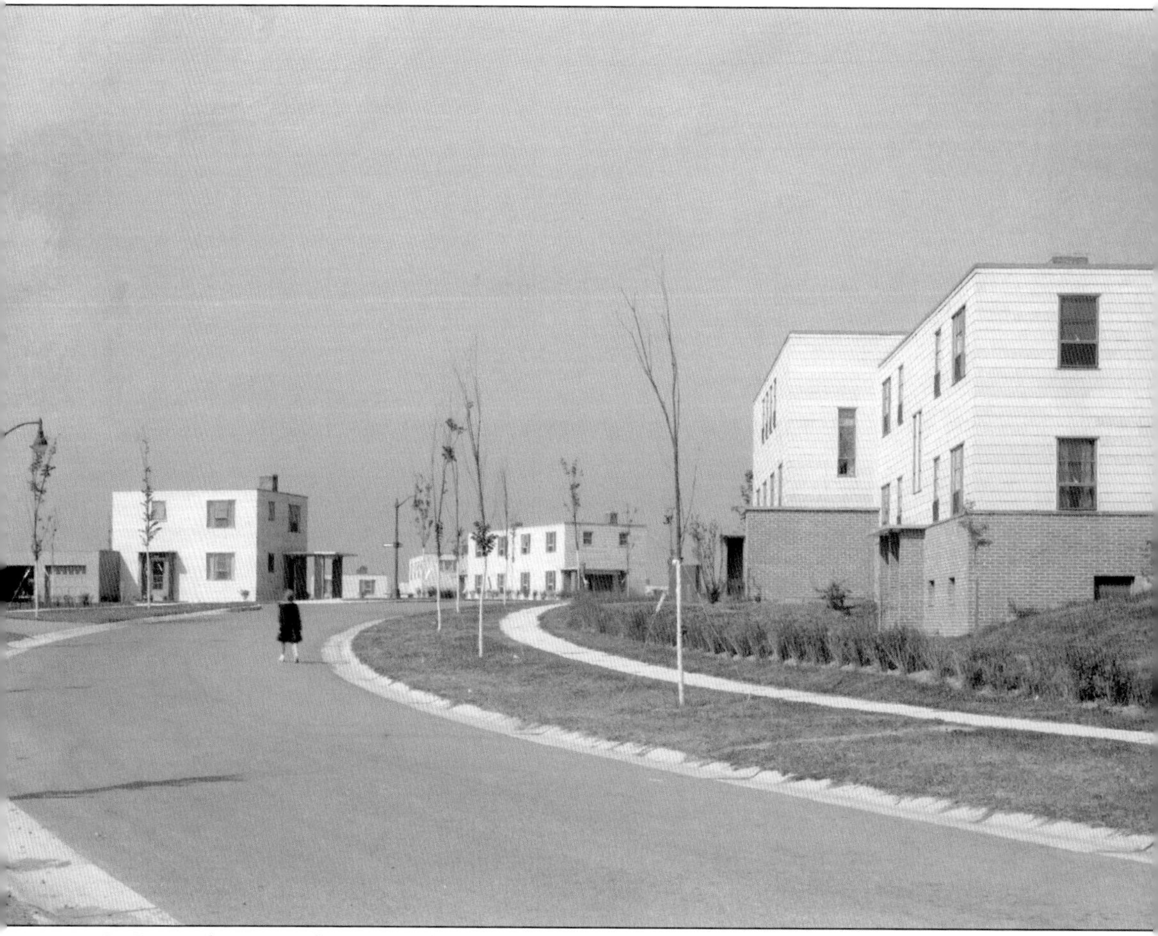

In September 2012, the National Park Service sent a team of historians to Greenhills to assess the historic district's possible designation as a National Historic Landmark. If approved, a process that takes several years, Greenhills would join an elite group of nationally significant properties in the Cincinnati area, including Union Terminal, the Carew Tower, the Roebling Suspension Bridge, and the villages of Glendale and Mariemont. As Greenhills approaches its 75th anniversary, village residents celebrate its fascinating history and look forward to the challenges and opportunities of the next 75 years. Here, a young girl walks boldly into the future along winding Burley Circle, with its bright new townhouses and freshly planted trees. (Courtesy of the Library of Congress.)

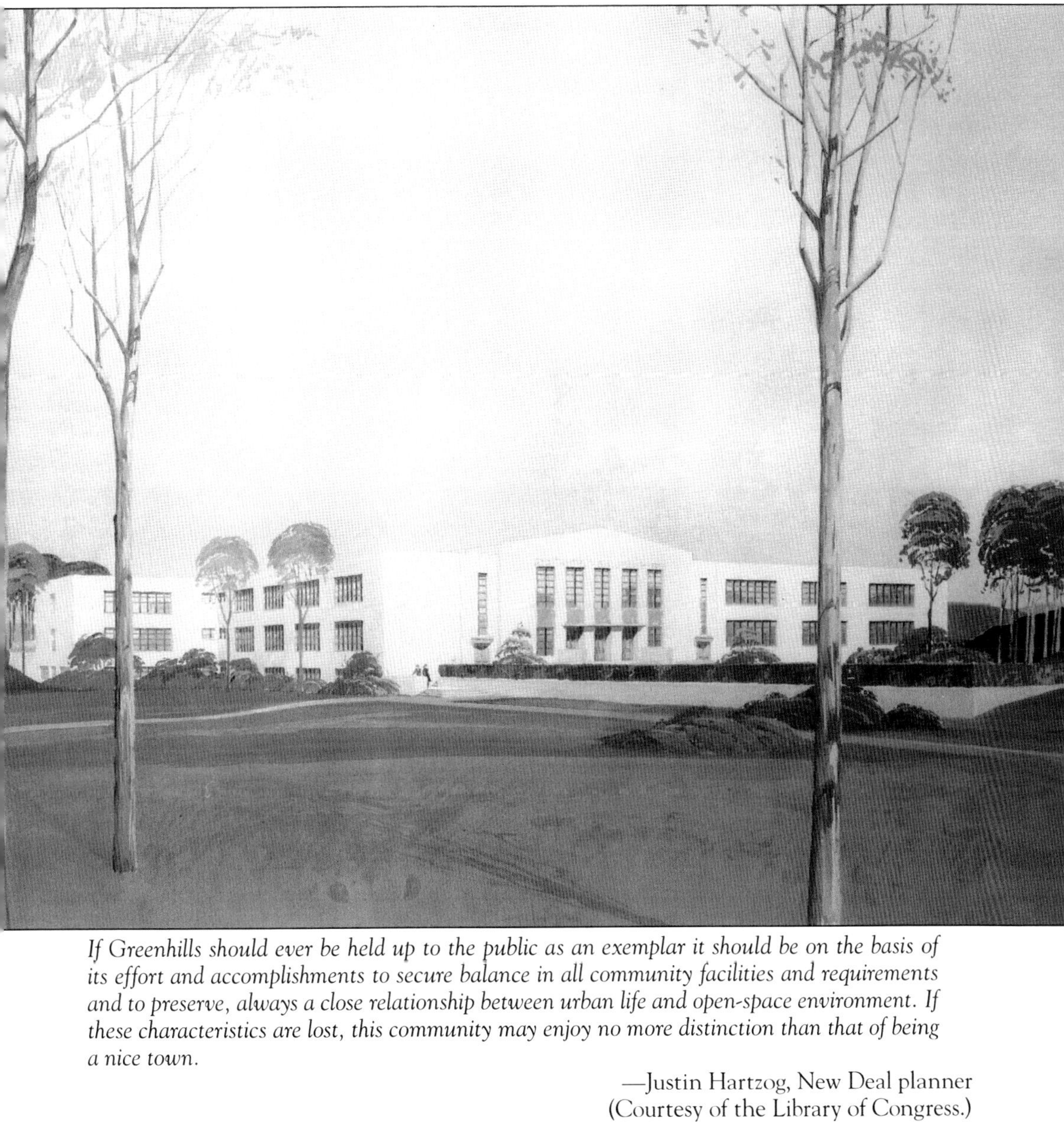

If Greenhills should ever be held up to the public as an exemplar it should be on the basis of its effort and accomplishments to secure balance in all community facilities and requirements and to preserve, always a close relationship between urban life and open-space environment. If these characteristics are lost, this community may enjoy no more distinction than that of being a nice town.

—Justin Hartzog, New Deal planner
(Courtesy of the Library of Congress.)